AFTERLIVES OF MODERNISM

RE-MAPPING THE TRANSNATIONAL
A Dartmouth Series in American Studies

The emergence of Transnational American Studies in the wake of the Cold War marks the most significant reconfiguration of American studies since its inception. The shock waves generated by a newly globalized world order demanded an understanding of America's embeddedness within global and local processes rather than scholarly reaffirmations of its splendid isolation. The series Re-Mapping the Transnational seeks to foster the cross-national dialogues needed to sustain the vitality of this emergent field. To advance a truly comparativist understanding of this scholarly endeavor, Dartmouth College Press welcomes monographs from scholars both inside and outside the United States.

For a complete list of books available in this series, see www.upne.com.

Lene M. Johannessen, *Horizons of Enchantment: Essays in the American Imaginary*
John Carlos Rowe, *Afterlives of Modernism: Liberalism, Transnationalism, and Political Critique*
Anthony Bogues, *Empire of Liberty: Power, Desire, and Freedom*
Bernd Herzogenrath, *An American Body|Politic: A Deleuzian Approach*
Johannes Voelz, *Transcendental Resistance: The New Americanists and Emerson's Challenge*

John Carlos Rowe

AFTERLIVES OF MODERNISM

Liberalism, Transnationalism, and Political Critique

DARTMOUTH COLLEGE PRESS
HANOVER, NEW HAMPSHIRE

Dartmouth College Press
An imprint of University Press of New England
www.upne.com

Manufactured in the United States of America
Designed by Katherine B. Kimball
Typeset in Sabon by Passumpsic Publishing

University Press of New England is a member of the Green Press Initiative. The paper used in this book meets their minimum requirement for recycled paper.

Library of Congress Cataloging-in-Publication Data appear on the last printed page of this book.

5 4 3 2 1

Rememory: Lindon Barrett: Friend

To borrow from Alex Haley's *Roots* (1976),
he helped "alleviate the legacies of the fact that
preponderantly the histories have been written
by the winners."

CONTENTS

PREFACE

All the chapters in this book were published previously as scholarly essays between 1983 and 2010. Three of the chapters were published outside the U.S. in Germany (chapter 2), Australia (chapter 7), and Italy (chapter 8) and thus have had little circulation in the U.S. The origins of most of these essays bear upon the central argument of the book and on my own cultural politics. All of the original essays, except for the essay on Gertrude Stein, were commissioned by editors of journals or books, usually on specific authors and in some cases specific texts. It is fair to conclude that these editors approached me because they considered my previous work to qualify me to write about these authors and texts. Some editors undoubtedly judged me to be a liberal capable of writing on liberal authors and texts. Others explicitly asked me, as Alice Hall Petry did when commissioning my essay on Harper Lee's *To Kill a Mockingbird*, to write a leftist interpretation of a liberal text. Alice was kind enough to express her admiration of my essay on Kate Chopin's *The Awakening*, which is a materialist analysis of the socio-economic relations in that novel.[1]

Dangerous as it is to judge one's own political or scholarly perspective, I identified myself as a leftist while writing all of these essays, except for the 1983 essay on Thomas Berger, which has been extensively revised for this book, in part because of the dated qualities of the original essay. I certainly began my scholarly career as a liberal, who wrote about primarily canonical, white male authors. Henry Adams and Henry James were the subjects of my first published book, *Henry Adams and Henry James*, an early example of the relevance of Continental deconstruction to American literature.[2] In the 1970s deconstruction was considered a radical philosophy, but its political significance was contested. During the Culture Wars of the late 1980s and early 1990s, neoconservatives frequently linked deconstruction, ethnic studies, "radical" feminism, and neo-Marxism to what these critics judged a "cultural relativism" that was generally permissive and falsified the truth. But in retrospect, I must conclude that although certain deconstructionists learned from their colleagues in ethnic studies, feminism, and on the political left, deconstruction was primarily liberal in its practical and academic politics.

My claim is contradicted by one of Jacques Derrida's major works, *Spectres of Marx*, in which he contends that the post-1989 legacy of Marxism might be pursued best in coordination with Derridean deconstruction.[3] But the connection between Marxism and deconstruction was always a difficult coalition between two inherently incompatible traditions. Marxism is built upon a thorough-going critique of an Enlightenment and idealist heritage that Marx himself insisted we must invert, if only to bring Kantian and Hegelian idealism down to the practical work of historical and dialectical materialism. Derridean deconstruction reinterprets that intellectual tradition, but in ways that are far more compatible with romantic idealism than traditional Marxism.

I will leave Jacques Derrida's legacy to the scholars who study his works in these contexts and are better qualified to judge it as either liberal or leftist. But I can write confidently that in my own contributions to those debates in the 1970s and early 1980s, my approach was liberal, even as my work attempted to broaden by way of deconstruction the very limited "liberal imagination" I identify in the introduction with Lionel Trilling and the New York Intellectuals of the 1950s. The rest of my intellectual trajectory from the late 1980s to the present has been a self-conscious effort to develop a leftist critique of liberalism, of the dominant U.S. literary canon, and to help broaden "American literature" by treating more radical challenges to its traditional definitions from ethnic minorities, women, lesbians and gays, and writers and intellectuals outside the United States in the broader Western Hemisphere.

My position as a left intellectual has not been rigorously faithful to a particular school or ideology, perhaps because much of my liberal background still clings to me. For some readers of this book, my liberal-leaning leftism or left-leaning liberalism will be annoying at best and contradictory at worst. Some readers may even praise me incorrectly for living up to Trilling's ideal of the individual capable of a "liberal imagination" that refuses ideology or academic labels. I prefer commitment in both practical politics and as a scholar-teacher, so I suppose I must offer myself up for criticism of my mixed intellectual heritage. My only apology is that such a legacy demonstrates that I am still capable of learning and do endorse Keats's "negative capability." I also still read liberal literature admiringly while recognizing its limitations.

I am grateful to my good friend Donald Pease for encouraging me to develop this book and then including it in his new series under the Dartmouth College Press imprint for the University Press of New England, and to Richard Pult at UPNE who has helped move this project from an idea to a published book. It is impossible for me to mention all the people who have influenced my thinking in this book, read portions of it, or just offered the sort of intellectual stimulation that makes scholarly books possible and valuable. My colleagues in the departments of American Studies and Ethnicity and English at the University of Southern California, including the superb graduate students in our PhD programs, have been inspirational. I thank them all without singling out anyone. Everyone I have met at the Futures of American Studies summer institutes I have attended, thanks to Donald Pease's generous invitations over many years, has contributed to this book. From the tough questions during the keynote lectures I have given to the exchanges in the workshops and subsequent emails I have had with scholars from around the world, I have benefited in countless ways. You remind me of what a privilege it is to learn I am wrong, to learn something new, and to think *with* others. I also want to thank everyone involved in our three-year research group, Transatlantic American Studies, which was sponsored by the Humboldt Foundation in Germany and Dartmouth College and the University of Southern California in the United States between 2006 and 2009. Although the collaborative research conducted by that international group is published in a separate volume, my work in this book benefited greatly from our conversations. A few good friends in addition to those already mentioned deserve thanks for general inspiration and good conversation: Nancy Armstrong, Colin Dayan, Edgar Dryden, Winfried and Birgitte Fluck, Cristina Giorcelli, Susan Griffin, Liam Kennedy, Katherine Kinney, Rüdiger and Eva Kunow, Günter and Ruth Lenz, Scott Lucas, Kevin

McNamara, Alan Nadel, Patrick O'Donnell, Mark Poster and Annette Schlichter, Marc Priewe, Ricky Rodriguez, and Gabriele Schwab.

My thanks to the editors and publishers for permission to reprint significantly revised versions of the essays that were first published by them: Chapter 1, "Naming What Is Inside: Gertrude Stein's Use of Names in *Three Lives*," first published in *Novel* 36:2 (Spring 2003), pp. 219–43; Chapter 2, "Interpellation, Urbanization, and Globalization in John Dos Passos' *Manhattan Transfer*," first published in *Toward a New Metropolitanism: Reconstituting Public Culture, Urban Citizenship, and the Multicultural Imaginary in New York and Berlin*, eds. Günter H. Lenz, Friedrich Ulfers, Antje Dallmann (Heidelberg: Universitätsverlag Winter, 2006), pp. 349–58; Chapter 3, "Faulkner and the Southern Arts of Mystification in *Absalom, Absalom!*" first published in *Blackwell's Companion to William Faulkner*, ed. Richard C. Moreland (Malden, MA: Blackwell Publishing, 2007), pp. 445–58; Chapter 4, "Our *Invisible Man*: The Aesthetic Genealogy of U.S. Diversity," first published in *Blackwell's Companion to the American Novel*, ed. Alfred Bendixen (New York: Basil Blackwell, 2011); Chapter 5, "Racism, Fetishism, and the Gift Economy in Harper Lee's *To Kill a Mockingbird* (1960)," first published in *On Harper Lee: Essays and Reflections*, ed. Alice Hall Petry (Knoxville: University of Tennessee Press, 2007), pp. 1–17. Used with permission. Chapter 6, "Alien Encounter: Thomas Berger's *Neighbors* as a Critique of Existential Humanism," first published in *Studies in American Humor*, special issue on Thomas Berger, ed. Brom Weber, II, new series (Spring 1983), pp. 45–60; Chapter 7, "Buried Alive: The Native American Political Unconscious in Louise Erdrich's Fiction," first published in *Postcolonial Studies* (Australia) 7:2 (July 2004), pp. 197–210; Chapter 8, "U.S. Literary Canons after Nationalism," first published in *Letteratura America* (Italy), special issue on U.S. literary canons, ed. Cristina Giorcelli, XXVII: 121–22 (2007–8), pp. 31–56.

Of course, the Rowe family has had to put up with my work on this book, as with all the others. My love and gratitude to you all: Kristin, Sean and Katherine and Fiona, Kevin and Karen and Leben, Mark and Angela. No, Ziggy, no!

Island Park, Idaho
August 2010

Notes

1. John Carlos Rowe, "The Economics of the Body in Kate Chopin's *The Awakening*," in *Kate Chopin Reconsidered: Beyond the Bayou*, eds. Lynda S. Boren and Sara de Saussure Davis (Baton Rouge: Louisiana State University Press, 1992); revised version in John Carlos Rowe, *At Emerson's Tomb: The Politics of Classic American Literature* (New York: Columbia University Press, 1997), pp. 200–221.

2. John Carlos Rowe, *Henry Adams and Henry James: The Emergence of a Modern Consciousness* (Ithaca, NY: Cornell University Press, 1976).

3. Jacques Derrida, *Spectres de Marx: L'État de la dette, le travail du deuil et la nouvelle Internationale* (Paris: Galilée, 1993).

AFTERLIVES OF MODERNISM

INTRODUCTION: THE INEVITABLE INTIMATE CONNECTION

These are not political essays, they are essays in literary criticism. But they assume the inevitable intimate, if not always obvious, connection between literature and politics.

—Lionel Trilling, *The Liberal Imagination: Essays in Literature and Society* (1950)

LIONEL TRILLING'S *The Liberal Imagination* was published sixty years ago, when post–World War II liberalism offered viable resistance to the conservative ideology defining the Cold War era. As recent scholars have re-evaluated the 1950s, they have acknowledged the social protest of a liberal culture often identified with the New York Intellectuals, including Trilling, and with some of his most influential students, such as Jack Kerouac and Allen Ginsberg.[1] Trilling was writing at the end of a venerable liberal tradition rooted in American transcendentalism and its secularization of Puritan theology. Only four years before the publication of *The Liberal Imagination*, Arthur Schlesinger Jr.'s *The Age of Jackson* won the Pulitzer Prize for History in 1946 by celebrating the social progressivism of Emerson, Thoreau, and other transcendentalists who challenged Andrew Jackson's reckless economic expansionism.[2] Less than a decade before *The Liberal Imagination*, F. O. Matthiessen's *American Renaissance: Art and Expression in the Age of Emerson and Whitman* (1941) canonized the liberal ideals of the transcendentalists and their continuing relevance for the modern age.[3]

Trilling sought to revive this liberal tradition in response to the political extremism on both the left and right that many feared in the postwar era. Western leftists had been divided since the late 1930s, when evidence of Stalin's show-trials and genocidal policies in the Soviet Union was publicized internationally. While some U.S. leftists, like W. E. B. Du Bois, defended Stalin and others tried to disconnect Western Marxism from the Soviet Union, others moved to liberal positions, like the *Partisan Review*'s editor, Philip Rahv. Trilling's anti-Stalinism and anti-Communism have been well documented, and he shared the anti-fascism that had driven the U.S. war effort.[4] Public revelations about the Nazi Holocaust confirmed anti-fascist views while indicating that both the Stalinist left and Nazi right had conducted genocidal policies unmatched in history.

Trilling's often-quoted view in the preface to *The Liberal Imagination* suggests that liberalism is the only possible *rational* position in an age threatened globally by the irrational positions of Stalinism and Fascism:

> In the United States at this time liberalism is not only the dominant but even the sole intellectual tradition. For it is the plain fact that nowadays there are no conservative or reactionary ideas in general circulation. This does not mean, of course, that there is no impulse to conservatism or to reaction. Such impulses are certainly very strong, perhaps even stronger than most of us know. But the conservative impulse and the reactionary impulse do not, with some isolated and ecclesiastical exceptions, express themselves in ideas but only in action or in irritable gestures which seek to resemble ideas.[5]

Later in the preface he warns us that "in the modern situation it is just when a movement despairs of having ideas that it turns to force, which it masks in ideology" (*Liberal Imagination*, 5; hereafter *LI*). On February 9, 1950, Senator Joseph McCarthy would make his infamous pronouncement that there were members of the Communist Party in the U.S. State Department, a claim he never proved, but which would lead to his anti-Communist witch hunts.[6] In his introduction to the *New York Times* Classic Edition of *The Liberal Imagination*, Louis Menand, another influential student of Trilling's, notes that Trilling never defines *liberalism*, preferring to specify what it is *not*.[7] Trilling's liberalism occupies the political "middle" between the extremes of Stalinism and Fascism. Trilling's novel *The Middle of the Journey* (1947) specifically invokes a middle course for U.S. postwar society, which complements the "centrist" position of his more conservative contemporary, Arthur Schlesinger Jr., in *The Vital Center: The Politics of Freedom* (1949).[8]

Today it is difficult to imagine "liberalism" as a political middle course, because since the anti-war, civil rights, and women's movements of the late 1960s, "liberalism" has moved steadily to the left in U.S. popular culture. The label "liberal" in political contests today inevitably designates a "left-leaning" person incapable of bipartisan cooperation in practical politics. Moderate Democrats running for political offices avoid the designation "liberal," and a politician like President Barack Obama, who endorses many liberal positions, has had a very hard time claiming the "middle ground" and "bipartisanship" that were hallmarks of his successful presidential campaign.

The Liberal Imagination was remarkably influential for a book that is an odd amalgam of literary and cultural essays previously published. The chapters do not develop a progressive thesis, even if they return to several central themes, and they do not offer even a clear "great literary tradition." As a specialist in late Victorian and early twentieth-century literary modernism, Trilling includes four influential but by no means representative modern U.S. writers: Theodore Dreiser, Sherwood Anderson, Henry James, and F. Scott Fitzgerald. Their works serve Trilling as examples of various sorts of modern realism, rather than radical avant-garde experimentalism. Henry James stands above the other three as a triumphant psychological realist best able to imagine the complexities of the liberal individual. Trilling's nineteenth-century literary authors include William Wordsworth, Mark Twain, and Rudyard Kipling, suggesting the importance of English influences on the American literary tradition. Other chapters on *The Partisan Review*, Freudian approaches to literature and culture and classical history may address various challenges to Trilling's humanist tradition, but there is no clear argument connecting the sixteen chapters of the book.

Trilling's preface is often quoted, but despite its involuted, scholarly style it relies on journalistic claims rather than analytic arguments. None of these aspects of *The Liberal Imagination* accounts for the book's substantial influence in scholarly and public intellectual circles over the next two decades. What does account for its impact is its overall invocation of a critical spirit of the age, at least in the United States, which had been building from the *fin de siècle* to the post–World War II era. Trilling's term for this critical attitude is aptly and quotably "the liberal imagination," the faculty Wordsworth famously contends the poet possesses in greater "degree" but not "kind" from the ordinary man.[9] Louis Menand is thus not entirely correct to claim that Trilling never defines the *liberal imagination*. Although Trilling only offers a negative definition of the phrase in his preface, each chapter offers an exemplification of the liberal imagination, especially those chapters devoted to great literary works and authors.

The qualities of the liberal imagination are clear and distinct. First, the liberal subject (author or citizen) is capable of imagining other positions and values than his own. A crucial function of this imaginative faculty is the "negative capability" Trilling admired in Keats's formulation of the ability to avoid settled ideas and recognize a certain ignorance or horizon to one's own knowledge, in order to keep the mind open to new ideas and experiences.[10] Second, the liberal imagination relies on a "critical spirit," which identifies "a discrepancy between . . . present particular manifestations" of liberalism and its ideal (*LI*, xxi). Trilling was influenced strongly by the English romantics' and American transcendentalists' criticism of the political liberalism that supported unregulated economic progress, territorial expansion, and personal freedom. Trilling feared liberalism itself could become an ideology without new ideas, as it had during the Presidency of Andrew Jackson (*LI*, xvi). Third, the liberal imagination depended upon a complex philosophical and psychological subject whose individualism was built upon both creative and analytic powers, such as those Coleridge named primary and secondary imaginations, and thus could not be reduced to his political or class affiliations.

Caught between being used by The Sun and Moon anarchist group as an assassin and the lure of aristocratic wealth and power, James's Hyacinth Robinson in *The Princess Casamassima* (1886) finally chooses suicide. In Trilling's interpretation of one of James's most politically explicit novels, Hyacinth represents the tragic fatality for the individual who is ideologically manipulated: "Hyacinth dies sacrificially, but not as a sacrificial lamb, wholly innocent; he dies as a human hero who has incurred a certain amount of guilt" (*LI*, 85). Unlike Hyacinth, Henry James can imagine both political extremes, weigh their respective intellectual and psychological appeals, and yet avoid their coercions. Fourth, the liberal imagination is characterized by modern cosmopolitanism and its apparent advocacy of universal human rights. Trilling's *Liberal Imagination* is transnational in a highly limited way, relying on Anglo-American modernism and invoking a European, Sigmund Freud, only insofar as he has entered into the dominant cultures of England and the United States. "Universality" for Trilling remains structured by the most civilized cultures and is in no way qualified by subsequent criticisms of Eurocentrism.

For Trilling, the West *is* the best because its cultural achievements, especially in literature, exhibit the best examples of the "liberal imagination." All of this suggests why the transnational Henry James, whose "international theme" was so important for Trilling's Columbia colleague Fred Dupee, would achieve such a central position in Trilling's book.[11]

What accounts for the success of *The Liberal Imagination* is in part the long legacy of such liberalism from Emerson to William James and John Dewey to Trilling and many of the New York Intellectuals, as well as the postwar cultural demand for a "middle ground" between the political impasses of Stalinism and European fascism. Trilling's version of liberalism is particularly conservative in its emphasis on bourgeois values, its defense of modernist realism over a more radical avant-garde, and its neglect of race, gender, and sexuality. Published four years before the landmark U.S. Supreme Court decision of 1954, Brown vs. Board of Education, and in the midst of the growing unrest among African Americans regarding their continuing lack of civil, social, and economic rights, *The Liberal Imagination* has virtually nothing to say about the issues of race and ethnicity, despite its invocation of an international romanticism marked by its commitment to abolition and universal human rights. There is one weird footnote in the essay "Art and Fortune" about the "question of whether the American attitude toward 'minority' groups, particularly Negroes and Jews, is not the equivalent of class differentiation" (*LI*, 250–53). Trilling's answer is clearly that "minority groups" do *not* suffer from the same discrimination as those relegated to a lower class, because "the excluded group" faces "no real cultural struggle, no significant conflict of ideals," insofar as it "has the same notion of life and the same aspirations as the excluding group" (*LI*, 250–3). By linking "Negroes and Jews," Trilling tacitly claims to know experientially what he is saying here, having faced discrimination as a Jewish professor at Columbia, but his assumption that all such "minority groups" share the concept of life and human aspirations with all other groups, especially the "excluding group," belongs to the ideology of American assimilation and consensus history. The fact that Trilling buries his one observation about ethnic minorities in a footnote under the urgent historical circumstances I have mentioned needs little further comment.

Trilling's hero in *The Liberal Imagination* is clearly Henry James, but Trilling has little to say about James's ability to imagine the social and psychological bondage of nineteenth-century women to patriarchal values and nothing to say about James's ambivalent sexual identity and its imaginary representation in his fiction. Is it possible to think liberally about Hyacinth Robinson, for example, without considering the extensive coding of *The Princess Casamassima* in reference to the gay subculture of Victorian London?[12] Because of the particularly repressive social climate for gays and lesbians in the United States in the 1950s, challenged aggressively by one of his best students, Allen Ginsberg, Trilling ought to have reflected critically on the politics of sexuality, as do three of his most important literary examples: Theodore Dreiser, Sherwood Anderson, and Henry James. For a book in which the cultural significance of Freudian psychoanalysis is addressed in three separate chapters—chapter 4, "Freud and Literature"; chapter 10, "Art and Neurosis"; and chapter 14, "The Kinsey Report"—Trilling's neglect of gender and sexuality is as noticeable as his disregard of race and ethnicity.

Of course, Trilling *does* address rather infamously "homosexuality" in his review of Alfred Kinsey, Wardell Pomeroy, and Clyde Martin's *Sexual Behavior in the Human Male* (1948). "The Kinsey Report" is the fourteenth essay in *The Liberal Imagination*, and it is one of the central examples of how Trilling's "literary criticism" might be applied to "society," as his subtitle promises. Trilling addresses homosexuality in the Kinsey Report by concluding that "these psychiatrists have thereby judged homosexuality to be an unexceptionable form of sexuality," but he himself cannot help but read into the report that "their opinion of the etiology of homosexuality as lying in some warp—as our culture judges it—of the psychic structure has not, I believe, changed" (*LI*, 232). This conclusion is certainly more subject to Trilling's interpretation than the report itself, but what is even more troubling is Trilling's waffling with regard to the conclusion we ought to draw from the report that homosexuality is "an unexceptionable form of sexuality": "There can be no doubt that a society in which homosexuality was dominant or even accepted would be different in nature and quality from one in which it was censured" (*LI*, 232). Trilling knows indubitably that in Anglo-American societies from the late Victorian period (his exact area of scholarly specialization) to the United States in 1950, homosexuality has been "censured" by severely punitive laws. Rather than engage the issue of the discrimination against homosexuals, Trilling prefers instead to *accept* the social constructedness of "liberal society" as one in which such discrimination is part of the social contract. Trilling then follows this odd, conservative conclusion with an indictment of what today we understand by the phrase "liberal permissiveness": "The Report has the intention of habituating its readers to sexuality in all its manifestations; it wants to establish, as it were, a democratic pluralism of sexuality. And this good impulse toward acceptance and liberation is not unique with the Report but very often shows itself in those parts of our intellectual life which are more or less official and institutionalized" (*LI*, 232–33). Trilling confesses that this "generosity of mind" is "to be admired," but "when we have given it all the credit it deserves . . . , we cannot help observing that it is often associated with an almost intentional intellectual weakness" (*LI*, 233). The "liberal imagination," it would appear, has certain limits for Trilling.

Trilling's *The Liberal Imagination* marks the turn of American liberalism from a progressive political position committed to specific social reforms to an aesthetic ideology. To be sure, nineteenth-century liberalism often suffered from a tendency to "aesthetic dissent" rather than to political criticism. The Emersonian tradition has often stressed philosophical and psychological changes over practical reforms, and Trilling fits squarely within this heritage.[13] Yet the great nineteenth-century social reform movements in the United States—abolition, women's rights, and Native American rights—were shaped profoundly by liberal activists. Although its publication in 1950 is too early to mark the beginnings of "neoliberalism," which does not appear until the so-called Culture Wars of the 1980s, *The Liberal Imagination* nonetheless provides a cultural milestone for the transformation of a liberal tradition that for a century had informed political critique and social reform in the United States.

The familiar story is that liberalism was hijacked by neoconservatives during the Culture Wars of the 1980s and that the "multiculturalism" of the late 1980s and early 1990s suffered from meliorist efforts to satisfy neoconservative demands of "equality for all," including those historically privileged, and in response to a vigorous campaign against "political correctness." One result was that neoconservatives cynically appropriated liberal positions and values in a neoliberal rhetoric unmatched by political action; the other consequence was that liberalism, now confused with neoliberal rhetoric, suffered from leftist critiques of its ineffectiveness and ideological co-optation. Some neoconservative intellectuals, often supported by private foundations, argued that they were "classical" liberals, tracing their values back to the eighteenth-century European Enlightenment and conveniently sidestepping contemporary social issues. Allan Bloom's *The Closing of the American Mind* (1987) exemplifies a neoconservative intellectual position that relied on "classical liberalism," which Bloom traced back to Plato's *Republic*, to condemn problems in contemporary education ranging from deconstruction and analytic philosophy to rock and roll.[14] Positively reviewed by the liberal political philosopher Martha Nussbaum and the conservative intellectual Harry V. Jaffa, *The Closing of the American Mind* was a best seller and mainstay of neoconservative attacks on higher education and its "tenured radicals." Despite the historical distance of nearly four decades separating Bloom's *Closing of the American Mind* and Trilling's *The Liberal Imagination*, the books have much in common, especially their advocacy of high culture as a defense against extremist political ideologies, their contempt for popular culture, and their neglect of race, class, and gender/sexuality as central social and political issues.

The decline of liberalism from Trilling's contention in 1950 that it "is not only the dominant but even the sole intellectual tradition" to its neoliberal cooptation and condemnation by the left in the 1990s tells only part of a much longer history from the nineteenth century to the modern period. I identify my own work with the political left, but I also recognize that the left has trivialized the work of liberal culture, either subordinating it to conservative politics or rejecting it as inadequately critical of the dominant ideology. But such a position is mistaken in terms of the functionality of liberalism in nineteenth-century and modern U.S. society. Working through liberal values may be the most effective means of achieving lasting change, as Martin Luther King Jr. understood in the civil rights movement and second-wave feminists did in the era of the National Organization of Women. Liberalism appeals to a popular base that can understand, even if it cannot fully share, the suffering of minoritized peoples. For this very reason, conservative interests have traditionally sought to appropriate the popular appeal of liberalism, turning its moral interests in the oppressed into political opportunities.

My aim is not to offer a defense of liberal culture and politics, as Lionel Trilling does in *The Liberal Imagination*, but instead to offer an oppositional interpretation of liberalism that respects its immense popularity, even defining function, in U.S. history. Without liberal culture, Barack Obama would never have been elected president. Dismissing or ignoring liberalism and treating it reductively as socialism or communism in disguise are equally inadequate responses to its social and cultural power. My goal is to respect what liberal culture has achieved while also recognizing how its genealogy can lead to genuinely conservative values, as it has in the neoliberal phase. By the same token, liberalism has much to recommend it, especially in its claims to "sympathetic" cultural recognition of others. This scholarly study focuses on modernist literary texts that engage issues of race, class, and gender/sexuality from Gertrude Stein's *Three Lives* (1909) to Ralph Ellison's *Invisible Man* (1952). Just how such liberalism could be transformed into a resource of neoliberals in the past twenty-five years is part of this story, which I attempt to tell through a series of literary interpretations of postwar writings by contemporary U.S. authors with strong liberal credentials—Harper Lee, Thomas Berger, Louise Erdrich, and Philip Roth—each of whom represents a different aspect of the spectrum that stretches from liberalism to neoliberalism.

Scholars commonly assume that avant-garde literary modernism in the United States relied on a political liberalism that marginalized issues of race, class, and gender/sexuality that would become the governing social issues in the post–World War II era. In this book, I contend that high modernism often addressed these questions in progressive ways, calling for specific reforms symbolically enacted in many literary works. Distinct from the deeply conservative politics of avant-garde modernists like Ezra Pound and T. S. Eliot, Gertrude Stein, John Dos Passos, William Faulkner, and Ralph Ellison took seriously the social inequities of U.S. racism, sexism, and classism. Each tried to identify with the situations of peoples marginalized in these ways and offered the literary *imaginary* as a possible means of calling for and proposing specific social, legal, and economic reforms. Employing avant-garde styles and forms to disrupt the conventional modes of cultural representation, they also worked to include minorities as participants in the debates of the avant-garde.

Whatever their political persuasions, avant-garde modernists responded to second-stage modernization as a transnational process that had specific consequences for discrete nation-states. With its twentieth-century emphasis on immigration and diversity, the United States claimed to incorporate new transnational forces into a sort of "super-nation" that would offer its democratic values, social inclusiveness, successful economy, and progressive politics as models to be exported around the globe. By our present moment, such hyper-nationalism has become a distinctive characteristic of U.S. neo-imperialism, evident in the countless ways international issues are transformed into domestic problems. Thus the global "war on terror" is in fact the U.S. fight against its enemies and often in pursuit of its own national self-interest. Women's rights in Afghanistan and Saudi Arabia are treated in terms appropriate to middle-class, white American women. Racial and ethnic conflicts in Africa and India are interpreted in terms of the U.S. civil rights movement.

Although attentive to this problem of nationalizing global issues, the U.S. literary avant-garde also contributed to the problem. In *Three Lives*, Stein treats the female, German-American, immigrant protagonists of "The Good Anna" and "Gentle Lena" as complements to Melanctha Herbert, the African-American protagonist of the central and best-known novella, "Melanctha." In doing so, Stein creates unexpected transnational affiliations but also risks treating racial and national questions in reductive ways. Dos Passos sets *Manhattan Transfer* (1925) in New York City as the new metropolitan center of global flows, treating the Russo-Japanese War, European colonial conflicts in Morocco, and other international news as equally important to the New Yorker as the local news. Faulkner's *Absalom, Absalom!* (1936) traces Sutpen's slaveholding fortune and ideology to the West Indies, where he traveled from poverty in Virginia to make his fortune and then fled during British emancipation. Ellison's *Invisible Man* acknowledges World Wars I and II as deepening racial conflicts when African Americans discovered that their military service did little to change their second-class citizenship at home. Nevertheless, Ellison rejects the internationalism of Communism to offer his ambivalent protest against U.S. policies in the novel.

I argue that modernism's characteristic liberalism survives in postwar fiction in two distinct ways: as a continuation of avant-garde modernism's efforts to represent political and cultural otherness and as a *neoliberalism* intent on neutralizing race, class, and gender/sexuality as real social issues. Both modes of modernist political protest depend on the elaboration of this notion of "internalizing" international issues in U.S. domestic policies. Harper Lee's small-town racial drama is interwoven with transnational dimensions, from the "missionary" work the First Purchase African M. E. Church in Maycomb does in Africa as an extension of its origins in international abolition to the traces of Cherokee culture on which the town of Maycomb is built. The class conflicts of the fractured middle class in Berger's *Neighbors* (1980) draws on Berger's Crazy in Berlin series, in which his characters witness in postwar Germany the collapse of the proletarian utopia crushed both by Hitler and by Allied troops. In Louise Erdrich's fiction about Euroamericans and the Ojibwe, the transnational drama acted out in North American history is that of European imperialism and the genocide of native peoples and destruction of their cultures. In Philip Roth, a new internationalism threatens the comfortable stability of Cold War–era, assimilated Jewish Americans, who ought to have provided the model for other immigrants and oppressed minorities, but somehow have been overwhelmed by the madness of multicultural differences, identity politics, and inassimilable foreign influences. To be sure, Roth's defense of U.S. nationalism seems the closest to contemporary neoliberalism.

Dismissed by the political left as merely an effort to appropriate race, class, and gender/sexuality by the white, male, bourgeois values of "classical" liberalism and demonized by the conservative right as leftist "fellow travelers," postwar liberal writers actually did substantial work in the interests of racial, class, and sexual justice. Other scholars have made similar arguments about avant-garde modernism, in particular Michael North in *The Dialect of Modernism* (1994) and Ann Douglas in *Terrible Honesty: Mongrel Manhattan in the 1920s* (1995), but they have generally exaggerated the abilities of modern liberal writers to internalize and engage the primary issues of race, class, and gender/sexuality.[15] Although I build upon their work, I also contend that modern liberalism always confronts a certain strategic limitation, a horizon that it cannot transcend when it comes to the task of representing and identifying with "otherness." In most of the works discussed in this book, that limitation is the U.S. nation, whose form is presumed to encompass cultural, racial, political, and sexual differences, but only as long they fit the national symbology.

The title of this book, *Afterlives of Modernism*, relies on the double meaning of *afterlives*: the heritage of liberal modernism in the post–World War II era; the shared motif in all of these novels that their authors live through characters whose "other" lives exemplify problems of race, class, and/or gender/sexuality identified by their authors as central to broader problems in U.S. society. Just how the authors manage to channel their characters to reach a better understanding of how social justice might be achieved is one of the organizing principles of this book. Trilling's "liberal imagination" treats uncritically the human ability to imagine another person's situation, especially when it differs from one's own. In the chapters that follow, I interpret both the possibilities and limitations of imaginative identification. What specific interests (race, class, gender/sexuality, nation) shape our identifications, especially in literary works in which characters' virtual individualities may disguise their broader social and political affiliations? We know that the imperial imaginary often works by projecting its own desires onto strange peoples and lands, so powerfully that European imperialists often fabricated people, animals, and lands that did not in fact exist.[16] We also know that well-intentioned efforts to help "save" nineteenth-century indigenous peoples attempted disastrously to remake them in the Euroamerican image. In the simplest possible terms, when is imaginative identification good and when is it bad? And does the timing of such identification change our ethical judgment? If we have today the benefit of historical perspective, then do we interpret differently the imaginative identifications of literature produced in an earlier period? And are there cases, rare to be sure, when such literary identifications transcend their times and places to achieve a measure of universality?

Afterlives of Modernism is divided into two parts: the first part treats U.S. literary texts from the first half of the twentieth century; the second part interprets U.S. novels since the 1960s. My focus on Trilling's *Liberal Imagination* suggests an approximate historical division of the two parts of the book into 1900–1950 and 1950–2000, even though I have chosen to include Ralph Ellison's *Invisible Man* (1952) in the first part, dealing as that novel does with racial issues in the U.S. between World War I and World War II. My choice of works in both parts is not meant to be representative, but exemplary. Whereas many other works and authors might have been considered, the works I have chosen provide good examples of the varieties of liberal responses to race, gender, sexuality, and class in these two broadly conceived historical periods. In addition, each work addresses the modern U.S. nation in relation to transnational issues that prefigure or in some cases coincide with contemporary processes of globalization.

Part 1, Liberal Modernism and Transnationalism, treats four avant-garde modernist U.S. narratives by authors who have had broad, international influence: Gertrude Stein's *Three Lives* (1909), John Dos Passos's *Manhattan Transfer* (1925), William Faulkner's *Absalom, Absalom!* (1936), and Ralph Ellison's *Invisible Man* (1952). The political position of each writer at the time she or he wrote the work considered is not self-evidently "liberal," but each exemplifies some of the key political problems resolved by liberalism in the first half of the twentieth century. Between 1905 and 1906, when she wrote *Three Lives*, Stein lived in Paris supported by an income from her family's investments, managed by her older brother, Michael Stein, after their parents' deaths in 1888. A student of William James's at Harvard, an early supporter of cubism, and a practitioner of avant-garde literary experimentalism, Stein was a cultural radical whose personal politics ranged from her advocacy of lesbianism to such bourgeois avocations as art collecting and gourmet cooking. John Dos Passos is by no means a liberal writer at any time in his career, establishing his reputation in the 1920s with works like *Manhattan Transfer*, deeply critical of class divisions, corporate exploitation of the working class, and sympathetic with the socioeconomic reforms of the Wobblies or IWW (Industrial Workers of the World). Disaffected in the 1930s from both socialism and communism, he was an early critic of Franklin Delano Roosevelt, a vigorous anti-Stalinist, and even in the 1950s a supporter of Senator Joseph McCarthy's anti-Communist crusade. William Faulkner has long been criticized for his "go-slow" statements during the civil rights movement, especially with regard to school integration in the South, even though his literary works deal centrally with slavery and its legacies of social and economic racism as major unresolved problems in the United States. Ralph Ellison's critique of the "Brotherhood" in *Invisible Man* is clearly directed at the Communist Party USA, and his opposition to Black Nationalism is well known. *Invisible Man* has long been praised and criticized for its invocation of the great American literary tradition, especially as it was established by white authors from Emerson to Faulkner. In effect, Ellison is the most obviously liberal of the four modern writers treated in Part 1.

Despite their overt political differences, Stein, Dos Passos, Faulkner, and Ellison in many respects fit Trilling's conception of the "liberal imagination," even as they treat the issues of race, gender/sexuality, and class that he avoids. Each stresses the individual's complexity and inability to be identified with a single group or position. Stein's Melanctha Herbert is and is *not* "Negro," both in terms of her mixed racial background and in her behavior. Melanctha is bisexual, and her characteristic "wandering" represents variously moral laxity, neurosis, and alternative knowledge. Dos Passos's Jimmy Herf identifies more closely with oppressed working-class immigrants than with his own white, middle-class family and friends. Faulkner's Thomas Sutpen scandalizes his white planter neighbors by fraternizing openly with his slaves, and Faulkner compares Sutpen's poor-white background in Tidewater, Virginia, with the oppressed conditions of African-American slaves. Ellison's protagonist remains an "invisible man" not only because of the systemic racism in the modern United States, but also because he cannot be identified in conventional ways: African American, Communist, or Black Nationalist.

Each author argues that the growing transnational forces of second-stage modernization ought to be regulated and organized by the United States, whose history of slavery and immigration suggests unresolved social problems and yet whose democratic principles offer the utopian promise of a society able to accommodate differences. Stein's two German-American characters, Anna and Lena, suffer from discrimination similar to what Melanctha endures, but it is in Stein's imaginary "Bridgepoint," a typical working-class eastern city, not cosmopolitan Paris or London, where Stein insists these problems must be overcome. Dos Passos sets *Manhattan Transfer* in the new metropolitan city of the emerging world-system, and he reminds us that everyday experience in New York mixes local and international news. New York City is obviously Dos Passos's "world-city," the site of either a frustrated or utopian cosmopolitanism. Faulkner's Yoknapatawpha County is deeply provincial in both the "Old" and "New" South, corrupted by a history of slavery and subsequent racism it could sustain only by excluding the outside world. But Faulkner's imaginative history suggests that the American South is the product of outside influences from the original slave trade with Africa to the subsequent slave trade and economic exchanges with the Caribbean. Ellison's *Invisible Man* addresses, only in order to reject, two of the most important international movements in U.S. modernity: international Communism and Black Nationalism, which draws upon Pan-African and diasporic African political and cultural affiliations in the interests of alternative, non-racist societies. Lingering as repressed subtexts are the two world wars, whose racial tensions for returning veterans, especially those of color, motivated Ellison's novel in the first place and yet occupy curiously marginal positions in the text.

Finally, these four modernists suggest that the cosmopolitan individualism their protagonists approach but do not quite achieve is best embodied in the figure of the literary author. All four works display a metafictional dimension that is a hallmark of avant-garde modernism, and in these particular narratives justifies their formal and stylistic experimentalism. Stein's problematic African-American dialect, Dos Passos's stream of consciousness and newspaper headlines, Faulkner's stream of consciousness and multiple narrators, and Ellison's fictional moments of absurdist fantasy revealing the violent contradictions of a deeply racist society—these all suggest authorial powers of the imagination to which their protagonists and readers should aspire. At the same time, these highly self-conscious narratives shatter conventional barriers of race, gender/sexuality, and class and thus enable their authors to achieve certain identifications with their protagonists.

Each work offers a different version of modern cosmopolitanism as an alternative to specific regional, class, ethnic, and sexual or gender identities that trap the fictional protagonists. Neither Anna nor Lena nor Melanctha ever escapes her specific subordination as working-class, minority woman, even though each rebels against these subaltern roles. But Stein's own Jewish-German-American and lesbian identities are combined with her Radcliffe education and European travels to create a cosmopolitanism firmly rooted in U.S. culture. At the end of Dos Passos's *Manhattan Transfer*, Jimmy Herf divorces Ellen, quits journalism, and leaves Manhattan, symbolically reversing the path of Whitman's "Brooklyn Ferry," suggesting his ambition to discover a new "Nature" for modern America, reinventing Whitman's nineteenth-century ideal in *Leaves of Grass*, perhaps emblematized more in the textuality of Dos Passos's novel than in any more transcendental Nature.

Dos Passos's cosmopolitanism remains firmly rooted in the United States, even if his techniques in *Manhattan Transfer* rely upon international modernism, including European cubism and Russian film montage, and would in turn have profound influences on such international modernists as Jean-Paul Sartre. Faulkner concludes *Absalom, Absalom!* with the famous narrative conversation between Quentin Compson and the Canadian, Shreve McCannon, in their cold dormitory room at Harvard. Faulkner's Southern "original sin" of slavery and its legacy of racial and sexual violence is broadened in the novel to encompass Thomas Sutpen's Caribbean experience (and marriage) and McCannon's Canada, one destination of the Underground Railroad and site of many communities founded by fugitive slaves. What appears in the traditional South to be racial "impurity"—the source of the complications in the novel's plot—is Faulkner's ideal of cosmopolitanism when viewed in the broader contexts of the Western Hemisphere. To be sure, Faulkner is not a fully committed advocate of a postnational conception of the Americas, because *Absalom, Absalom!* concludes with Shreve's prediction of an eventual "amalgamation" of the races, full of Shreve's (and perhaps Faulkner's) own racist fantasies.[17]

Ellison's cosmopolitanism in *Invisible Man* is somewhat more difficult to represent than in these other moderns. After all, the protagonist goes "underground" in the final pages, claiming to live both in Dostoevsky's existentialist and the U.S. racial Unconscious. Ellison deleted from the published novel those passages from the merchant seaman Leroy's diary, which the protagonist reads in Mary Rambo's boarding house, in which Leroy opens the broader world of the black Atlantic and exposes the racial provincialism of modern America. In deleting those passages and marginalizing the international significance of the African-American riots in New York City that stemmed in part from African-American veterans' disappointments on their return to racist America, Ellison truncates the cosmopolitanism of his novel, letting it speak primarily through a protagonist finally trapped in the underground of New York City. Yet from his broader, authorial perspective Ellison claims a more encompassing U.S. identity, at least for the aesthetic powers he represents so effectively in the style and form of his novel.

Part 2, Postwar Liberalism and the New Cosmopolitanism, treats novels by three white, middle-class writers and one German-Ojibwe writer who are rarely treated together but whose works suggest the divided political legacy of postwar liberalism. Harper Lee's Pulitzer Prize–winning novel, *To Kill a Mockingbird* (1960), is a well-known liberal critique of race and class relations in the New South, made into a famous film in 1962 directed by Robert Mulligan and starring Gregory Peck as Atticus Finch.[18] Both the novel and film are frequently studied in U.S. high-school English and history classes, but for all their popularity have rarely been treated seriously in scholarly discussions of twentieth-century U.S. culture. Often dismissed as "adolescent" or "popular" literature, *To Kill a Mockingbird* may well have been ignored because its racial politics are rooted in white liberalism. My interpretation links Lee's racial politics with class issues, specifically her criticism of the impact of modern capitalism on Southern society, especially in the changing small towns Lee knew so well. By linking race and class, Lee actually goes far beyond the identity politics that would overtake subsequent debates within various ethnic studies. Yet by focusing primarily on her white protagonists, she also paves the way for the neoliberal appropriation of racial/ethnic discourse, often by invoking related class concerns, as conservatives in the 1990s did in various states by insisting that class deprivation and racial discrimination be linked in such programs as affirmative action.

Much of the appeal of Lee's novel stems from its Southern regionalism, with the town of Maycomb, Alabama, exhibiting the charm of a vanishing Southern ruralism while hiding the ugly history of the displaced Creek people, slavery, and racism. Yet Maycomb is a small town undergoing inevitable changes as a consequence of second-stage modernization, and it cannot avoid contact with transnational forces beyond its region. Aunt Alexandra's missionary group cares for the poor "Mrunas" of Africa, even as white middle-class residents continue to exploit African-American locals. "Dark" strangers, like two traveling salesmen who visit Maycomb oddly selling furs are suspected of being "Syrians" and accused of stealing furniture. Lee employs these transnational touches both to stress the impact of modernization but also to suggest that Americans ought to look first to their own diverse peoples, rather than worrying about the rest of the world. Innocent as Lee's moral advice appears, it is also part of a growing "nationalization" of international issues, internalizing complex foreign-policy issues in a culture of American isolationism.

Thomas Berger's *Neighbors* (1980) and its sequel *The Feud* (1983) also internalize international relations, but they do so after more than three decades of Cold War stalemate between the United States and the Soviet Union. Berger's purpose in focusing on the thinly repressed violence of bourgeois life in suburban America is not to deflect readers from transnational concerns, but to show the continuation of World War II's violence in the Cold War and its unresolved tensions in Western bourgeois economic, political, and social values. Like Harper Lee, Thomas Berger is not a Marxist, but a thoroughly bourgeois writer criticizing the failures of U.S. democracy governed by the middle class. Berger's novels mark the end of the modernist critique of bourgeois values we identify with philosophical and literary existentialism. Continental existentialism was itself a bourgeois philosophy, even when such foundational figures as Jean-Paul Sartre claimed to be leftists, even members of the French Communist Party. Yet Sartrean existentialism rejected *l'esprit de serieux* that Sartre judged to be international Communism's fatal flaw. Berger moves toward a new theory of an aesthetic avant-garde in these two novels that builds upon what he understands as the internal contradictions of late capitalism and bourgeois family values.

The theoretical framework for my interpretation of Berger is drawn from the left aesthetics of the Frankfurt School, notably the work of Theodor Adorno, even though Berger probably had not read any Frankfurt School theorists when he wrote these novels. Nevertheless, much of Berger's criticism of existentialism draws on his own familiarity with the main traditions of European philosophy, which he addresses in his Crazy in Berlin tetralogy, three parts of which were published before *Neighbors*.[19] In *Crazy in Berlin* (1958), Carlo Reinhart rediscovers his German background while serving in the Army of Occupation in postwar Berlin and wrestles with a variety of ideologues, ranging from the African-American officer Splendor Mainwaring to Reinhart's chief nemesis, the Jewish-American Communist Nathan Schild. *Crazy in Berlin* is a devastating critique of liberal pieties and what today would be termed "political correctness," but the novel's conclusion is unmistakably existentialist, in keeping with the U.S. counterculture of 1958: "All we have in this great ruined Berlin of existence, this damp cellar of life, this constant damage in need of repair, is single, lonely, absurd-and-serious selves, and the only villainy is to let them pass beyond earshot."[20]

By the early 1980s, Berger realizes that the existentialist critique of *la vie quotidienne* has been commodified as part of the liberal culture it once challenged. Translating the transnational and interethnic conflicts of *Crazy in Berlin* to suburban America, Berger wants to expose the deep human conflicts thinly covered by liberal tolerance. At the same time, Berger struggles in the early Reagan years to find a post-existentialist critical perspective that can resist the appeal of bourgeois anomie and "property ownership" to those Americans who elected Reagan. Anticipating such ideological slogans of the Reagan Administration as "the ownership society" and "trickle-down economics," Berger looks for aesthetic means to simulate his own "culture wars" well before they became popular in the late 1980s.

Louise Erdrich's *The Last Report on the Miracles at Little No Horse* (2001) and *The Master Butchers Singing Club* (2003) deal centrally with Ojibwe and Euroamerican social and cultural conflicts and relations in the Upper Midwest. Both of these works focus on liberal Euroamericans attempting to cope with the repressed memory of the genocide and terror Native Americans suffered from Euroamerican imperialism. The "back story" of Father Damien Modeste's origins as a white woman who cross-dresses as a priest on the Little No Horse Reservation in *The Last Report* is neatly complemented by the adventures of Fidelis Waldvogel, the German World War I sniper who emigrates to Argus, North Dakota, on the edge of the Ojibwe reservation and begins a successful business as a butcher. As she has done throughout her remarkable career, Erdrich begins with the assumption that native peoples must negotiate Euroamerican culture in order to survive and thus preserve their lifeways, even though her own social and political models are based on pre-national Ojibwe traditions. Erdrich's fiction is thus structured in terms of liberal discourse, often causing more radical Native American writers, such as Leslie Marmon Silko, to criticize Erdrich for capitulating to the dominant culture. But Erdrich successfully refunctions liberalism in ways that make Native American issues unavoidable and thus integral to any social reforms and appeals for political justice invoked by liberal culture. Because these two works mark the beginning of Erdrich's more direct incorporation of Anishinaabeg (Ojibwe language) into her texts, they have particular value in the language politics of the late 1990s and early 2000s.

Lee operates within the rhetoric and ideology of postwar liberalism in the manner of Trilling's liberal imagination, even as she addresses issues of racial conflict that Trilling ignores. Berger recognizes the growing contradictions within the liberal tradition that includes his earlier existentialism, performing a self-criticism that he now directs at the social and personal consequences of a liberal culture that tolerates the conservatism of the Reagan administration. Erdrich recognizes that liberal culture is, as Trilling claimed, "the sole intellectual tradition," increasingly appropriated by neoconservatives to increase their political and economic powers (*LI*, xv). She employs that "liberal imagination" successfully in ways she hopes will transform it from a Eurocentric tradition to one that might include indigenous peoples, their lifeways, and their expressive forms. To accomplish this work, she must *change* liberal culture without slipping into what she considers the impractical extremes of postnational or antinational Native American movements. Erdrich also must change traditional Ojibwe lifeways to include their contact with Catholicism, broader changes in gender and sexual mores, and second-stage modernization. Although she includes Anishinaabeg words and phrases, she still writes primarily in English; her prose fictions resemble Euroamerican novels or short-story collections, but they also draw upon the non-linear forms of narrative she adapts from the oral-formulaic culture of the Ojibwe.

The final chapter turns to one of the most fascinating literary stories of the past fifteen years: Philip Roth's voluminous productivity since the mid-1990s and reinvention of himself as what he considers a "classical liberal" and others have condemned as "neoliberal."[21] The novels he has written in this period are among his most ambitious and politically relevant, as well as technically superb in formal conception and stylistic execution. In *Operation Shylock* (1993), *I Married a Communist* (1998), and *The Plot against America* (2004), Roth levels his liberal rage at neoconservativism in the guise of right-wing defenders of Israel, Cold War McCarthyism, and American neo-Nazis from Charles Lindbergh to George W. Bush. Roth's wrath against right-wing madness is genuine and focused, but it is also recognizably liberal, as *American Pastoral* (1997) and *The Human Stain* (2000) demonstrate. The latter novels mount withering indictments against the 1960s' counter culture and ethnic "political correctness," thus situating Roth in a liberal middle that turns out to be far more conservative than he thinks.

Roth's productivity and popularity in this period are symptomatic of why liberal culture should not be dismissed; its appeal to a wide reading audience, even in an age when traditional literary forms are slowly dying, is greater than ever before. The problem of challenging the "American literary canon"—the "canon debate" was a skirmish in the Culture Wars of the late 1980s and early 1990s—is today far more difficult than scholars once imagined. Today the literary canon is defended vigorously not simply by reactionary scholars, whose works have little public circulation, but by highly visible authors like Roth, who employ their status as public intellectuals both to bolster their claims to inclusion in the American canon and thus to defend cultural canons in general. Because this chapter broadens the discussion of specific authors and literary texts to a wider consideration of literary canons as being crucial to the heritage of political and cultural liberalism, it serves as a conclusion to the book.

The liberal imagination persists in the twenty-first century as a "classical liberalism" and "neo-liberalism" committed to the revival of traditional white, bourgeois privilege and to the repression of social, economic, and cultural diversity. But the liberal imagination has also been redefined by ethnic minority writers and intellectuals, who like Erdrich and Trilling are opposed to the political extremes on the left and the right. Maxine Hong Kingston, Amy Tan, Le Ly Hayslip, Sandra Cisneros, Toni Morrison, Alice Walker, Jamaica Kincaid, James Welch, Bharati Mukherjee, Walter Mosley, and many other U.S. ethnic writers have enjoyed wide popularity thanks to their liberal engagement of the issues of race, gender/sexuality, and class in contemporary U.S. society. Open to the insights of leftist intellectuals, but often vigorously anti-Communist, these writers are also critical of unregulated capitalism while defending small-business opportunities and the principles of free enterprise.

In *Cosmopolitanism: Ethics in a World of Strangers* (2006), the philosopher Kwame Anthony Appiah has developed an explicitly liberal cosmopolitanism more appropriate to the global and multiethnic contexts in which most of us live today.[22] Appiah carefully distinguishes his cosmopolitanism from modern cosmopolitanism of the sort we recognize in James's fictional sophisticates. Leaving their Eurocentrism behind, Appiah proposes a new cosmopolitanism in which individuals might try to imagine other peoples and cultures while respecting regional, religious, linguistic, and historical differences. Incorporating his own experiences growing up in Ghana, his education in London, and his academic career in the United States, Appiah appeals for a liberal cosmopolitanism that is fundamentally postnational. Criticized by both the left and right for his liberalism, which his severest critics attribute to Appiah's life of privilege, his *Cosmopolitanism* nonetheless offers a helpful contrast to Trilling's *Liberal Imagination*.

Although Appiah does not mention Trilling's *Liberal Imagination*, he invokes many of the key features of Trilling's liberalism: the thinking, critical individual who is capable of "negative capability" in his interest in the lives and experiences of people different from him, and the commitment to a certain universality or "human rights" shared by all. The cosmopolitan is thus a psychologically and socially complex individual who learns from his/her experiences; the cosmopolitan takes the entire globe as the field for education, even if his/her particular experiences tie that subject to a specific region or nation. Some of these predicates of Appiah's cosmopolitanism broaden Trilling's, especially the global scope of the cosmopolitan's knowledge. Trilling's liberal individual was singularly "American" and male, drawing on his English and European cultural heritage but superior to other cultures. Thus the "other" cultures to which Trilling's individual was exposed were highly limited and very familiar, whereas Appiah's cultural encounters offer drastic challenges to his (and many readers') social conventions. Finally, as Ghanaian, English, and American, Appiah differs radically from Trilling's restricted idea of the "liberal" intellectual, modeled as it was on his colleagues in the primarily male, white, and Anglo-American circle of the New York Intellectuals.

I won't risk my oppositional stance to modern liberalism by concluding that Appiah's cosmopolitan has "progressed" from Trilling's liberal imagination while preserving many of its chief qualities: they are simply different while sharing some qualities typical of Western bourgeois culture. But it is a difference worth noting at the beginning of this cultural study of the literary representation of "liberalism" from the first decade of the twentieth century to the first decade of the twenty-first century. Kwame Anthony Appiah's position as a Princeton professor of philosophy, addressing a broadly based, English-speaking world on the subject of liberal cosmopolitanism tells us a great deal about the transformation of a political and cultural concept in the past six decades. Whether we understand it as a utopian ideal or as a practical political position, liberalism is a concept we ignore or trivialize at our peril. It continues to shape our values.

Notes

1. Leerom Medovoi, *Rebels: Youth and the Cold War Origins of Identity* (Durham, NC: Duke University Press, 2005).

2. Arthur M. Schlesinger, Jr., *The Age of Jackson* (Boston: Little, Brown and Co., 1945).

3. F. O. Matthiessen, *American Renaissance: Art and Expression in the Age of Emerson and Whitman* (New York: Oxford University Press, 1941).

4. Russell Reising, "Lionel Trilling, *The Liberal Imagination*, and the Emergence of the Cultural Discourse of Anti-Stalinism," *boundary 2*, 20:1 (Spring 1993), pp. 94–124.

5. Lionel Trilling, *The Liberal Imagination: Essays in Literature and Society* (New York: Viking Press, 1950), p. 5.

6. "'Communists in Government Service,' McCarthy Says," February 9, 1950, U.S. Senate History Web site (www.senate.gov).

7. Louis Menand, introduction to *The Liberal Imagination: Essays on Literature and Society* (New York: New York Review of Books, 2008), p. viii.

8. Lionel Trilling, *The Middle of the Journey* (New York: Viking, 1947); Arthur Schlesinger Jr., *The Vital Center: The Politics of Freedom* (Boston: Houghton Mifflin Co., 1949).

9. William Wordsworth, "Preface to the Second Edition of *Lyrical Ballads*," in *Critical Theory since Plato*, rev. ed., ed. Hazard Adams (New York: Harcourt Brace Jovanovich, 1992), p. 441.

10. John Keats, Letter to George and Thomas Keats (Dec. 21, 1817), in *Critical Theory since Plato*, p. 494; Lionel Trilling, introduction to *Selected Letters of John Keats*, ed. Lionel Trilling (New York: Farrar, Straus, and Young, Inc., 1951).

11. F. W. Dupee, *Henry James: His Life and Writings*, 2nd ed. (Garden City, NY: Doubleday and Co., Inc., 1956), pp. 91–92, where Dupee refers to the "international subject." Dupee first published this book in 1951, one year after Trilling's *Liberal Imagination*.

12. See Wendy Graham, *Henry James's Thwarted Love* (Palo Alto: Stanford University Press, 1999), pp. 177–206.

13. On "aesthetic dissent" and "Emersonianism," see John Carlos Rowe, *At Emerson's Tomb: The Politics of Classic American Literature* (New York: Columbia University Press, 1997), pp. 1–3.

14. Allan Bloom, *The Closing of the American Mind* (New York: Simon and Schuster, 1987).

15. Michael North, *The Dialect of Modernism: Race, Language, and Twentieth-Century Literature* (New York: Oxford University Press, 1994); Ann Douglas, *Terrible Honesty: Mongrel Manhattan in the 1920s* (New York: Farrar, Straus and Giroux, 1996).

16. Mary Louise Pratt, *Imperial Eyes: Travel Writing and Transculturation* (New York: Routledge, 1992).

17. William Faulkner, *Absalom, Absalom!* (New York: Random House, 1964), p. 378.

18. *To Kill a Mockingbird*, dir. Robert Mulligan, screenplay by Horton Foote (Universal Pictures, 1962).

19. Berger's tetralogy consists of: *Crazy in Berlin* (1958), *Reinhart in Love* (1962), *Vital Parts* (1970), and *Reinhart's Women* (1981).

20. Thomas Berger, *Crazy in Berlin* (New York: Charles Scribner's Sons, 1958), pp. 319–20.

21. See Ross Posnock, *Philip Roth's Rude Truth: The Art of Immaturity* (Princeton: Princeton University Press, 2006).

22. Kwame Anthony Appiah, *Cosmopolitanism: Ethics in a World of Strangers* (New York: W. W. Norton and Co., 2006).

[I]

LIBERAL MODERNISM AND TRANSNATIONALISM

[1]

NAMING WHAT IS INSIDE: GERTRUDE STEIN'S USE OF NAMES IN *THREE LIVES*

People if you like to believe it can be made by their names. . . . Generally speaking, things once they are named the name does not go on doing anything to them and so why write in nouns. . . . As I say a noun is a name of a thing, and therefore slowly if you feel what is inside that thing you do not call it by the name by which it is known. —Gertrude Stein, "Poetry and Grammar" (1934), *Lectures in America*

THE CURIOUS FIRST NAME Gertrude Stein gives her protagonist, Melanctha Herbert, has attracted little comment, despite the prominence of this name in the title of "Melanctha: Each One as She May," the second and arguably central narrative in *Three Lives* (1909).[1] The critical neglect of this character's name is not surprising, considering Stein's criticism of given names, along with other proper nouns, as conventional uses of language and her insistence that "more and more one does not use nouns."[2] A traditional onomastic study of Gertrude Stein's use of characters' names would thus appear to be a quixotic project, based on an assumption about the symbolic significance of proper nouns antithetical to Stein's avant-garde use of language and its special emphasis on verbal action and stylistic performance.

Yet the significance of the name *Melanctha* offers one part of the solution to the intellectual puzzle concerning Stein's literary representation of race, ethnicity, and sexual identity in *Three Lives*. Was Stein adopting the persona of her African-American protagonist, Melanctha Herbert, for purely aesthetic purposes, thus implicating her version of modernism in other forms of popular blackface minstrelsy? Was Stein exposing the social construction of racial and ethnic identities, perhaps of all identities, and thereby deconstructing *avant le lettre* "race" and "ethnicity" as essential categories? Was Stein equating her own social marginality as a lesbian with that of German immigrants and African Americans, and was this imaginative identification sympathetic or manipulative?

The larger issue, of course, is Stein's relationship to other avant-garde modernists, including the high moderns (Yeats, Pound, Joyce, Eliot, Stevens, for example) and artists of the Harlem Renaissance (Du Bois, Johnson, Cullen, Toomer, and Hurston, for example).[3] Stein's cultural politics are not really in dispute in the period (1905–1906) when she was writing *Three Lives*. In this period, she is certainly a liberal, upper-middle-class U.S. writer, just beginning her career and living as an expatriate in Paris. Stein hardly deserved the "lost generation" tag given to so many of her expatriate U.S. friends in Europe. She chose carefully her foreign place of residence, preferring the cultivated society and language of the French, even though she would write primarily in her own version of English. Certainly she was somewhat of a radical in her public declaration of her lesbian sexual identity, but she was hardly a political radical and by no means even a fellow traveler with international Communists. Living comfortably with her brother, Leo, on an allowance from the family trust, managed ably by their brother, Michael, Stein could buy paintings, indulge her interests in *haute cuisine*, and otherwise appreciate the "civilized" pleasures of pre–World War I Paris.

Stein's expatriatism was not only deeply liberal but was also profoundly U.S. centered, despite her lifelong residence in France, including the period of the Nazi Occupation and the Vichy Government. *Three Lives* exemplifies her inclination to write about U.S. subjects and characters while enjoying the aesthetic distance of France. My purpose in this chapter is not to address the broader significance of these paradoxes for the entire U.S. "lost generation," but instead look more closely at how Stein's liberalism was represented in a distinctively American modernist work produced in the context of European avant-garde modernism, especially that of Paris. In sum, what is the meaning of Stein's particular, perhaps *peculiar*, Euroamerican authorial identity as expressed in one of her best-known narratives, *Three Lives*?

Among the literary modernists at the beginning of the twentieth century, Stein is notable for her rejection of the "surface"-versus-"depth" relationship typical of high modernism. James Joyce's *A Portrait of the Artist as a Young Man*, T. S. Eliot's *The Waste Land*, and Ezra Pound's *Hugh Selwyn Mauberley*, for example, offer quasi-naturalistic representations of the modern alienation and fragmentation of Dublin and London in order to suggest the "deeper meanings" organized by their aesthetic forms and language. Names are connotatively rich in these works—Stephen Dedalus, Tiresias, the Fisher King, Mauberley—and have attracted extensive commentary. While sharing many characteristics of these moderns, Stein stresses consistently writing as a surface without depth. Verbal complexity for Stein is the result not of deep, unconscious, symbolic, or otherwise "hidden" meanings but of the "natural" tendency of language to proliferate, refuse control and form, and exceed the intention of a discrete sender (author) or receiver (reader).[4] Indeed, much of Stein's recent critical reputation as one of the modernists who best anticipates the central concerns of postmodern writing depends on her fundamentally post-structuralist understanding and use of language.[5] Thus the literary symbolism that such post–World War II scholars as William York Tindall and Charles Feidelson Jr. celebrated as a distinctive aesthetic feature of modernism is usually absent from Stein's practice and often rejected in her theoretical statements.[6]

Stein's literary use of Melanctha's given name does not so much involve a "secret" or "hidden" meaning, then, as establish relationships between otherwise discrete "universes of discourse" and by transgressing their boundaries *produce* new meanings and new ways of understanding. As Stein suggests in "Poetry and Grammar" (1934), people's "names . . . generally speaking" do "not go on doing anything to them," so that people are imprisoned or caricatured by such names. When she continues by asking rhetorically, "so why write in nouns," she means that poetic writing should use "names" differently and more in the manner of *verbs*, as if they were actions capable of producing new results, rather than commodifying existing meanings.[7] Stein approximates this idea when she recalls in "Poetry and Grammar" how much she enjoyed "diagramming sentences" when she was in school—a startling, if not preposterous, claim for the reader recalling his or her own agonizing experience with this mind-deadening school exercise. What Stein means, of course, is that poetry offers a radically different way of "diagraming sentences" and thereby "learning grammar" by embodying language, which leads ultimately to what Stein suggests is a "way one is completely possessing something and incidentally one's self" ("Poetry and Grammar," 126; hereafter PG). In Stein's linguistic universe, the "self" becomes visible in and through the acts of expressive language, not by way of a "name" parentally or legally assigned to a "body." The latter is a noun, a proper noun, and "nouns are not really interesting" (PG, 126).

Stein's efforts to distinguish poetic, emancipatory language from ordinary, conventional language led her throughout her career to rely on a wide variety of metaphors to call attention to the ways poetic language invests humans with identity and ordinary language commodifies us. Sometimes these metaphors are closely related, as in Stein's use of "sentence diagraming" in "Poetry and Grammar," in order to force the reader to choose and thereby activate a certain potential for poetic expression or conventionality lurking in every linguistic performance. Two of the metaphors she uses most frequently for the constitutive powers of language are masking and painting, suggesting that language is not just words on a page but encompasses a broader range of signification including visual and iconic representation. In his intriguing interpretation of Stein's "Melanctha" and Picasso's early cubism in *Portrait of Gertrude Stein* (1906) and *Les Demoiselles d'Avignon* (1907), Michael North has argued that early literary and visual modernism relied on rhetorical and pictorial versions of "masking" drawn from the folk art of African masks: "Placing a painted mask over his naturalistic portrait [of Gertrude Stein], Picasso duplicates the linguistic mask Stein was devising for herself. By rewriting her own story for black characters, Stein anticipates, and perhaps even motivates, Picasso's use of African masks in *Les Demoiselles d'Avignon*. In each case, in painting and in literature, the step away from conventional verisimilitude into abstraction is accomplished by a figurative change of race."[8] As North implies elsewhere in his discussion of "Melanctha," a name is also a kind of verbal mask, compatible with the early modernists' emphases on "personae, metamorphoses, doubles, and mythic parallels," all of which are metonymies for literary representation itself as a masked or disguised "doubling."[9]

In the two framing narratives of *Three Lives*, "The Good Anna" and "The Gentle Lena," the characters' names seem obviously drawn from the German-American immigrant communities that neighbor and interact with the Irish- and Italian-American communities in which the dramatic actions are explicitly set. Anna Federner and Lena Mainz are the protagonists of their respective narratives, and they are surrounded by characters with similarly explicit German names: Mrs. Lehntman, Mrs. Drehten, Bertha Haydon, and Herman Kreder. Although Stein does not comment on Melanctha Herbert's given name, Stein's emphasis on Melanctha's racial hybridity—"She had not been raised like Rose [Johnson] by white folks but then she had been half made with real white blood"—makes it difficult for the reader to trace her given name to any specific regional or ethnic custom of naming.[10] The dramatic actions of all three narratives are set in the fictional "Bridgepoint," which is usually assumed to be Baltimore, Maryland, where Stein was attending Johns Hopkins Medical School and claims to have first encountered the real-life models for her central characters in *Three Lives*.[11] Stein fictionalizes and abstracts Bridgepoint so that it could be a city anywhere on the Eastern seaboard, and she enacts her dramas in modern, albeit unspecified, times probably intended to be proximate with Stein's composition of the stories between 1905 and 1907.[12]

One of Stein's possible purposes in making Melanctha Herbert "a graceful, pale yellow, intelligent, attractive negress" is to expose the social fiction of racial or ethnic identity by stressing the process of hybridity in the "making" of any "American" (*Three Lives*, 78; hereafter *TL*). The narrator may refer to Melanctha's "real white blood," but she is only "half made" with it. The artifice of the phrase "real white blood" suggests an ironic comment on racial purity, which anticipates Stein's association of "white" with a patriarchal ideology in *Tender Buttons* (1914): "Suppose a man a realistic expression of resolute reliability suggests pleasing itself white all white."[13] The reader tempted to conclude that Melanctha's intelligence comes from her "real white blood" learns from Rose Johnson that "Melanctha . . . is so bright and learned so much in school, she ain't no common nigger . . . , though she ain't got no husband to be married to like I am to Sam Johnson" (*TL*, 78). Rose herself claims, "I ain't no common nigger, . . . for I was raised by white folks" (*TL*, 78). Even as Rose Johnson endorses popular racist clichés, she calls attention to the fact that the distinction between "a common nigger" and a respectable person depends on environmental influences, like proper upbringing "by white folks," education, and marriage. To be sure, the attentive reader does not miss Stein's association of a good education and marriage with white values, a point she will make even more tellingly in her characterization of Melanctha's relationship with Dr. Jeff Campbell.

In the two other narratives in *Three Lives*, Stein also challenges prevailing stereotypes of African-American and immigrant identities as racially or ethnically hereditary or essential. She makes several connections between her German-American protagonists and African Americans, sometimes by way of their shared working-class conditions and at other times in terms of their racial coloring. Thus Lena Mainz's American cousins hate her, "who was to them, little better than a nigger" and "as far below them as were Italian or Negro workmen" (*TL*, 223, 222). Stein describes Lena as "brown," but distinguishes her from "the yellow or the red or the chocolate brown of sun burned countries," but in the very course of making this seemingly essentialist contrast Stein stresses the artifice of color: "[B]ut brown with the clear colour laid flat on the light toned skin beneath, the plain, spare brown that makes it right to have been made with hazel eyes" (*TL*, 218). Even Stein's racialization of regions ("sun burned countries") suggests the variety of colors of the peoples inhabiting them (yellow, red, chocolate brown), as if to cause the reader to look with new eyes on the variety of peoples living *anywhere*.

In *Tender Buttons*, Stein uses colors to "paint" or compose objects and spaces in relationship to other aspects of her verbal compositions or collages; color is thus performative and verb-like, rather than serving adjectivally to designate some essential characteristic of a thing, a space, a person. One of the objects she represents in *Tender Buttons* is "A Piece of Coffee": "A single image is not splendor. Dirty is yellow. A sign of more in not mentioned" (*Tender Buttons*, 463; hereafter *TB*). Dangerous as the effort is to "translate" Stein's verbal assemblages, I want to suggest that in this passage she departs from what would become the Imagists' stress on the discreteness of the poetic image—"an intellectual and emotional complex presented in an instant of time," as Pound defined it[14]—to call attention to the ways a successful "image" always exceeds its boundaries, already includes other colors (as well as shapes and connotations), in order to signify what lies prior to and beyond it in the "not mentioned." One characteristic of this anti-formal "image" is its mixture of colors, which Stein borrows from the painter's technique of combining colors both on the palette and then layering them on a canvas to get precisely the right effect. "A piece of coffee is not a detainer. The resemblance to yellow is dirtier and distincter. The clean mixture is whiter and not coal color, never more coal color than altogether" (*TB*, 463). Perhaps Stein is representing in "A Piece of Coffee" spilled coffee (with cream?) on the dining-room table ("A place in no new table"), which is a connotation reinforced by the apparent pun on the English "detain" and the French "à détenir." The French infinitive can be used as a cognate of the English "detain," but it can also mean to "withhold, hold, or possess," and these different meanings combine both the coffee outside its cup (having materialized as a stain) and the tendency of language always to defer and imply another connotation. Just as she must use two different languages to express the true qualities of "a piece of coffee," so Stein struggles to approximate the color of the stain by claiming that its approximation to "yellow is dirtier and distincter," being "whiter" than that and not the underlying "coal color" of black coffee (463). My point is not to offer a "translation" of Stein's prose here, which would be contrary to the aesthetic purpose of *Tender Buttons*, but to suggest what Stein knew well from painters: that any color's apparent singularity is the result of many different characteristics, some of which might be other colors. To be sure, there is nothing racial in her discussion of colors in this passage from *Tender Buttons*, but the mixture of "whiter" and "not coal color" to which she refers anticipates the famous episode in Ralph Ellison's *Invisible Man* when his protagonist discovers while working at Liberty Paints that white paint includes ten drops of black liquid, in order to produce what his boss terms "the purest white that can be found. . . . This batch right here is heading for a national monument!"[15]

Thus Stein's interesting description in "The Gentle Lena" of Lena Mainz's skin color as if it were paint on canvas anticipates Stein's poetic uses of color in *Tender Buttons* while calling attention to the "compositional" quality of racial designations. In this instance, Stein's verbal portraiture reminds us explicitly of the stories told first by Stein and repeated in various contexts by many scholars about how Cézanne's portrait *Mme. Cézanne, 1881* inspired her to write *Three Lives*. Stein and her brother Leo purchased the portrait from the Parisian art dealer Vollard in 1904. As Stein writes in *The Autobiography of Alice B. Toklas*: "It was an important purchase, because in looking and looking at this picture Gertrude Stein wrote Three Lives. She had begun not long before as an exercise in literature to translate Flaubert's Trois Contes and then she had this Cézanne and she looked at it and under its stimulus she wrote Three Lives" (*The Autobiography of Alice B. Toklas*, 39; hereafter *ABT*). Reclining in a red, high-backed chair and holding a fan, Mme. Cézanne turns her face one quarter of a turn toward the viewer and her downturned mouth, short brown hair, and round face suggest a mask, accentuated by the white paint used to frame the face down the left and up the right sides. Abandoning a realistic shadow effect on the right-hand side of the face, except for the barest suggestion in the right-hand corner of the mouth, Cézanne makes the face stand out starkly from the red chair and his wife's green skirt, an effect intensified by the relationship between her white blouse and its collar with the white paint laid on her face. Almost bearded by the white paint, the rest of the face and neck are painted in contrasting flesh tones. The mask-like quality of Mme. Cézanne's face lends it a mysterious quality, which nearly mocks the conventions of femininity in the barely visible, closed fan and the green skirt and matching jacket.[16]

Stein observes that "the Cézanne portrait had not seemed natural it had taken her some time to feel it was natural," anticipating remarks she would make in later writings, notably "Composition as Explanation," regarding the curious combination of the artificial and the natural in Stein's own work.[17] The art-dealer Vollard "said of course ordinarily a portrait of a woman always is more expensive than a portrait of a man but, said he looking at the picture very carefully, I suppose with Cézanne it does not make any difference" (*ABT*, 38). This portrait occupies a singular place in what would become Stein's significant collection of modern art. In the many photographs of Stein in her Paris residence at 27 rue de Fleurus, notably those taken by Man Ray, the portrait often figures prominently, hanging just above Stein seated in her chair by the fire or above Stein at her long worktable in her study. However we interpret Stein's remarks about *Mme. Cézanne, 1881*, they suggest Stein's identification with the style of the painting and its transgression of conventional femininity.

Picasso must have noticed the resemblance between Cézanne's portrait and Stein, at least as Picasso imagined her, because his 1906 *Portrait of Gertrude Stein* is heavily influenced by Cézanne's portrait. The two figures share short, brown hair and white blouse and collar. The whitened face of Mme. Cézanne is replaced by the famous African-inspired "mask" Picasso composed for Stein's face, and the red touch on Mme. Cézanne's lips is displaced to a red brooch holding together Stein's blouse. Mme. Cézanne's fan has vanished from Picasso's Stein, but the hands in both portraits are posed in virtual mirror images of each other.[18] The story of how Stein posed for "some eighty or ninety sittings" for Picasso, only to have him paint out her face before leaving for Spain, then returning to Paris to paint quickly the African-inspired "mask" of her face in the final portrait, was made legendary by Stein herself in *The Autobiography of Alice B. Toklas* (*ABT*, 53). Stein connects Picasso's completion of her portrait with his transition to cubism and her own "invention" of literary modernism:

> It had been a fruitful winter. In the long struggle with the portrait of Gertrude Stein, Picasso passed from the Harlequin, the charming early italian period to the intensive struggle which was to end in cubism. Gertrude Stein had written the story of Melanctha the negress, the second story of Three Lives, which was the first definite step away from the nineteenth century and into the twentieth century in literature. (*ABT*, 61)

Stein also stresses how she "meditated and made the sentences . . . of her negro story Melanctha Herbert" on her walk home from sessions posing for Picasso and how "the poignant incidents she wove into the life of Melanctha were often these she noticed in walking down the hill from the rue Ravignan," where Picasso's Paris studio was located (*ABT*, 56).

Michael North interprets Stein's celebrated account of modernism's beginnings in the twinned revolutions of literature and painting as the origin of a "calligraphy" shared by verbal and visual images and thus tacitly an anticipation of Derridean *écriture* and the more general poststructuralist "language model." What North finds extraordinary is the role of African forms, especially that of the mask, in exposing the conventionality of all representational systems, whether pictorial or visual: "The African mask is convention embodied, the sign of signs. As such, it inaugurates Western abstraction by exposing the conventional nature of all art. Instead of revealing what lies behind the face, the mask grinningly exposes a void where the face should be."[19] In this context, Stein's experimentalism in "Melanctha" challenges a conventional, naturalistic literary portrait of Melanctha Herbert's ethnic dialect and identity. For Stein, language performs the work of visual identification, and she uses words to "shape" the face of her character, Melanctha. In this way, Stein's style replaces Melanctha's character with that of the author, who relies on the forms of language she is able to imagine and employ, just as Pablo Picasso depends on his cubist forms.

Stein's use of Melanctha Herbert as one persona for Stein's own literary identity poses a wide range of problems, but I want to state clearly that what "inspired" Stein (and perhaps Picasso, or at least Stein's version of Picasso) in Cézanne's *Mme Cézanne, 1881*, was the relationship among the artificially "colored," mask-like quality of Madame Cézanne's painted face, the conventionality of "proper names" and thus identities, and language as a convention-based system.[20] In what would become typical of the high-modernist aesthetic, Stein argues in *Three Lives* that only the deformation or "estrangement" accomplished by the originality of literary language enables linguistic conventionality—and the related conventions of race, gender, sexuality, and other forms of identification—to become "visible" and change thus possible. Like other moderns, Stein claims for such strategic distortion—Russian Formalist *ostranenie* and later Brechtian *Verfremdungseffekt*—a special cognitive dimension, so that modern art enables us to know differently than the customary practices of technocratic rationality so abhorred and envied by the cultural avant-garde.

Melanctha's "learning" and special "knowledge" are themes that Stein uses to organize the narrative, and Stein moves the reader toward the conclusion that Melanctha's mysterious appeal for many characters (and the cause of many of Melanctha's personal problems) has to do with her alternative knowledge. Sometimes this knowledge is represented as simply a coded way of describing her sexual openness with men and women—a Biblical "knowledge" that Stein represents also with the term "wandering." At other times, Melanctha's special knowledge is associated with religion, which Stein suggests Melanctha gradually learns "how to use": "Rose Johnson and Melanctha Herbert had first met, one night, at church. Rose Johnson did not care much for religion. She had not enough emotion to be really roused by a revival. Melanctha Herbert had not come yet to know how to use religion" (*TL*, 79). This passage occurs early in the story, when Stein is still introducing Rose and Melanctha to the reader. Much later in the narrative, Dr. Jeff Campbell, who is strongly attracted to Melanctha but profoundly confused by her behavior as well as his desire for her, compares his love for her with a religious feeling:

> "And then certainly sometimes, Melanctha, you certainly is all a different creature, and sometimes then there comes out in you what is certainly a thing, like a real beauty. I certainly, Melanctha, never can tell just how it is that it comes so lovely. Seems to me when it comes it's got a real sweetness, that is more wonderful than a pure flower, and a gentleness, that is more

tender than the sunshine, and a kindness, that makes one feel like summer, and then a way to know, that makes everything all over, and all that, and it does certainly seem to be real for the little while it's lasting, for the little while that I can surely see it, and it gives me to feel like I certainly had got real religion." (*TL*, 126)

Jeff Campbell, the medical doctor, represents in most of the narrative the aspirations of middle-class African Americans to socio-economic status as respected professionals. Appealing to the conventions of enlightenment rationality as his standards for judging experience, he usually typifies African Americans who imitate white culture and favor assimilation. In this passage, however, Jeff Campbell approaches the "wandering" rhetoric both of Melanctha's own dialogue and Stein's prose style. In his discussion of Melanctha *as* religion, rather than merely a devout representative of the church, he reminds us of the Greek classical association of divinity with "wandering" as suggested by the term for philosophical truth, *aletheia*, which is derived from the Greek roots *alea* and *thea* and may be approximately translated as the "wandering divine."[21]

Lisa Ruddick has traced the influence of Stein's teacher William James on *Three Lives*, especially with respect to Stein's use of the term *wandering*. Ruddick cites James's discussion of "mind-wandering" and "wandering attention" in his *Psychology: The Briefer Course* as typical of children and some adults who never outgrow "this sensitiveness to immediately exciting sensorial stimuli" and for whom "perceptual life continues to consist of immediate, aimless sensation."[22] As Ruddick points out, "this description fits the case of Stein's Melanctha" extremely well, but with the difference that Stein does not appear to treat Melanctha as a case of arrested development but rather as a character with different epistemological methods.[23] Dr. Jeff Campbell is the "model of mental growth, conceived in Jamesian terms," but Stein's Melanctha obviously baffles Jeff and represents an alternative knowledge that for Stein goes beyond the traditional rationalism and its psychological models represented by William James.[24] For Ruddick, Stein develops in Melanctha special sensitivities to the body, its sensuous and affective processes, and other modes of knowing "distinct from James's instrumental knowledge."[25] Quoting one of Stein's notebooks for *The Making of Americans*, Ruddick refers to what Stein considered her own "Rabelaisian, nigger abandonment."[26]

Stein's deliberate vulgarization of her own identification with a racial alter ego is typical of many white moderns' desires for the adventure of "passing" and the identification of their own avant-gardism with non-European figures and experiences. Michael North points out: "Like her friend [Carl] Van Vechten, who began passing for black as an undergraduate, Stein had toyed with such notions from the time of her days at Radcliffe. The 'dark-skinned' alter ago named Hortense Sänger who appears in one of the themes she wrote there lives a life that is strangely mirrored in the racial genre pieces written the day before and the day after."[27] For Stein, the fantasy of "passing" is realized in her fictional character, Melanctha, and the racialized German immigrant characters, Anna and Lena. Melanctha takes form as a character from Stein's critique of racial essentialism, claims for the "compositional" aspects of "color" in both people and things, and the extension of these ideas to encompass identity as a "mask" or persona either imposed on the subject or *performed* by her. In all of these respects, of course, Melanctha serves as Stein's double, a fictional projection of Stein's aesthetic aims and authorial identity.

Stein's gestures at imaginary racial "passing" include the alternative knowledge she terms "wandering" in "Melanctha." Cynthia Ann Sarver has argued that Stein may well be alluding to W. E. B. Du Bois's notion of African-American "double consciousness," which he uses to begin *The Souls of Black Folk* (1903), "published just one year before Stein began writing 'Melanctha.'"[28] Although there is no solid evidence Stein ever read Du Bois's writings, the connection between *The Souls of Black Folk* and *Three Lives* is especially intriguing because William James had taught both Du Bois and Stein. Sarver suggests that Du Bois's "double consciousness" offers a critical reading of James's conception of self-consciousness in *Principles of Psychology* (1890) by arguing that James's "true self-consciousness" is "a privilege Negroes cannot . . . enjoy because of their constant awareness of the visibility of their racialized bodies and, hence, their inability to escape fully the object status of 'Me.'"[29] Of course, Du Bois gives "double consciousness" an appropriately double meaning, suggesting that cultural schizophrenia can also be understood as special knowledge: "The Negro is . . . born with a veil, and gifted with second-sight in this American world" and what might seem to some "like the absence of power, like weakness" is also "not weakness," but it is "the contradiction of double aims."[30] Whether or not Stein alludes directly to "double consciousness" by way of Melanctha's "wandering," there are close relations between Du Bois's effort to transform "the black man's turning hither and thither in hesitant and doubtful striving" into a positive ability to understand "doubly" and Stein's attempt to transform Melanctha's apparent irresponsibility into a new, anti-rational epistemology.[31]

These preliminary interpretations of *Three Lives* and its place in Stein's developing avant-garde poetics in the first decades of the twentieth century are necessary to contextualize the onomastic significance of Melanctha's name. It is a scholarly commonplace to note that Melanctha's given name combines the Greek roots for black, *melas* and *melanos*, with the Greek root for earth (as in "ground"), *chthon*. Many of the interpretations of the story as a racist fantasy by a high-modernist white author depend on the racial essentialism suggested by this odd name. On the other hand, Stein's associations of Melanctha with alternative knowledge, epistemological "wandering," and some unconventional religious sense or spirituality encourage the learned reader to trace her given name back to Philipp Melancthon (also spelled "Melanchthon") (1497–1560), the German reformer, theologian, and educator, who was Martin Luther's friend and collaborator in the Protestant Reformation. Born Philipp Schwarzerd ("black earth"), he adopted the name "Melancthon" as a testament to his classical learning and heritage. His teacher at the Pforzheim Latin School, Johannes Reuchlin, himself a famed Hebraist and humanist, first used this Greek version of Philipp's surname in his dedication of a Greek grammar he gave to the twelve-year-old student in 1509, but Philipp did not formally adopt the name until 1531, after having tried several other variants, such as *Pullisolus* and *Melas Brittanus*. Even in Melancthon's classical humanist circles and times, his adopted name was repeatedly misspelled and mispronounced.[32]

The simplest identification of Stein's Melanctha with the most obvious historical figure to whom her name alludes is, then, through the meaning of a name: "black earth," which denotes a natural essence. The allusion appears to reinforce a tendency in Stein's narrative to rely on certain double meanings that divide the reader's understanding between the matter-of-fact, highly racialized experiences of the characters and the sophisticated meaning built into the narrative by the literate, upper-middle-class author. This impression is reinforced by a narrative style that imitates African-American vernacular speech patterns, even though it cannot be said to specify a regional or otherwise identifiable African-American dialect. The fact that no one in the dramatic action comments on Melanctha's name suggests that its historical significance is reserved for the sophisticated, rather than casual, reader.

The double meaning of Melanctha's name recalls antebellum practices by the white slavocracy of naming slaves after national leaders such as George Washington or Thomas Jefferson, or classical figures such as Caesar or Cato, to lend an aura of grandeur to the white owner's plantation while further demeaning his slaves. Eugene Genovese points out that southern slaves "rarely" chose themselves "those pompous, classical, or comical names which masters sometimes inflicted on them. Very few Caesars, Catos, and Pompeys survived the war; the freedmen divested themselves of these names so quickly that one wonders if they had ever used them among themselves in the quarters."[33] The Greek root of *Melanctha*, even though it involves the potentially racist pun on "black earth," is not characteristic of such slave names. Indeed, the oddity of the name recalls the fact that many of the strange or unusual slave names were selected by slaves themselves and had "African origins," probably as ways of resisting white culture.[34] Stein seems to underscore the point that Melanctha is *not* a slave name by contrasting this proper noun with Dr. Jeff Campbell's full given name, Jefferson, which Stein uses for apparent variation on several occasions in referring to: Dr. Jeff Campbell, Jefferson, Jeff, Campbell, et al.[35] In short, Stein suggests thereby that Jeff Campbell's uncritical endorsement of the dominant culture's scientific epistemology, especially his insistence on *understanding*, is a sort of racial sell-out that Melanctha rejects.

Stein may not succumb to the racism of exploiting pretentious and comical slave names, but she still seems to be employing a double, even duplicitous, style much like Stephen Crane's mock-heroic in his Bowery stories, such as "Maggie: A Girl of the Streets" and "George's Mother."[36] Critics have commented frequently on this division between dramatic content and narrative tone since *Three Lives* was privately published in 1909. Marianne De Koven terms the narrative voice "consciously naive" and stresses the disparity between its "innocent, straightforward, mildly jolly" tone and the "often grotesque, sinister, ridiculous" circumstances facing these three women.[37] In fact, the narrative voice in all three stories seems distant and detached from the obviously terrible fates her three protagonists must endure, rather than naive or comic in tone. Despite their claims to "good educations," Rose Johnson, Melanctha Herbert, and even Dr. Jeff Campbell fall short of the elite education and opportunities shared by Stein and her ideal reader.

However inadequate the formal educations of the characters in "Melanctha," they far exceed the educational levels of Anna Federner in "The Good Anna" and Lena (née Mainz) Kreder in "The Gentle Lena." In choosing for herself an alter ego or persona, Stein certainly does not select either Anna or Lena, despite the German heritage they share with her. Several recent critics have emphasized the literary ways Stein transforms her own scientific inclinations as a medical student into the character Dr. Jefferson Campbell, pitting his rationality against the "alternative" knowledge of Melanctha Herbert.[38] In part relying on their interpretation of "Melanctha" as a rewriting of Stein's novel about a lesbian triangle, *Q.E.D.*, written in 1903, these critics stress Stein's need to "work through" her unresolved psychological response to her frustrated affair with May Bookstaver, thereby reinforcing the popular image of Stein as "mannish" or "butch."[39]

Useful as such critical approaches have been in emphasizing the relationship between the neglected *Q.E.D.* and *Three Lives*, they distract us from the racial and ethnic issues in the latter work. First, they mistakenly reduce *Q.E.D.* to Stein's biographical relationship with May Bookstaver, assuming that Adele is Stein and Helen Thomas is May. Yet all three women characters in *Q.E.D.* display characteristics of Stein's actual and ideal self-conception around 1903. The fictionalization in *Q.E.D.* involves just this sort of "splitting" of authorial identity into multiple characters, some of whom are clearly modeled on Stein's friends and lovers but who are also versions of Stein's projected subjectivity. Just what Adele, Mabel Neathe, and Helen Thomas have in common seems to describe Stein's self-conscious identity at the time and to anticipate that which links the otherwise diverse protagonists of *Three Lives*: "They were distinctly American but each one at the same time bore definitely the stamp of one of the older civilisations, incomplete and frustrated in this American version but still always insistent" (*Q.E.D.*, 4).

The second problem with the critical treatment of "Melanctha" as a rewriting of *Q.E.D.* is the tendency to interpret Dr. Jeff Campbell as the former text's "version" of Adele in *Q.E.D.* Yet neither narrative emphasizes an overtly "butch-femme" narrative of lesbian relations. Adele and Helen Thomas are different character types, but each is at certain times vulnerable and at other times self-assertive. By the same token, Dr. Jeff Campbell's confidence in scientific rationality conventionally represents the assumptions of middle-class, modern culture, including its patriarchal attitudes. While agreeing with previous critics who view Jeff Campbell as Stein's alter ego in "Melanctha," Michael North suggests a more complex approach to this problem by insisting upon Stein's sexual ambiguity and its influence on her own methods of composition. Citing Picasso's reference to Stein as "hommesse" and his representation of her in his *Portrait of Gertrude Stein* in the form of "a physical bulk and power not at all conventionally feminine," North concludes that such references underscore Stein's "sexual ambiguity," rather than her masculinity or femininity.[40] North's hint allows me to conclude that Stein represents herself in *Three Lives* by way of a fictional "splitting," already evident in *Q.E.D.*, in which characteristics, tendencies, and idealizations of her identity are variously represented in all of the characters, but especially the protagonists.

There is yet a third problem raised by the critical association of "Melanctha" with *Q.E.D.* that bears directly on the use of high-cultural allusions and symbolic expression. The use of the African-American contexts in "Melanctha" to work out a coded story about the special "knowledge" that comes from lesbian-feminist identity and relations risks either equating the minority status of the racial and homosexual subject or simply appropriating racial situations for a coded lesbian narrative in a variation of the white minstrelsy so prevalent in this period of U.S. culture. Allusion and symbolic representation, especially to high-cultural pretexts, would only reinforce this tendency of the upper-middle-class lesbian narrative in *Q.E.D.* to exploit the African-American working-class contexts of "Melanctha" and contribute as egregiously as many popular "blackface" narratives of the late nineteenth and early twentieth centuries did to the cultural colonization of African Americans.

Q.E.D. relies in many ways on the pretenses typical of many first novels, including rather clumsy high-cultural allusions. At the end of Book 1, for example, Adele shares a wordless epiphany with a young Spanish woman in Granada, then lies on "the ground reading again Dante's *Vita Nuova*," which is "now divinely illuminated" (*Q.E.D.*, 14). In Book

3, Adele compares her relationship with Helen to Henry James's Milly Theale and Kate Croy in the recently published *The Wings of the Dove* (1902): "Like Kate Croy she [Helen] would tell me 'I shall sacrifice nothing and nobody' and thats just her situation she wants and will try for everything, and hang it all, I am so fond of her and do somehow so much believe in her that I am willing to help as far as within me lies" (*Q.E.D.*, 54). Although Stein provides here an insightful and extremely early interpretation of the gay subtext in James's novel, the allusion is forced and pretentious. In such cases, Stein is far too anxious to display her learning and be taken for a "cultured" writer. Traveling through Europe, dawdling at the Alhambra and in Granada, taking tea in Florence, the characters of *Q.E.D.* are self-indulgent and superficially cosmopolitan.

Three Lives is remarkably free of literary allusions, symbolic expressions, and displays of learning, which is why the knowledge represented by Melanctha's "wandering" seems a genuine alternative to traditional rationality. Unlike high-modern contemporaries like Pound, Eliot, and Joyce, each of whom would insist on redirecting the reader from conventional knowledge to the alternative canons of knowledge they variously advocated, Stein represents in Melanctha a "wandering" that departs significantly from the Euroamerican traditions of knowledge. In the rare cases when Stein does make literary allusions in *Three Lives*, the reader is disturbed and the allusion itself seems nearly inappropriate. As far as I can tell, there are only three major literary references in *Three Lives*: the work's French epigraph from Jules Laforgue, roughly translated, "Then I am unhappy, and it is neither my fault nor the fault of life" (*TL*, 66; my translation); a single use of the English idiom "Struldbrug," drawn from Swift's *Gulliver's Travels*, in reference to "a dog that's old and so cut off from all its world of struggle, is like a dreary, deathless Struldbrug, the dreary dragger on of death through life" in "The Good Anna" (*TL*, 68); and the given name "Melanctha."[41] Taken together, the three allusions appear to work against Stein's innovative intentions in *Three Lives* to provide a verbal account of human lives that are subtle and nuanced but without depths, symbolic secrets, or profundities. In general, Stein offers the reader three narratives about three characters without essences but whose lives still matter.

Even if the allusions are contrary to Stein's intention of representing simple yet significant lives, I still do not wish to dismiss them as simply aesthetic mistakes. It is quite possible that they are poor choices, but they have significance for that very reason, even if only to suggest how Stein struggled in such early works as *Q.E.D.* and *Three Lives* to strip her prose of the allusive mode characteristic of late Victorian (Robert Browning), decadent (Wilde and Swinburne), and Anglo-Irish symbolist (George Moore, W. B. Yeats, early T. S. Eliot) styles. As mistakes, these allusions help us judge Stein's attitude toward her narrative voice and its apparent distance from her humble subjects. Her epigraph from Jules Laforgue in the original French smacks of the mock-heroic strategies of Stephen Crane I mentioned earlier; neither the French symbolist Laforgue nor his metaphysical skepticism are likely to be familiar to the German-American or African-American communities of Bridgepoint. Her affected reference to the aging dog as an instance of Swiftian "Struldbruggery" has a similar effect and recalls the overly literate prose in *Q.E.D.*, even as the reference reminds us of Stein's lifelong affection for dogs. Both allusions fail, because they are not integrated into the larger narrative development or argument. They do not help the reader understand better the significance of the three lives represented; they hold those characters at a distance, nearly in contempt. The possible allusion to Philipp Melancthon also threatens to widen the distance between these characters and their author and readers, but it differs from the other two insofar as it comments directly on the narrative in which it appears and even suggests ways to link "Melanctha" with "The Good Anna" and "The Gentle Lena."

With these problems and contexts in mind, then, I want to return to the possible significance of the allusion in Melanctha Herbert's name to Philipp Melancthon and more generally to the Protestant Reformation and Melancthon's contributions to German educational reform. Melancthon came to Wittenberg University, where he first met Luther, in order to teach Greek, and four days after his arrival delivered an inaugural address, *De corrigendis adolescentiae studiis* (*On Correcting the Studies of Youth*), in which he defended classical learning as basic to modern education, responding in part to students' protests that Greek and Hebrew were not educationally useful.[42] In general, Philipp Melancthon is associated with the fusion of Renaissance humanism with Christian theology and Scripture. As a humanist, he drew on the Aristotelian tradition, but as a theologian he insisted upon the limits of human rationality and thus the need for faith. His defense of Scripture against the authority of the Pope laid the foundation for the Protestant Reformation, and his lectures on St. Paul's Epistle to the Romans (1521), *Loci communes rerum theologicarum seu hypotyposes theologicae* (*Commonplaces of Theology*), was a sixteenth-century bestseller and established him as a leader of the Reformation. Although this work is famous for its rigorous presentation of reformation theology, it also expresses well Melancthon's lifelong commitment to a mystical appreciation of God's transcendence of human reason, especially in the often quoted sentence: "We would do better to worship the mysteries of the Godhead than research them."[43]

Philipp Melancthon's greatest achievements were the founding of preparatory schools and the reorganization of Germany's university systems, which earned him the informal title of "Preceptor of Germany." His *Unterricht der Visitatoren* (*Instructions for Visitors*) of 1528 served as a guide for inspectors of religious and educational conditions in Saxony and as a model for other German principalities. Enacted into law in Saxony, Melancthon's plan established the Protestant public school system. By 1555 more than 135 plans based on his model had appeared and more than fifty cities had requested his help in founding their schools. He helped to establish the universities of Marburg, Königsberg, and Jena and instituted reforms at Greifswald, Wittenberg, Cologne, Tübingen, Leipzig, Heidelberg, Rostock, and Frankfurt.[44] In many respects, the modern "Enlightenment" German university we identify with Immanuel Kant (Königsberg) and G. W. F. Hegel (Jena and University of Berlin), to which the U.S. university model of liberal education is so indebted, is traceable back to Melancthon's educational reforms.

Reading the general outlines of Melancthon's sixteenth-century educational reforms in Germany in terms of Melanctha Herbert's alternative knowledge in the early-twentieth-century United States, we might draw more positive conclusions about Stein's allusion than the coding of her otherwise "naturalist" narrative about African Americans at first suggests. Philipp Melancthon brought together religion and humanism in ways that coordinated their respective contributions to what he considered the well-educated subject. In Stein's story, Dr. Jeff Campbell is obviously too captivated by the rational principles of white middle-class society and its work ethic. What attracts him to and at times repels him from Melanctha is her alternative knowledge of sexual and interpersonal relations, human emotions, and life itself. As Jean Toomer would represent

African-American women in *Cane* (1923), so Stein uses Melanctha to epitomize a certain contact with "Nature," including our emotional and affective natures, that today we condemn rightly as racial and gender essentialisms.[45] Nevertheless, Stein gathers together in the term *wandering* all the different affective, sexual, linguistic, and cognitive practices that cannot be controlled or understood by ruling-class reason.

The history of the African-American Church as a place of spiritual, political, and communal organization suggests that African-American religion has supported this sort of "alternative" knowledge, albeit without the emphasis on *sexual* knowledge Stein adds to the formula. Albert Raboteau writes: "To describe slave religion as merely otherworldly is inaccurate, for the slaves believed that God had acted, was acting, and would continue to act within human history and within their own particular history as a peculiar people just as long ago he had acted on behalf of another chosen people, biblical Israel. Moreover, slave religion had a this-worldly impact, not only in leading some slaves to acts of external rebellion, but also in helping slaves to assert and maintain a sense of personal value—even of ultimate worth."[46] In this respect, there is a subtle link between Melanctha's "wandering," her identification with religion, and Philipp Melancthon's reform of education, role in the Reformation, and insistence on God as mystically beyond rational understanding. In *The Souls of Black Folk* (1903), W. E. B. Du Bois reproaches himself and other contemporaries for a secular humanism that trivializes the social powers of religion, especially of the African-American church. One important trajectory of the narrative development that organizes the essays in *Souls* is Du Bois's dawning awareness that African-American progress and modernity must be built upon the foundations of African-American political activism and religious solidarity.[47] Stein's *Three Lives* cannot be compared, of course, with Du Bois's sustained effort in *Souls* to create a unified African-American cultural heritage, but the analogy between "Melanctha" and *Souls* suggests a contemporary context in which the religious connotation of Melanctha Herbert's alternative knowledge has specific relevance for the African-American heritage and its departure from the European traditions of modernity.

By including Melanctha's wayward sexuality with various men and with Jane Harden as part of her different "knowledge," Stein risks equating African-American spirituality with a neo-primitivism often figured from the late nineteenth century to the present in terms of "Congo dances" and the sort of eroticized spirituality bound up with the dominant culture's demonization of voodoo, Santería, Candomblé, and related African, African-American, and Afro-Caribbean alternatives to Euroamerican Christianity. By the same token, Stein finds the risk worth taking in order to identify the fatal limitation in Dr. Jeff Campbell's complete devotion to reason and science. In addition, Stein risks such neo-primitivism in part to strengthen her own identification with different cognitive practices that anticipate what today we identify with "queer" theories and their practices of social critique.

The Greek and German cultural allusions in Melanctha's name involve another set of possible connotations that link more closely the three narratives composing *Three Lives*. Because it is the longest and stylistically and thematically the most complex of these narratives, "Melanctha" tends to be treated separately from *Three Lives*. To be sure, "Melanctha" is more explicitly modernist than "The Good Anna" and "The Gentle Lena," both of which have strong resemblances with the prevailing literary naturalism of the period. But there are good reasons to reconsider the three narratives as part of a unified work, albeit one typical of Stein's anti-formalist aesthetic. The subtitle of "Melanctha," "Each One as She May," seems to be a commentary, perhaps even a moral, for all three lives, just as one connotation of "black earth" may be that all three characters share a common human nature, as in the more conventional idiom, "the salt of the earth."

I mentioned earlier how Stein subtly links working-class, racial, and national identifications in *Three Lives*, connecting German-American immigrants with racially stereotyped African Americans. Lena comes to America after her aunt Mathilda Haydon invites her during a visit to Haydon's extended family in Germany, where they are "middling farmers," but "not peasants" (*TL*, 220). Nevertheless, Mrs. Haydon's daughters Mathilda, who "was blonde, and slow, and simple, and quite fat," and Bertha, who "was dark, and quicker, and . . . was heavy, too," treat Lena with contempt and repeatedly compare her to "a nigger" (222).[48] In particular, these spoiled and idle young women dislike the "ugly and dirty" and "all rough and different" qualities of their German relatives, rejecting thereby the honest toil that has led to their privileged positions. Indeed, Lena's rural background in Germany links her directly with the "black earth" in Melancthon's name and with the racialization of Melanctha Herbert. Unlike her American cousins, Lena is "patient, gentle, sweet and German" and "had been a servant for four years and liked it very well" (*TL*, 217). Stein does not idealize or sentimentalize Lena, who is described as dreamy and unfocused, "mind-wandering" in William James's sense. If she lacks self-consciousness and directed interests, Lena nonetheless feels "a gentle stir within her" on repeated occasions, particularly when she is gently teased by her friends among the other servants with whom she sits in the park (*TL*, 225). Whatever this "gentle stir within her" means for Stein, it is not explicitly erotic and yet carries within it some element of affective and physical pleasure. By no means as complex as Melanctha's "wandering," the "gentle stir within" Lena is usually associated with her sense of belonging to a community. Thus when the Irish- and Italian-American serving women "[laugh] at her and always [tease] her," she is "happy," probably because their jibes are signs of their friendship and care for her (225). Despite their gentle provocations, her friends never succeed in getting Lena to express herself. It is not "self-consciousness" she lacks; it is the language by which to express that "gentle stir within her," or the unrealized imaginative potential each person possesses.

Instead of learning how to express herself and her social companionship with other working-class women, Lena is pushed by her aunt into an arranged marriage with Herman Kreder.[49] Mrs. Haydon assumes that the two are made for each other, because both are "very saving," in keeping with stereotypes about German immigrants (*TL*, 227). But if Lena prefers the company of other serving women, Herman prefers that of men: "He liked to be with men and hated to have women with them. He was obedient to his mother, but he did not much prefer to get married" (228). Stein suggests that Lena's and Herman's respective preferences for members of their own sex are entirely social preferences, but the boundary dividing social and sexual relations is as unclear in *Three Lives* as it is in *Q.E.D.*

Their preferences mean nothing to Lena's aunt or Herman's parents: "Old Mrs. Kreder did not discuss the matter with her Herman. . . . She just told him about getting married to Lena Mainz . . . , and Herman made his usual grunt in answer to her" (*TL*, 230). In fact, Herman objects mightily, even though he is as incapable as Lena of expressing those objections, so he runs away to stay with his married sister in New York, where his father eventually tracks him down and brings him back to be married. Once married, Herman and Lena move in with his parents, who utterly ignore Lena; after all, her father-in-law understands marriage simply as "a bargain just like the one you make in business," so that Lena is little more than an exchangeable commodity (*TL*, 239). His brief rebellion quelled by his parents and his sister, "who did not want him not to like to be with women," Herman performs his role as father as if he were an automaton (241). With each new baby, Lena loses interest in her life and personal appearance, so that her death giving birth to their fourth child is hardly noticed.

"The Good Anna" is less obviously related to "Melanctha" than "The Gentle Lena." In many respects, the "small, spare, German woman," Anna, whose "face was worn, her cheeks were thin, her mouth was drawn and firm" appears to be an orderly, hard-working, provincial South German Catholic—the stereotypical opposite of the "wandering" African-American, even the mulatto, Melanctha Herbert (*TL*, 11). Yet in her "arduous and troubled life," in which she appears to be the opposite of her German surname, "Federner," or "flexible," Anna actually ends up adapting to a wide range of different life experiences (*TL*, 9). At first, she does not appear to like children and never has any of her own, but she acts as a surrogate mother to many younger servants and the children of her employers. Although her character type is "very saving," Anna "in the kindly fashion of the poor" lends money to "many friends, who . . . used up her savings and then gave her promises in place of payments" (*TL*, 20). As Stein observes: "Even a thrifty German Anna was ready to give all that she had saved. . . . Save and you will have the money you have saved was true only for the day of saving, even for the thrifty German Anna" (*TL*, 60). Stein further subverts the stereotype of the "solid lower middle-class south German" by substituting Anna's friendships for the strong family ties of the German immigrant family. Although she has a half-brother who is a successful baker in Bridgepoint, she does not feel close to him and is disliked by her sister-in-law (*TL*, 21). Her real "family" is the extended group of indebted friends, employers, their children, and her dog, aptly named "Baby" (and the object of the allusion to Swift's Struldbrugs), for whom she works and worries herself to an early death.

Anna often lends her savings for noble purposes, such as her friend Mrs. Lehntman's home for unwed mothers. "The widow Mrs. Lehntman was the romance in Anna's life," Stein writes, but the exact nature of this romance is never explained (*TL*, 27). It appears to involve far more their close friendship and commitment to common ideals than any erotic relationship. As a midwife, Mrs. Lehntman "loved best to deliver young girls who were in trouble. She would take these into her own house and care for them in secret, till they could guiltlessly go home or back to work, and then slowly pay her the money for their care" (*TL*, 27). The surname Lehntman seems clearly composed of the German verb *lehnen* and impersonal pronoun *man*, as in "one leans upon." In the early stage of their friendship, Anna's romance with the widow Lehntman involves their common "goodness": their embodiment of Christian caritas and selfless devotion to others. Later in the narrative, when the widow Lehntman becomes romantically and professionally involved with a male doctor who appears to be doing abortions at her home for unwed mothers, Anna judges them as "doing things that were not right to do," but remains a faithful friend to widow Lehntman through these troubles (*TL*, 59). And when her employer and friend, Dr. Shonjen, who medically treats the poor in their community, marries a snobbish woman who dislikes Anna and urges him to move uptown, Anna judges Dr. Shonjen for neglecting her friends "so now I never see him any more" (*TL*, 67).[50]

Anna's charitable, morally good character is flawed by her inability to express clearly her ethical views of the world. Her devout German Catholicism—"Anna really did believe with all her might"—is an inadequate substitute for her own words to represent herself and her relations with the world (*TL*, 56). Jayne Walker has pointed out how "Anna's speeches are frequently introduced by descriptions that call attention to their abrupt, jerky rhythms" and how "the narrator surrounds Anna's quoted speech with descriptions and interpretations of her body language, which emphasize the inadequacy of her language to her emotions." Walker concludes that this "story simply presents Anna's difficulty with language as a naturalistic character trait."[51] Anna's difficulties with language, especially the substitution of her own body's labor either in the sublimation of self-expression or in the actual complement of body language, seem related to her physical decline and rapid death, which are recounted in the spare twenty-five paragraphs composing part 3, "The Death of the Good Anna."

Lisa Ruddick argues convincingly that the three narratives are related by the common feminine experience of abjection and masochism, that "the book gives a picture of a world that prompts self-punishing behavior in women."[52] Lena is crushed by a patriarchal world, which does not always work through men. Mrs. Haydon and her daughters are made in the image of such patriarchy, just as Mrs. Kreder typifies masculine assertiveness and control far better than her son Herman, despite his preference for male company. In a different sense, Melanctha identifies "with strong men," as Ruddick points out, only to end up being victimized by them.[53] In "The Good Anna," Anna is exploited by her friends, who rely on her hard work, thrift, and sense of responsibility at the cost of her physical and emotional powers. All three characters suffer from many deficiencies that prevent them from realizing their potential: Lena's modest sociability, Anna's charity and responsibility, and Melanctha's imagination and passion.

Of the three, Melanctha comes the closest to expressing herself in and through language and inspiring others, however briefly, to approximate a discourse that brings self and other into a vital, performative relationship. In the end, she fails in part because she does not know how to control her discourse and in part because those around her don't know how to share, rather than "understand," that language. Much as Jeff tries to participate in her "wandering," he is too much the rationalist, too committed to the instrumentality and referentiality of language. Stein, of course, claims not only to share Melanctha's discourse but to know how to create and control it. At its best, it is a discourse that combines cognitive, psychological, and sensuous contact between human beings, as in the following, highly eroticized passage:

> Melanctha sometimes now, when she was tired with being all the time so much excited, when Jeff would talk a long time to her about what was right for them both to be always doing, would be, as if she gave way in her head, and lost herself in a bad feeling. Sometimes when they had been strong in their loving, and Jeff would have rise inside him some strange feeling, and Melanctha felt it in him as it would soon be coming, she would lose herself then in this bad feeling that made her head act as if she never knew what it was they were doing. And slowly now, Jeff soon always came to be feeling that his Melanctha would be hurt very much in her head in the ways he never liked to think of, if she would ever now again have to listen to his trouble, when he was telling about what it was he still was wanting to make things for himself really understanding. (*TL*, 147–148)

By no means conventionally realistic, Stein's prose in this passage nevertheless manages to express powerfully the sorts of confused emotions, half-realized thoughts, and tacit eroticism in arguments between partners. Such prose helps explain why the most logical and irrefutable rational argument can work counterproductively in such situations, and how we are compelled to "keep talking" until someone's head hurts or another limit is reached. The conversation in such circumstances and in this passage is performative, constituting in its fragile threads and unrealized intentions the relationship itself.

The dialect in *Melanctha* is not so much a faithful representation of African-American vernacular speech as what Jayne Walker terms a "new mode of realism" that "is grounded in a fundamentally different valuation of language." For Walker, this new realism of language involves a "shift of focus from the 'realism of character' to the 'realism of the composition of . . . thoughts,' language like Cézanne's patches of color" and becomes thereby "a property shared, at least to some extent, by the object and the medium."[54] I would add that what is shared in language is the common responsibility of speaker and interlocutor to keep this "speech" alive or conversely to let it lapse into silence, so that what *makes* character or identity is not so much the authoritative utterance of the author as it is the mutual participation in the ceaseless flow of language that *makes us* as speakers and listeners, authors and readers.

There is much in this view that anticipates the post-structuralist "language-model" of reality and of subjectivity. We are effects of language, which in its convention-based system cannot be "changed" easily or permanently, even by our most radical, willful, and individual efforts to change it. As de Saussure pointed out at around the same time, language is fundamentally conservative in this regard, even as its conservative qualities depend upon variation and distortion to function as such.[55] Walker makes a similar observation about *Three Lives*: "Stein's project of modeling the actual 'composition' of thought in language necessarily entailed not only disrupting this normative discourse but also challenging its authority to represent the reality of human consciousness."[56]

There are other aspects to our experience, Melanctha Herbert's character seems to suggest, and these include not only sexual and religious "knowledges," but also the alternative knowledge that many different modern artists identified with aesthetic understanding or what Stein terms in the title of her famous essay "Composition as Explanation." Anglo-American New Criticism was in large part founded on the special cognitive functions of literature and how they could be distinguished from instrumental rationality, but the New Critics never considered the possibility of productive analogies between this "logic of metaphor" and the different epistemologies offered by cultures and subjects minoritized by ethnic, class, and sexual identifications. Rather than being taken as a literary naturalist's account of German-American and African-American experiences written in a style that imitates their dialects, *Three Lives* can also be read as the avant-garde experimentalist's effort to draw upon the poetically and rhetorically rich qualities of their language patterns, even as Stein recognizes the difference between the instrumental use of dialect by the characters and her own control of such dialect for purposes both of representation and metapoetic reflection. Zora Neale Hurston would make similar claims for her narrative and stylistic revisions of the folklore composing *Mules and Men* (1935).[57] It is equally significant that a white, upper-middle-class, and avant-garde writer like Gertrude Stein could claim in the first decade of the twentieth century to have learned from African-American culture and to have articulated its relationship with European immigrant cultures, such as her own German-American heritage. Stein's achievement in this regard helps explain the enthusiastic recognition of *Three Lives* by Richard Wright, Nella Larsen, and Carl Van Vechten.[58]

We can conclude that Melanctha Herbert is a misguided, confused, and socially or naturally determined woman, who concludes her pathetic life in "a home for poor consumptives," where she "stayed until she died" (*TL*, 215). Or we can read her as a prophetic figure who does for her own time and place what Philipp Melancthon did for sixteenth-century Saxony by coordinating religion and reason, by insisting upon a revolutionary approach to both areas of human experience, and by inspiring a mode of discourse—call it Stein's modernism—that had an influence far beyond either prophetic figure's powers. Even while acknowledging the limitations of this position, including its tendency to romanticize certain aspects of African-American culture and personal experience at the beginning of the twentieth century, Stein's view calls for the recognition of African-American contributions to U.S. culture that would transform rationalist and technocratic social values. There is an aura of neo-primitivism in Stein's use of the African-American figure for such a recognition and the risk that "reason" is thus understood to be the property of white Europeans. I do not wish to dismiss, even diminish, this characteristic, because it inflects all three lives in this narrative and because it is an identifiable feature of the high-modernist experimentalism in which Stein participated. Insofar as Melanctha Herbert represents the "unrealized" potential of an expressive ideal and "new" knowledge achieved by Stein herself, Stein also contributes to the liberal politics of "sympathy" through which she legitimates herself at the expense of her character types, whatever their sources of social marginalization. Such an aesthetics of sacrifice is familiar to readers of Henry James, in which his feminine protagonists never quite succeed in achieving the insight and thus power he always reserves for himself.[59]

In conclusion, I want to answer explicitly my opening questions about Stein's literary representation of race, class, gender, and sexuality in *Three Lives*. Stein's modernism is indeed changed by her racial "passing" and working-class fantasy, and the curious combination of literary naturalism and experimentalism helped destabilize prevailing racial and ethnic stereotypes at the time of its composition. Stein's identification with her characters, ambivalent as it often is, functions in both sympathetic and manipulative ways, reminding us how little we understand about the complexities and consequences of literary and imaginative identification with others. As another version of the "tragic mulatto," Melanctha Herbert is part of the unfortunate literary history of black minstrelsy of early modernity.[60] As a figure that crosses African-American and Euroamerican cultural traditions, warning us of the limitations of either tradition in and for itself, Melanctha Herbert is used by Stein to represent, along with the two other immigrant women, Anna Federner and Lena Mainz in *Three Lives*, the missed opportunities for the modern, hybrid subjectivity of the American.

Stein's argument in favor of such hybridity includes her own identity, both her family background and the choices she made in her own life. But even in Paris, Stein remains a decisively U.S.-centric writer. Anna and Lena's gently counter-cultural identities are unimaginable in their country of origin, Germany. Melanctha's transnational identity is shaped by Stein in terms of a suite of ironic allusions to European high culture, not to Africa, even if Du Bois and other pan-African activists were in this same period arguing vigorously for an "Ethiopianism" we recognize today as the background to Afrocentrism. Stein may have left the United States on account of its lack of culture, even its discrimination against the working class, people of color, Jews, and lesbians, but she still believes passionately in the United States as an ideal democracy where diversity is most likely to be accepted in the future.

Stein's liberal imagination is well represented in her later work, *The Making of Americans* (1934), which offers her own avant-garde and fictional version of her family history.[61] For all of its stylistic experimentalism, *The Making of Americans* remains, like *Three Lives*, a hopeful, even sentimental book by reinforcing the conventional narrative of successful immigration and adaptation, if not complete assimilation, to the settler society of the United States. Alluding to Stein's monumental family history, Maxine Hong Kingston includes a chapter entitled "The Making of More Americans" in her own imaginary history of Chinese immigration to the States, *China Men* (1980).[62] Although Kingston recalls *The Making of Americans* out of respect for Stein's contributions to modernism, Kingston is also reminding her readers that Stein's account is Eurocentric and excludes the contemporary immigration from China (and many other Asian countries) occluded not only by the Chinese Exclusion Laws but also by the U.S. cultural bias in favor of Europe. Still another literary work, Monique Truong's *The Book of Salt* (2003) challenges Stein's and U.S. modernism's Eurocentrism by telling the story of Binh, the gay Vietnamese immigrant to Paris, who becomes Stein's and Toklas's live-in cook.[63] Thus even Stein's love of French *haute cuisine* is challenged by Truong's story and the implication that during French colonial rule of Indochina French cuisine and culture were influenced both by social and political contacts with Southeast Asia. Kingston and Truong are Chinese-American and Vietnamese-American liberal writers in their own rights, but their own "liberal imaginations" take us far beyond Stein's Euroamerican framework, even as both encourage their readers to re-read Stein's writings and her biography, in effect keeping Gertrude Stein in our cultural perspective even as we broaden our view to include other peoples, lands, and issues.

Notes

1. I wish to thank James Zeigler with whom I first discussed the idea for this chapter during his attendance in my graduate seminar at the University of California, San

Diego in the spring of 2000. I did most of the research and wrote the essay while a Gastprofessor in the Amerika-Institut at Ludwig Maximilians Universität in München, where I was very ably assisted in the research by Anne Stadler and Katrin Windolf.

2. Gertrude Stein, "Poetry and Grammar," *Lectures in America* (New York: Random House, 1935), p. 210.

3. The following scholarly studies are of particular significance in the task of understanding Stein's relationship to high modernism and the Harlem Renaissance: Marianna Torgovnick, *Gone Primitive: Savage Intellects, Modern Lives* (Chicago: University of Chicago Press, 1990) and *Primitive Passions: Men, Women, and the Quest for Ecstasy* (Chicago: University of Chicago Press, 1996); Michael North, *The Dialect of Modernism: Race, Language and Twentieth-Century Literature* (New York: Oxford University Press, 1994); Sieglinde Lemke, *Primitivist Modernism: Black Culture and the Origins of Transatlantic Modernism* (New York: Oxford University Press, 1998).

4. Stein's insistence upon the "naturalness" of language is not that of the romantics but of decadents, like Oscar Wilde in "The Decay of Lying," and symbolists, like Baudelaire and Mallarmé, all of whom insist upon the ways artifice (especially poetic language) and fiction are integral to any understanding of "Nature." See Stein, "Composition as Explanation," *Writings 1903–1932* (New York: Library of America, 1998), p. 527: "The time of the composition is a natural thing and the time in the composition is a natural thing it is a natural thing and it is a contemporary thing."

5. See, for example, Marianne De Koven, *A Different Language: Gertrude Stein's Experimental Writing* (Madison: University of Wisconsin Press, 1983), and Janice L. Doane, *Silence and Narrative: The Early Novels of Gertrude Stein* (Westport, CT: Greenwood Press, 1986). Randa Dubnick, *The Structure of Obscurity: Gertrude Stein, Language, and Cubism* (Urbana: University of Illinois Press, 1984) stresses Stein's anticipations of the structural linguistics of Roland Barthes and Roman Jakobson. Georg Schiller, *Symbolische Erfahrung und Sprache im Werk von Gertrude Stein*, (Frankfurt: Peter Lang, 1995) tries to locate Stein's work somewhere between a modernist symbolic mode, typified by Ernst Cassirer's *Philosophy of Symbolic Forms*, the late structuralism of Roland Barthes, and the post-structuralism of Jacques Derrida. Schiller focuses exclusively on the late writings of Gertrude Stein and pays little attention to such early works as *Three Lives*.

6. William York Tindall, *The Literary Symbol* (New York: Columbia University Press, 1955), pp. 3–27; Charles Feidelson Jr., *Symbolism in American Literature* (Chicago: University of Chicago Press, 1957), pp. 47–74.

7. Stein, "Poetry and Grammar," *Writings and Lectures, 1909–1945*, ed. Patricia Meyerowitz (Harmondsworth, UK: Penguin Books, 1971), pp. 125–126. Interestingly, Stein links the "naming" of people with their formal educations in this same passage: "nouns are the name of anything and just naming names is alright when you want to call a roll but is it any good for anything else. To be sure in many places in Europe as in America they do like to call rolls" (124–125).

8. North, *The Dialect of Modernism*, p. 61.

9. Ibid., p. 67.

10. Gertrude Stein, *Three Lives* (Harmondsworth, UK: Penguin Books, 1979), p. 78.

11. Gertrude Stein, *The Autobiography of Alice B. Toklas* (Harmondsworth, UK:

Penguin Books, 1966), p. 90: "It was then that she had to take her turn in the delivering of babies and it was at that time that she noticed the negroes and the places that she afterwards used in the second of the Three Lives stories, Melanctha Herbert, the story that was the beginning of her revolutionary work."

12. James R. Mellow, *Charmed Circle: Gertrude Stein and Company* (Boston: Houghton Mifflin Co., 1974), pp. 70–71.

13. Stein, *Tender Buttons*, in *Selected Writings of Gertrude Stein*, ed. Carl Van Vechten (New York: Random House, Inc., 1962), p. 476.

14. Ezra Pound, "A Retrospect," *The Literary Essays of Ezra Pound*, ed. T. S. Eliot (London: Faber and Faber, Ltd., 1954), p. 4.

15. Ralph Ellison, *Invisible Man* (New York: Random House, Inc., 1952), pp. 152, 153.

16. My verbal description is, of course, inadequate. Paul Cézanne's *Mme Cézanne, 1881*, which is now in the Sammlung E. G. Bührle in Zürich, is conveniently reproduced on the cover of the Penguin edition of *Three Lives* used in this essay.

17. Stein, "Composition as Explanation," *Writings 1903–1932*, p. 522, appears to be describing her own method of stylistic repetition when she writes: "Beginning again and again is a natural thing even when there is a series. Beginning again and again and again explaining composition and time is a natural thing."

18. Once again, my description is inadequate to the painting. Pablo Picasso's *Portrait of Gertrude Stein* (1906), which is now in the Metropolitan Museum of Art (as a bequest of Stein in 1946), is conveniently reproduced on the cover of the Penguin edition of *The Autobiography of Alice B. Toklas* used in this essay.

19. North, *The Dialect of Modernism*, p. 63.

20. Like Pound's theorization of the poetic image in the various *Des Imagistes* manifestoes and anthologies he edited and to which he contributed, Stein's theoretical reflections on language and visual imagery as semiotic share a certain zeitgeist, albeit no possible influence, with Ferdinand de Saussure's theorization of the sign and the beginnings of structural linguistics in his lectures at Geneva between 1909 and 1911. See my *Through the Custom-House: Nineteenth-Century American Fiction and Modern Theory* (Baltimore: The Johns Hopkins University Press, 1982), pp. 172–173.

21. Frank Kermode, *The Genesis of Secrecy: On the Interpretation of Narrative* (Cambridge, MA: Harvard University Press, 1979), pp. 39–40, discusses *aletheia* in relation to hermeneutic issues relating to the interpretation of philosophical truth and, following Heidegger, the necessity for an interpretive "outside" to truth in order to reveal it as such. Kermode's intriguing treatment of the relation of inside and outside posed by the necessity of interpreting, rather than merely recognizing, truth is yet another instance of such "wandering." Kermode's treatment of *aletheia* and his most important source, Heidegger's *Der Ursprung des Kunstwerkes* (1935/1936), in *Holzwege* (Frankfurt am Main: Vittorio Klostermann, 1950), pp. 36–43, obviously come after Stein's "Melanctha" and cannot thus be considered influences, but the tradition of thinking about the relationship between philosophical truth and religious meaning in the Greek term *aletheia* may well have relevance for Stein's narrative.

22. Lisa Ruddick, *Reading Gertrude Stein: Body, Text, Gnosis* (Ithaca, NY: Cornell University Press, 1990), pp. 17–18.

23. Ibid., p. 18.

24. Ibid., p. 25.

25. Ibid., p. 32.

26. Ibid., p. 33.

27. North, *The Dialect of Modernism*, pp. 65–66.

28. Cynthia Ann Sarver, "Seeing in the Dark: Race, Representation, and Visuality in Literary Modernism," Ph.D. Dissertation (University of Southern California): 2004, p. 84.

29. Ibid., p. 88.

30. W. E. B. Du Bois, *The Souls of Black Folk* (New York: Penguin Books, 1989), pp. 5, 6.

31. Ibid., p. 6.

32. Heinz Schieble, *Melanchthon: Eine Biographie* (Munich: Verlag C. H. Beck, 1997), pp. 15–16.

33. Eugene D. Genovese, *Roll, Jordan, Roll: The World the Slaves Made* (New York: Random House, 1974), p. 447. Genovese also notes that "classical or whimsical names appeared on the slave lists much less frequently than generally believed. Most large plantations sported a few, but the great majority of names were straightforward" (448).

34. Ibid., p. 448.

35. See *Three Lives*, pp. 164–172, for an especially good example of Stein's variations on Jeff Campbell's different names, syncopated in accord with his changing opinions in his intense conversation with Melanctha, his reading of a letter from her, and concluding with his formally signed letter of reply.

36. See my discussion of Crane's use of the mock-heroic and bathos in *Literary Culture and U.S. Imperialism: From the Revolution to World War II* (New York: Oxford University Press, 2000), pp. 158–159.

37. De Koven, *A Different Language*, p. 29.

38. Ibid., p. 31; North, *The Dialect of Modernism*, p. 75; Ruddick, *Reading Gertrude Stein*, pp. 25–28; Jayne L. Walker, *The Making of a Modernist: Gertrude Stein* (Amherst: University of Massachusetts Press, 1984), pp. 28–38. As I note above, however, Ruddick goes on to show that Melanctha is Stein's real alter ego in *Three Lives*, displacing the character Dr. Jeff Campbell, who epitomizes William James's model of reason.

39. Stein, *Q.E.D.*, in *Writings 1903–1932*. In their notes to this edition, Catharine R. Stimpson and Harriet Chessman point out that the manuscript is dated "October 24, 1903," but not published until after Stein's death in 1946, when Alice B. Toklas discovered the untyped manuscript and published it in 1950 with the Banyan Press in Pawlet, Vermont, as *Things As They Are* in a limited edition of 516 copies (928). Stein refers to *Q.E.D.* in *The Autobiography of Alice B. Toklas*, p. 93, as a "short novel she completely forgot about . . . for many years" and "must have forgotten about it almost immediately."

40. North, *The Dialect of Modernism*, p. 69.

41. The *Oxford English Dictionary* lists "Struldbrug" (and several variant spellings) as an idiom referring to the Struldbrugs, or "immortals," in Jonathan Swift's *Gul-*

liver's Travels, chapter 9, in the kingdom of Luggnagg, who are incapable of dying but after the age of eighty continue in miserable decrepitude, are regarded as legally dead, and yet still receive a small pension from the state. Swift was satirizing Anglo-Irish social policies toward old-age pensioners. As an idiom, a "struldbrug" refers to a person or animal that is past its prime, anachronistic, or "living death."

42. Schieble, *Melanchthon*, pp. 31–32.

43. Ibid., p. 34. My translation of Schieble's German translation of the original Latin: "Mysteria divinitatis rectius adoraverimus quam vestigaverimus."

44. Ibid., pp. 34–56.

45. Jean Toomer, *Cane*, ed. Darwin T. Turner, Norton Critical Edition (New York: W. W. Norton and Co., Inc., 1988), especially in the opening sections—"Karintha," "Becky," "Carma," "Fern," and "Esther"—stresses what Turner in his preface terms "the need of Afro-American women to liberate themselves from repressive, middle-class, Anglo-Saxon morality" (viii).

46. Albert J. Raboteau, *Slave Religion: The "Invisible Institution" in the Antebellum South* (New York: Oxford University Press, 1978), p. 318.

47. W. E. B. Du Bois, *The Souls of Black Folk* (New York: Penguin Books, 1989), pp. 154–217. From chapter 10, "Of the Faith of the Fathers," through chapter 14, "The Sorrow Songs," Du Bois organizes the final movement of *Souls* as an appeal to his readers to revive the political and religious coherence of African-American culture exemplified by its churches and such religious leaders as Alexander Crummell, the subject of chapter 12.

48. Mellow, *Charmed Circle*, pp. 18–19, notes that Gertrude "had little concern" for her older sister, Bertha, whom she considered "a little simple minded."

49. The surname "Kreder" seems derived from the German *kreden*, to "serve" or "offer," which is certainly what this obedient young man does most of the time.

50. Dr. Shonjen's given name is odd for the German-American community, but it is probably an agglutination of the German "schon," "already," and "je," "always," in reference to his years as a dutiful bachelor doctor serving his community. Spelled as it is, it has a Japanese sound, whose oddity may serve a modest alienation effect for the reader, making that reader work to figure out the name's significance in the narrative.

51. Walker, *The Making of a Modernist*, pp. 21–22.

52. Ruddick, *Reading Gertrude Stein*, p. 48.

53. Ibid., p. 50.

54. Walker, *The Making of a Modernist*, p. 17.

55. Ferdinand de Saussure, *Course in General Linguistics*, eds. Charles Bally and Albert Sechehaye, in collaboration with Albert Reidlinger, trans. Wade Baskin (New York: McGraw-Hill Book Co., 1966), p. 112.

56. Walker, *The Making of a Modernist*, p. 17.

57. See my interpretation of *Mules and Men* as a narrative of educating the protagonist "Zora" about her African and Afro-Caribbean heritage in *Literary Culture and U.S. Imperialism*, pp. 253–270.

58. In *Selected Writings of Gertrude Stein*, ed. Carl Van Vechten (New York: Random House, 1990), p. 338, Van Vechten includes an account of Richard Wright's review of Stein's *Wars I Have Seen* in *PM* (March 11, 1945), in which Wright tells the

story of how he discovered *Three Lives* in the Chicago Public Library and read it aloud to "a group of semi-literate Negro stockyard workers" in "a Black Belt basement," contending that they "understood every word" and "enthralled, they slapped their thighs, howled, laughed, stomped, and interrupted me constantly to comment upon the characters." John Malcolm Brinnin, *The Third Rose: Gertrude Stein and Her World* (Reading, MA: Addison-Wesley Publishing Co., Inc., 1987), p. 121, quotes Larsen's letter to Stein: "I never cease to wonder how you came to write it and just why you and not some one of us should so accurately have caught the spirit of this race of mine." In Van Vechten's novel about Harlem, *Nigger Heaven*, "an up-to-date young black woman, collects African sculpture and quotes a long stretch of 'Melanctha' from memory," as North, *The Dialect of Modernism*, p. 62, points out.

59. See my *The Other Henry James* (Durham, NC: Duke University Press, 1998), pp. 11–12, 55.

60. On the literary function of the "tragic mulatto/a," see Barbara Christian, *Black Women Novelists: The Development of a Tradition, 1892–1976* (Westport, CT: Greenwood Press, 1980), pp. 35–61, and Hazel V. Carby, *Reconstructing Womanhood: The Emergence of the Afro-American Woman Novelist* (New York: Oxford University Press, 1987), pp. 88–91. On Stein's use of "the racist stereotypes of the 'tragic mulatta' for her literary camouflage" of feminist purposes, see Sabine Broeck, "Gertrude Stein's 'Melanctha' in den Diskursen zur 'Natur der Frau,'" *Amerika Studien* 37:3 (1992), 515–516.

61. Gertrude Stein, *The Making of Americans: The Hersland Family* (New York: Harcourt Brace and Co., 1934).

62. Maxine Hong Kingston, *China Men* (New York: Random House, 1980), pp. 163–221.

63. Monique Truong, *The Book of Salt* (Boston: Houghton Mifflin, 2003).

[2]

JOHN DOS PASSOS'S IMAGINARY CITY IN *MANHATTAN TRANSFER*

When I look at the newspapers today I wonder why the pundits don't acknowledge that we're in the middle of World War III. I'm sure that some future historians will say so. —Walter Mosley, *Known to Evil* (2010)

RECENT CONCEPTIONS of the postmodern city as a transnational site with a unique "global-local" relationship often imply some radical departure from the modernist city so crucial to the legitimation of, and thus dependent on the form of, the nation-state. Fredric Jameson claims that contemporary Los Angeles constitutes a "postmodern hyperspace," which "has finally succeeded in transcending the capacities of the individual human body to locate itself" in "the great global multinational and decentered communicational network in which we find ourselves caught as individual subjects."[1] Of course, the postmodern, postindustrial city in first-world nations must follow global flows of capital through corporate channels that are no longer restricted by national borders. The protests at the World Trade Organization Ministerial Conference in Seattle in March 1999, when 600 people were arrested and the conference prematurely ended, were prompted in part by the awareness that corporate modes of controlling workers as both laborers and citizens are no longer subject to the regulatory authority of national governments. A decade later, in the summer of 2009, when the Group of Twenty organization of Finance Ministers and Central Bank Governors met in Pittsburgh, concerns about protests were so extreme as to empty a downtown barricaded with tanks and military personnel. The postmodern city has become a site of contestation between global corporatism—advocates of so-called "free-trade" like the WTO, G20, and World Bank—and transnational activists concerned about the global exploitation of labor.

Postmodern cities, like Los Angeles and Berlin and New York, have become sites of contestation between diasporic subject-citizens and corporate authorities who are otherwise stateless and often ingeniously "invisible." By the same token, multinational corporations may often benefit from their national affiliations. In the recent massive leak of oil from the explosion of the Deepwater Horizon platform in the Gulf of Mexico, BP could claim both its local affiliations on the U.S. Gulf Coast while trying to appease outraged citizens and at other times seek the legal safety of its home base in the United Kingdom.[2] Culturally diverse, often disparate metropolitan populations pose special problems of ideological control, but they are also less capable of organizing resistance to inequitable social and economic practices, despite special appeals for coalition politics and cultural hybridities. Yet, just how new are these social and economic conditions of the postmodern city? In *Terrible Honesty: Mongrel Manhattan in the 1920s* (1995), Ann Douglas argues that modern New York was an aesthetically, intellectually, and culturally diverse city, and its modernist vanguard worked self-consciously toward aesthetic coalitions and cultural hybridities that crossed conventional boundaries of race, class, gender, and sexuality.[3] Part of a general critical and scholarly effort to redeem high modernism from criticism of what Lukács long ago termed "the ideology of modernism," Douglas's argument should be treated with caution, but it helps remind us how crucial it is to understand the *similarities*, as well as the differences, between modern and postmodern cities.[4]

What I would term the *visibility* of the city in global social, political, and economic disputes is by no means historically new or unique in the postmodern era. Second-stage industrialization relied on processes of urbanization whereby cities throughout the industrialized world became the principal sites of transnational populations, imported primarily as cheap sources of labor that dramatically changed the demographics and sociologies of the nations employing them. Unionization and other labor organization in these metropolitan centers also focused attention on national and international issues. The demonstrations in 1999 in Seattle against the World Trade Organization Ministerial Conference were prompted in part by the passage of the North American Free Trade Agreement in 1993 and what were widely perceived as its negative consequences for U.S. workers in global contexts. But this activism by workers in a postindustrial era can be traced back to that of the Industrial Workers of the World

(IWW), the "Wobblies," founded in Chicago in 1905 as the first union with a global scope in efforts to organize rank-and-file industrial workers. Originally gathering together socialists, anarchists, and radical trade unionists in Chicago in 1905, the IWW would have over 100,000 members at its peak in 1923, and expand its international organizations to Australia, the United Kingdom, Germany, Switzerland, and Austria.[5] Diminished in membership and power by anti-Communist persecution in the 1950s, the IWW nevertheless continues as a powerful union today, as recently as 2007 forming the Food and Allied Workers from New York City warehouse and IWW Starbucks Workers Union.[6]

The IWW is just one example of how the concentration of labor in metropolitan centers in industrialized nations prompted transnational organization of labor interests. Whether labor unions fought for protectionist tariffs and isolationist foreign policies or advocated genuine international cooperation among workers to prevent exploitation on a global scale, the very organization of labor in metropolitan centers called attention to transnational issues long before our contemporary era of "globalization." In *The New Imperialism* (2003), David Harvey argues that many of the key features of U.S. neo-imperialism in the post–World War II era can be traced directly back to the early twentieth-century and "second-stage industrialization," especially the imperial consequences.[7] Beginning with traditional Marxist analyses of how imperialism and capitalism are inextricably bound together, Harvey complicates Lenin's rather straightforward argument in *Imperialism, the Highest Stage of Capitalism* (1916) and rejects Rosa Luxemburg's argument in *The Accumulation of Capital* that "underconsumption" at home motivates territorial expansion in the quest of new markets, according to the insatiable need for capital accumulation. Harvey agrees with Lenin and Luxemburg that capitalism and imperialism are necessary complements, but contends that capitalism's need for "endless" (and we might add, ever-accelerating) capital accumulation depends on an equally "endless accumulation of political power," which the "territorial logic" of traditional imperialism frustrates (Harvey, 140). Trying to control nineteenth-century India, Harvey argues, the British struggled to extract surplus capital from the Subcontinent, whereas "the open dynamic of the Atlantic economy" with its mercantilism and slave trade did far more to allow the British and other colonial participants to extract economic surpluses (Harvey, 140).

Despite his disagreements with modern leftists like Lenin and Luxemburg, Harvey assumes that neo-imperialist political economies are built upon the imperialist practices of the second-stage industrialization. Despite the manifest differences of modern imperialism based on industrial superiority and late-modern neo-imperialism based on postindustrial superiority in research and development, the processes of accumulating political power remain quite similar. Metropolitan centers remain central means of acquiring and increasing such power, especially when such cities are the sites of labor immigration and its necessary division into work for the "national" interest. The long history of the exclusion and exploitation of foreign workers in the United States supports Harvey's notion that modern and postmodern imperialisms are closely related. The legal "exclusion" of Chinese immigration between 1869 and 1943, the importation of temporary contract workers from Mexico during the Bracero Program (1942–1964), and recent efforts to restrict undocumented workers in the United States belong to the same history, in which foreign workers are used to "modernize" the United States and yet are deprived of basic civil and economic rights.

In the modern period, metropolitan centers are sites of contact between internal and external imperial practices and thus especially good places to study "glocal" phenomena. John Dos Passos's *Manhattan Transfer* (1925) typifies both U.S. modernist techniques in prose fiction and attitudes toward the possibilities and dangers of urban social and economic organization. Departing from the familiar modernist critique of the city as the site of alienation and universalized spiritual death, Dos Passos stresses the cultural, ethnic, class, and sexual variety of New York as a source of both urban vitality and new social problems.[8] Dos Passos's political views changed dramatically throughout his long career, ranging from his radical socialism and support of the IWW in the 1920s to his vigorous anti-Communism in the 1930s and support of Joseph McCarthy's post–World War II persecution of leftists.[9] Dos Passos wrote *Manhattan Transfer* in support of socialist labor organizations, especially the IWW.

In the novel's final chapter, "The Burthen of Nineveh," Ellen Herf stops by Madame Soubrine's dress shop and witnesses a fire that badly burns Anna Cohen, one of the garment workers, who joins her partner Elmer in efforts to organize other garment workers.[10] This brief episode, only five pages from the end of the novel, alludes to the Triangle Shirtwaist Factory

Fire on March 26, 1911 in New York, when 146 women garment workers died after a fire broke out and they were trapped behind factory doors locked by the owners. The event galvanized early efforts at labor organization in New York, leading to the organization of the International Lady Garment Workers Union and strengthening the fledgling IWW. As Anna Cohen is carried out of Madame Soubrine's on a stretcher, Ellen "tries to puzzle out why she is so moved," reflecting that "it is as if some part of her were going to be wrapped in bandages, carried away on a stretcher" (*Manhattan Transfer*, 399; hereafter *MT*). As it turns out, Ellen is late for a party, so hurries away—"Go to the Algonquin, please" (399)—but this moment of identification with the injured worker, Anna, herself a labor activist, suggests one way to overcome "a horrible tired blankness" Ellen feels "inside her" (399).

In *Manhattan Transfer*, Dos Passos endorses the importance of stronger unions and the need for the international organization of labor to contest the growing transnational power of modern capitalism. In 1925, such views are clearly associated with the political left, not with liberalism, but from our postwar perspective belong interestingly to the "liberal imagination." *Manhattan Transfer* does not advocate a Communist internationalism, as Alfred Döblin's *Berlin Alexanderplatz* (1929) does in interwar Germany, a work often considered to have been strongly influenced by Dos Passos's *Manhattan Transfer*.[11] Dos Passos advocates labor organization but does not stress any particular political party, preferring instead to emphasize the diversity of ethnic and national backgrounds, the complexity of individual lives, and the entanglement of identity and party politics. His enthusiasm for the promise of multicultural New York anticipates the liberal endorsement of multiculturalism in the 1980s and early 1990s; both are subject to similar criticisms of their idealization of both cultural differences and hybridities. By emphasizing interpersonal and cultural changes over practical political reforms, Dos Passos anticipates the "critical" function of the liberal imagination that Trilling would codify a quarter of a century later in *The Liberal Imagination* (1950).

Dos Passos satirizes the idea of the United States as a "classless society" by demonstrating both the arbitrariness and yet power of class divisions in New York. The class mobility of characters like the actress Ellen Thatcher, or Gus McNiel, the milk truck driver who wins a damage settlement of $12,500 arranged by the struggling attorney George Baldwin early in the novel, depends variously on luck, publicity, and their acceptance of the basic social Darwinism that drives individual destinies.[12] To be sure, Dos Passos follows his literary naturalist models by treating class divisions in terms of the relative success or failure of characters' adaptations to the laws of the urban jungle, but he complicates familiar social Darwinist arguments by foregrounding a wide range of sexual identities and behaviors that shape not only interpersonal relations (and thus domesticity) but also the public sphere. Women wield real power in the novel, ranging from sexual power over men (as Ellen Thatcher, Nevada Jones, and Nellie McNiel do) to economic independence (Emile Loustec's wife owns a boulangerie, and Frances, the Flapper Bandit, is sentenced to a twenty-year sentence with her partner, Dutch Robertson). Such bisexual characters as JoJo (John) Oglethorpe (Ellen Thatcher's first husband) and Tony Hunter represent the flexibility and social constructedness of sexual identity.[13] Painful as Tony Hunter's confession of his homosexuality is for him personally—"I hate myself"—Jimmy Herf suggests that modern urban society is tolerant: "Ther're lots of people in the same boat. The stage is full of them" (*MT*, 234). When the drunken Stan Emery collapses in Ellen's bathtub, thoroughly soaking himself, Ellen and Milly make him put on one of Ellen's dresses to get past the doorman. Theatricality, transvestism, and urban life complement each other; urban anonymity and the accelerated pace of modern life encourage role-playing as much as they contribute to alienation, as Ellen suggests when they sneak the cross-dressed Stan past old Barney, the doorman: "You can get away with anything if you do it quick enough" (*MT*, 215).

Dos Passos clearly links the arbitrariness of class distinctions and sexual identities with the fiction of national identification. The French emigré Congo Jake leads anarchists and socialists in New York behind the slogan, "A workingman has no country" (*MT*, 227), and the young Dos Passos seems to agree that only those who recognize the flexibility of the boundaries of class, sexuality, gender, and nation have any chance of avoiding the illusions that trap or destroy most of the characters. Influential mass media, like the newspaper and film, work either as propaganda to convince individuals to accept the artifices of city, nation, and class as true and natural or as potentially emancipatory media promoting class-consciousness, the demystification of urban naturalness, and international organization. Jimmy Herf is eventually disillusioned with the deceitful words he uses as a journalist, but Dos Passos incorporates journalistic prose and forms into a modernist montage that allows the reader to understand journalism as simply one among several representational media of modernity. By refusing the monologic, consensus-driven discourse of the mass media, Dos Passos approximates the heteroglossia of a multicultural society. In so doing, he lays claim to the multimedia effects of high-modernist technique by combining cubist abstraction in painting, cinematic montage, poetic imagism, and the modern novel's perspectivism.[14]

One purpose of the news stories in the novel is to remind us that New York City is now a major metropolitan center in an increasingly connected globe, long before Marshall McLuhan coined the phrase in the 1960s of the coming "global village."[15] Dos Passos represents the city as dependent on new economic aspects of the globalizing process in which the United States plays an increasingly central role in the years following the Spanish-American War (1898). At times, Dos Passos suggests that New York City is a synecdoche for a larger, unrepresentable global society, which effectively transgresses any clear boundary between domestic and foreign policies, between local and global news, the plight of U.S. workers and the aims of international labor. George Baldwin's first concern when he hears news of the assassination of Archduke Ferdinand in Sarajevo is that the stock market will be negatively affected, and he urges that the New York Stock Exchange be closed pending international negotiations (*MT*, 217). On the other hand, Gus McNiel considers the war an economic opportunity, because "A panic's the time for a man with a cool head to make money" (*MT*, 225).

New York is repeatedly compared with legendary dynastic cities of the ancient world, such as Babylon, Nineveh, Rome, Athens, Constantinople, and the "slave civilizations of Egypt and Mesopotamia" (*MT*, 263).[16] The novel begins well before the outbreak of World War I, suggesting that U.S. global authority antedates the war. Dos Passos accurately traces U.S. global and imperial authority to the Russo-Japanese War (1904–1905), which was concluded by the Portsmouth (New Hampshire) Treaty negotiated by Secretary of State John Hay.[17] Bud Korpenning first reads of the Japanese siege of Port Arthur together with the unrelated local story of Nathan Sibbetts, fourteen years old, who has killed his mother (*MT*, 17). As George Baldwin rushes to the hospital to get the McNiel personal injury case, he reads the red headline, "JAPS THROWN BACK FROM MUKDEN" (*MT*, 60). And Jimmy's mother, Lily, writes him while he is away at school that she took out his toy soldiers, the same "ones that used to be in the taking of Port Arthur," as sentimental reminders of him (*MT*, 97). Once again, newspaper headlines blare international news in specious efforts to simulate national or global consensus, but Dos Passos connects colonial struggles between world powers, like Russia and Japan, with more local, domestic struggles that begin at the level of family and interpersonal relations and extend to encompass working and other class divisions in the United States.[18] Dos Passos consistently establishes isomorphisms among the domestic, public, national, and international domains throughout the novel.

Dos Passos pays special attention to European colonialism in Africa in the years leading up to World War I, following contemporary left political arguments that the "scramble for Africa" among the European powers contributed significantly to the outbreak of World War I.[19] Dos Passos's references to several well-publicized events of Eurocolonialism in Africa seem intended to warn U.S. readers that the wage-slavery of U.S. capitalism is not as remote from the situation of the colonial subaltern in Africa as they might think. W. E. B. Du Bois had made a similar argument in *Darkwater*, published in 1920, five years before *Manhattan Transfer*, albeit focusing on the shared fate of African-American workers under urban modernity and that of Africans under the yoke of European imperial control.[20] Dos Passos refers variously and in apparent passing to several important political crises of Eurocolonialism in Africa, including the British "burning of Magdala," Ethiopia by Sir Robert Napier in 1867–1868 (*MT*, 87) and the "Agadir Incident" that pitted Germans, French, and British colonial powers against each other in their efforts to control Morocco in 1911–1912 (*MT*, 238) that would eventually include the uprisings in the Spanish Zone of Morocco that were underway in the year *Manhattan Transfer* was published.[21]

In many respects, *Manhattan Transfer* is typical of modernist literary representations of how urban, national, and global concerns are interrelated in the 1920s and 1930s. These territories are complicated by further intersections with psychological, interpersonal, and kinship relations in both their private and public aspects. In many respects, then, *Manhattan Transfer* represents complex, multicultural *stories*, whose overall narration is competitively claimed by the mass media, the dominant ideology, and the avant-garde artist. Dos Passos, the experimental socialist writer, criticizes journalistic accounts of "progress" and U.S. democratic emancipation as false stories hiding inequitable social relations. In his own use of journalistic devices, such as the famous headlines in the novel, Dos Passos offer an alternative reportage capable of revealing the Unconscious of U.S. modernity: its class distinctions, its neo-imperialism, and its social inequalities. Dos Passos connects internal class divisions to the global politics of European colonialism and the interpersonal difficulties of New Yorkers with the subaltern status of colonized peoples, especially those living in the colonial Black and Brown Belts of modernity (that is, Africa, Asia, and the Pacific Islands). In so doing, he connects the emerging global authority of the United States with a long tradition of European imperialism that anticipates both the insights of current cultural studies and the critical methods and theories of recent postcolonial studies.

Despite his critique of U.S. racism and the affinity of his postcolonial argument with that of major African-American intellectuals like Du Bois, Dos Passos does not include African Americans and other peoples of color as major voices or agents of the plot in the novel. There are some notable exceptions, including the African-American nurse who cares for Ellen Thatcher's baby and expresses the concern and care for the child that Ellen is often too busy to provide, and Achmet, Phineas P. Blackhead's South Asian servant, who spits contemptuously on the face of his dead employer, whose Import-Export firm, Densch and Blackhead, has profited from the "opportunity" of World War I and then failed as a consequence of the postwar recession (*MT*, 392). Dos Passos hints that Achmet's rebellion against his abusive employer might lead to an international proletariat revolution, which Dos Passos hints might begin in New York as well as in colonial India. Nevertheless, Dos Passos provides no macropolitical basis for such speculation, certainly not a conventional Communist appeal for a global workers' revolt. Dos Passos refers to Achmet as "the Hindu," perhaps ironically echoing Phineas Blackhead's use of this patronizing tag-name, but also oblivious to the fact that Achmet is an *Islamic*, not Hindu given name and thus contributing to the very cultural colonialism Dos Passos criticizes in the character Blackhead.

In general, however, people of color are represented by Dos Passos according to racial stereotypes of the African-American male as a violent criminal inclined to rape and murder, or as his opposite, the obliging, abject servant. Although issues of race, gender, and sexuality are clearly linked with the false divisions of class, Dos Passos treats these marginalized groups as virtually powerless, or at best capable of merely symbolic gestures, like Achmet's, or violent *ressentiment*, like that of the African-American criminals. The same ideology of disempowerment and sacrifice informs Dos Passos's treatment of the working-class characters, and it is reinforced by his technique of representing these characters primarily from the outside, without significant interiority. Middle-class characters are thoroughly criticized and their corruptions satirized, but Dos Passos portrays them as psychologically complex, giving them significant parts in the plot and disproportionate shares of the dialogue. Dos Passos seems to rely on a familiar liberal paternalism, in which *concern* for the working class is complemented by a desire to "raise" them to the level of the liberal bourgeoisie.

The promise of a postcolonial critique and the utopian prospect of multicultural (and ethnically diverse) New York are not fully realized in Dos Passos's *Manhattan Transfer* because Dos Passos subordinates what we term today the "identity politics" of women, ethnic minorities, and gays to a class-consciousness that turns out to be the work of an enlightened bourgeoisie, especially its artists and intellectuals, rather than organized political parties or even labor unions. Dos Passos's techniques of cubist composition, cinematic montage, and narrative perspectivism do not finally encompass the *differences* of the modern metropolis but instead become the predicates of a newly empowered middle-class aestheticism. Leaving New York City at the end of the novel, Jimmy Herf takes Whitman's famous ferry in the opposite direction, apparently toward a new natural ideal. Alone at first on the ferry, he is joined by "a brokendown springwagon loaded with flowers, driven by a little brown man with high cheekbones" (*MT*, 403). At first curious about where this man of color "is going with all those flowers," Jimmy "stifles" the impulse to ask him, in apparent obedience to his newfound aesthetic sense. Instead, he simply enjoys "a rich smell of maytime earth . . . , of wet flowerpots and greenhouses" and "walks to the front of the ferry" (*MT*, 403). It is this same ferry that in the previous paragraph appears to Jimmy as "looming big with its lights in a row like a darky's smile" (*MT*, 403).

This concluding and very metaliterary scene reorganizes and rationalizes the troubling disparities of class, race, gender, and sexuality that have threatened throughout the novel to erupt in a political revolution against capitalist oppression. Just before Jimmy leaves his apartment in the city, a "shrill drunken voice" calls out, "you're suspected of being the bobhaired bandit" and a girl in his building asks, "Why don't you take up a career of crime, Jimmy?" But when Jimmy replies, "How do you know I'm not?" we already know the answer he will give us as he exits the city on that very romantic ferry (*MT*, 402). Anna Cohen and her partner Elmer, the labor organizers, are quickly forgotten in favor of more romantic "bandits," so that Jimmy Herf misses his connection with the workers of the world as easily as Ellen does when she heads to her party at the Algonquin Hotel, "dressed up like a Christmas tree, like an Effenbee walking talking doll" (*MT*, 399).

In his surrender to an aesthetic ideology, Jimmy denies the actual city of New York as a viable site of political, social, and cultural contestation. Like Whitman, Dos Passos identifies with oppressed and exploited minorities, workers, and immigrants, but he ends up using them to construct his own ideal literary landscape, much as Jimmy Herf can metaphorize the ferry's lights as a "darky's smile" or the "little brown man's . . . high cheekbones" as an allusion to native America (*MT*, 403). Jimmy Herf does not head out across the Atlantic to align himself with the several international movements in revolt against capitalism in the 1920s, but instead he follows the poetic tracks of Walt Whitman into the heart of "America," a United States still imagined by Dos Passos to offer the utopian answers that have eluded Jimmy in the metropolis of New York City. Jimmy Herf forecasts aesthetic modernism's failure to come to terms with the multicultural urbanism and its transnational consequences already well underway in the course of modernization. Such a conclusion does not change our conventional understanding of John Dos Passos in the 1920s as an avant-garde socialist, critical of U.S. capitalism, but it does help us understand why Dos Passos might have been able to swerve so drastically from this apparently leftist position to right-wing anti-Communism. Dos Passos's politics in *Manhattan Transfer* are proleptically *liberal* and thus subject to internal contradiction and unexpected transformation; his politics in this period are anticipations of how post–World War II liberalism could be converted into today's neoliberalism.

Notes

1. Fredric Jameson, *Postmodernism or, The Cultural Logic of Late Capitalism* (Durham, NC: Duke University Press, 1991), p. 44.

2. BP's corporate name, formally changed from "British Petroleum" to "BP," suggests an effort to acknowledge its global operations and transnational identity, even as it continues to rely on its home base in the United Kingdom.

3. Ann Douglas, *Terrible Honesty: Mongrel Manhattan in the 1920s* (New York: Farrar, Straus and Giroux, 1995). Douglas is somewhat evasive about just how much the Harlem Renaissance and the New York avant-garde actually influenced each other in the 1920s and how much this cross-fertilization is the result of recent comparative scholarship on these two aspects of U.S. modernism. My argument in this essay is that a definitive characteristic of the "postmodern" is its engagement of multiple cultures, ethnicities, genders, sexualities, and classes. Whatever fails to take into account these now inescapable social forces is "modern"—or something else—but not postmodern.

4. Douglas somewhat defensively argues that high modernism, at least in New York, was always already postmodern, as if to chastise critics of modernism, especially cultural critics, for their failures to read carefully or comprehensively. Other scholars of modernism, however, have argued that U.S. high modernism must be put into conversation with other modernisms—the Harlem Renaissance, the 1930s Left, the pan-Indian movement of the 1920s and 1930s, European modernisms, and the Latin American literary "Boom"—in order for us to understand both its limitations and its historical and cultural frames of references. In this latter group, I include Andreas Huyssen, *After the Great Divide: Modernism, Mass Culture, Postmodernism* (Bloomington: Indiana University Press, 1986); Cary Nelson, *Repression and Recovery: Modern American Poetry and the Politics of Cultural Memory 1910–1945* (Madison: University of Wisconsin Press, 1989); Walter Kalaidjian, *American Culture between the Wars: Revisionary Modernism and Postmodern Critique* (New York: Columbia University Press, 1993); Michael North, *The Dialect of Modernism: Race, Language, and Twentieth-Century Literature* (New York: Oxford University Press, 1994); Sieglinde Lemke, *Primitivist Modernism: Black Culture and the Origins of Transatlantic Modernism* (New York: Oxford University Press, 1998); and John Carlos Rowe, *Literary Culture and U.S. Imperialism: From the Revolution to World War II* (New York: Oxford University Press, 2000).

5. Howard Zinn, *A People's History of the United States: 1492–Present* (New York: HarperCollins, 2003), pp. 330–38.

6. For the recent coalition of the IWW and Starbucks' workers, see the Web site for the IWW Starbucks Union (www.starbucksunion.org).

7. David Harvey, *The New Imperialism* (New York: Oxford University Press, 2005), pp. 139–40.

8. For example, T. S. Eliot, *The Waste Land*, in *The Waste Land and Other Poems*, ed. Frank Kermode (New York: Penguin Books, 1998), p. 57, complains:

Unreal City,
Under the brown fog of a winter dawn,

A crowd flowed over London Bridge, so many,
I had not thought death had undone so many.
Sighs, short and infrequent, were exhaled,
And each man fixed his eyes before his feet.

9. Townsend Luddington, *John Dos Passos: A Twentieth Century Odyssey* (New York: Dutton, 1980), pp. 200–202.

10. John Dos Passos, *Manhattan Transfer* (Boston: Houghton Mifflin Co., 1925), pp. 395–400.

11. Luddington, *John Dos Passos*, pp. 200–202.

12. McNiel rises to prominence in the corrupt Tammany Hall political machine of New York in part thanks to the financial seed-money provided by his insurance settlement.

13. Interestingly, Dos Passos does not seem to treat homosexuality, as so many other white male moderns would, as an "effect" of corrupt urban modernity.

14. Donald Pizer, *Dos Passos' U.S.A.: A Critical Study* (Charlottesville: University Press of Virginia, 1988), p. 15: "He would conceive of New York, not as constituting a single story (comparable to the traditional representationalist device of a single perspective on an object), but as comprising many stories (the cubist's multiple angles of vision). And he would combine these stories, which constituted the inherent form and meaning of the city, through montage, through the constant juxtaposition of a portion of one story and a portion of another."

15. McLuhan uses the term in both *The Gutenburg Galaxy: The Making of Typographic Man* (1962) and in *Understanding Media* (New York: Gingko Press, 1964), p. 6, where he specifically identifies the "global village" with the coming of electronic communications. McLuhan's son, Eric, contends that his father adapted the phrase from his study of James Joyce and Wyndham Lewis, thus establishing a continuity with avant-garde modernists in "The Source of the Term 'Global Village,'" *McLuhan Studies*, II, pp. 12–30.

16. In a letter of September 1920, quoted in Luddington, *John Dos Passos: A Twentieth Century Odyssey*, pp. 200–201, Dos Passos describes New York City as "magnificent" and comparable to "Nineveh and Babylon, or Ur of the Chaldees, or the immense cities which loom like basilisks behind the horizon in ancient Jewish tales. . . ."

17. For a detailed discussion of John Hay's development of U.S. foreign policy as foundational for U.S. global authority in the rest of the twentieth century, see *Literary Culture and U.S. Imperialism*, pp. 166–93.

18. Dos Passos relates family abuse, such as Bud Korpenning's father's abuse of him as a child, to the escalating violence that reaches its culmination in global warfare. The artist's task is in large part to demonstrate a connectedness to such social forces that the news can only represent in spatial contiguity, rather than in any sort of connected narrative or history.

19. Dos Passos, like Du Bois, is following Lenin's argument in *Imperialism, the Highest Stage of Capitalism* (1916).

20. See my discussion of Du Bois's *Darkwater* as a critique of U.S. imperialism in *Literary Culture and U.S. Imperialism*, pp. 200–215.

21. For a more detailed discussion of the Battle of Magdala, Emperor Theodore II of Ethiopia, and the British commanding general, Robert Cornelius Napier, who earned the title "1st Baron of Magdala" for his victory there, see my *The Other Henry James* (Durham, NC: Duke University Press, 1998), pp. 147, 224–225nn62–63. The Agadir Incident was precipitated when Germany sent the cruiser *Panther* to Agadir to protect the concessions of German financiers and was supported by local tribal leaders opposing French colonialism. The French had occupied Oujda in 1907, after the French national, Dr. Emile Mauchamp, had been murdered in Marrakech. Great Britain supported France, and there was a diplomatic crisis among the three powers that was settled by two agreements. The first agreement, signed on November 4, 1911, virtually recognized a French protectorate in Morocco, but assured German interests equal treatment in trade and commerce, ceding to Germany about 100,000 square miles in the northern French Congo. The second agreement was the Franco-Moroccan Treaty of March 30, 1912, signed at Fez, whereby the Sultan of Morocco recognized a French Protectorate. The French General Louis H. G. Lyautey was appointed "resident general" and began to "pacify" the countryside, which had rebelled against the Sultan. While Dos Passos was writing the novel, uprisings under the Riffian leader, Abd-al-Karim, were still underway against the Spanish in the Spanish Zone of Morocco, and in 1925 the rebel leader carried the fighting into French territory. He was defeated by combined French and Spanish troops and surrendered on May 26, 1926, whereupon he was exiled to the Atlantic island and French colony of Réunion.

[3]

FAULKNER AND THE SOUTHERN ARTS OF MYSTIFICATION IN *ABSALOM, ABSALOM!*

How exquisitely human was the wish for permanent happiness, and how thin human imagination became trying to achieve it. —Toni Morrison, *Paradise* (1998)

FAULKNER IS OFTEN PRAISED as a Southern writer who drew upon the region's rich traditions of storytelling, just as he is admired for his powerful indictment of the moral corruption that resulted from slavery and fueled the economic failures and social inequities of the New South. Storytelling and the sins of slavery are usually treated as separate and distinct legacies, the former representing all that is good about the region and the latter containing its evil. I will argue in this chapter that Faulkner recognized his own perverse complicity in a storytelling tradition in the South that was deeply involved in the rationalization of the many different fantasies on which slavery and Southern racism relied. Faulkner's obsessive fascination with Southern storytelling as crucial to regional culture is evident in all of his writings, but *Absalom, Absalom!* displays in the greatest detail his personal struggle to draw upon that culture while distinguishing his own narrative from its inherent immorality.

My thesis is treated in the complexities of Faulkner's modernist style and multiple narrative perspectives, but my conclusion can be simply drawn in terms of the popular idiom, "liberal guilt." The phrase usually refers to individuals who address historical injustices not by identifying with the victims, but with the victimizers. The aesthetic logic of liberal guilt has a more venerable definition in Aristotle's theory of tragic action, in which we identify with the tragic hero in order to purge ourselves of his inclination to error, which for Aristotle is the equivalent of "sin." My purpose in this chapter is not to reconsider or even add a small point to the immense legacy of Aristotelian scholarship, but merely to use the familiar concept of tragic catharsis to indicate how "liberal guilt" functions in aesthetic identification.

Aristotle renders tragic drama socially important, because it provides a moral context in which we might reflect upon the basic process of human knowledge. We look at the world, Aristotle contends, and "recognize" an outer world, much as we recognize another person: "Ah, that is *he*."[1] What Aristotle means is that we recognize another human being—"he"—by way of our own identification with him *as* human. Knowledge depends upon shared reason and thus the implicitly social human domain. In tragic drama, recognition (*anagnorisis*) does not occur between audience and hero on the basis of similarity, but rather because of the radical difference between the hero's actions and our own. When Sophocles's Oedipus kills his father and sleeps with his mother, however unwittingly, he is violating familiar social taboos and thus disobeying the gods, either literally or metaphorically. Our reaction in viewing such tragic action is to exclaim, "Oh, no," but still to recognize our human inclination to violate crucial social taboos, "There but for the grace of the gods, go I." Aristotle's notion of "catharsis," then, is intended to offer us a way to recognize our inclinations to social deviance—error and sin—and figure out the means to avoid such mistakes. Although each great tragedy involves its own specific kind of catharsis, I would generalize that the function of catharsis is to reawaken and strengthen the social bond. Oedipus ignores advisors, acts on his own, and fails to read adequately numerous signs he is given. The audience should leave the theater thinking that they should obey reasonable social rules and reaffirm their social bond, which the theatrical experience itself has reinforced. We, Athenians, have just watched a play about tragically misguided leadership in Thebes; let us not let this happen to us or our state.

The aesthetic politics of Aristotelian tragedy are thus inherently conservative, although the process through which the individual viewer undergoes his/her catharsis is apparently liberal. As an individual, I develop my own personal relationship to the tragic hero, interpreting how I might avoid his mistakes in my own life. My "civic virtue" depends on using my own powers of reason to think through the double bind in which the tragic hero finds himself. My identification occurs primarily in relation to the victimizer, not the victim. Oedipus draws our emotional response, not his father King Laius, who is laid low early in the dramatic action and is merely a dramatic device to focus our attention on his son's tragedy. What Aristotle does not take into account, I think, is our fascination, even obsession with the tragic hero, the character who challenges social laws, in effect rebelling against the gods. We know that Milton's Satan epitomizes sin, but Milton tempts us with Satan's powers, even his charms. The problem with such charismatic tragic heroes is that they draw us by way of their political, rhetorical, and erotic powers. We may in the end condemn them, "purging" ourselves of their faults, but along the way we have forgotten to identify with their victims, whose wrongs may continue into the present social situation.

This problem of identification with the tragic hero is central to Faulkner's success as a Southern novelist and to the morality of his work. Faulkner's literary corpus is described well by the phrase "liberal guilt," in which readers are encouraged to immerse themselves in the intricate psychological problems of white Southerners attempting unsuccessfully to come to terms with—to purge themselves of—the fundamental sin of slavery. African Americans victimized by slavery and its legacy of racism are difficult to identify with in Faulkner. They are stoic, comic, abused, violated, murdered, raped, but rarely "embodied" as complex, psychologically vital characters whom we recognize as ourselves. There is a way of reading against this rhetoric of tragic identification, but it requires readers like James Snead and Toni Morrison who refuse the imperatives of the Faulknerian text. I will return to Snead and Morrison's alternative hermeneutics at the end of this chapter, but at this point want to address Faulkner's poetic logic of tragic identification, or what I have more casually termed Faulkner's "liberal guilt."

The issue is an old one facing imaginative writers, who tell stories whose moral truths seem opposed to their fictional forms. Creative writers ask their readers to suspend their disbelief for the sake of some higher truth, but in so doing, authors identify themselves at least initially with the characters they criticize and morally condemn—those characters who lie, deceive, or are merely self-deluded. Faulkner's predecessor, Mark Twain, struggles to distinguish his work from the "lies" eloquently and skillfully told by the rich, powerful, and corrupt.[2] Joseph Conrad's Marlow infamously declares his hatred of "a lie," even as the reader knows him to be a pathological liar, leaving Conrad's own status as the author of *Heart of Darkness* in considerable doubt. Whom do we trust when the narrator of the story betrays an immoral unreliability? Is the "author" lurking somewhere in the blank places of the text, impossibly *between* the words, giving us hints of the truth? Although this problem has attracted many scholars, the ethical status of unreliable narration remains a troublesome one for readers of all competencies and thus an attractive option for writers precisely because such unreliability poses the fundamental question of literary authority: how do we know when to trust an absent author dealing in ostensibly fictive situations?

In Faulkner, such unreliability is usually integral to a culture built upon systematic deception and the constant labor of maintaining fragile social illusions of honor and respectability. In his *Narrative of the Life of Frederick Douglass*, Douglass describes in vivid detail the deceptiveness of the slave-master Covey, who is called "the Snake" by the other slaves. Douglass and his fellow workers know how slavery is maintained by trickery, even though they do not have the obvious means to overturn the system of laws and everyday practices through which such illusory power is maintained.[3] In the longer history of the South covered by Faulkner's Yoknapatawpha narratives, the symbolic system of racial, gender, and class discriminations has developed into an even more elaborate order of *fables*, often told and retold by individuals from all segments of that society as a means of internalizing and thus giving reality to its lies. "Unreliable narration," then, is much more than merely a technical device for Douglass and Faulkner, but an integral part of a deluded society. Yet if this is the moral situation of the South for both authors, then why can't they simply tell the truth?

In a certain sense, of course, such truth-telling is precisely what we identify as the task of great literature, but how a literary work accomplishes this work by way of imagined forms—character, plot, setting, and style—remains another one of the enduring problems for literary theorists. One compelling answer is that the literary text's obsessive interest in its own formal and communicative means can be used to mimic and sometimes expose the broader social modes of producing accepted meanings. The otherwise self-indulgent "metaliterariness" or "self-consciousness" of a literary text can thus be turned into a representation of the symbolic machinery of the culture that prompted it. Just how the internal commentary on literary possibility is transformed into an effective political critique, even potential *reform*, of social discourse and behavior is a more complicated question that can only be addressed in individual cases.

Absalom, Absalom! is one of the best possible test cases for how narrative unreliability and literary self-consciousness might serve the political and moral criticism of social reality. The novel is narrated formally by Rosa Coldfield, Quentin Compson's father, and Quentin Compson in parts that overlap and often offer different versions of the Sutpen family's history. Each of these narrators, of course, relies on numerous other sources and on auditors, like Quentin, who listens to "Miss Coldfield's" and his father's versions, and Quentin's Canadian classmate at Harvard, Shrevlin McCannon, whose questions and comments end up forming parts of the narrative. The purpose of this multiple narration is ostensibly realistic: to imitate the diverse ways in which we apprehend historical events, especially those involving scandal distorted by repression, which are prone to existing in different versions. The traditional assumption has been that such realism renders the psychological complexity of scandalous events in ways far more truthful than any historical chronicle, and that the different narrations allow responsibility for the repressed past to be shared by the community.[4]

The repressed, scandalous event cannot be overcome simply by uttering it, in part because its very repression makes literal statement impossible. As every reader of the novel is aware, the "secret" past of the Sutpen family has many different versions: Thomas Sutpen disavowed his son, Charles Bon, who is African (Haitian) American; Thomas Sutpen's son, Henry Sutpen, murdered his half-brother, Charles Bon; Charles Bon and Judith Sutpen, half brother and half sister, were incestuous lovers; and so on (there are still other versions). Each family "scandal" in Faulkner's South derives from the deeper sin of slavery, which for Faulkner has an even more profound source: ownership. So what is the *real* scandal to be "revealed" in the course of the novel: miscegenation, incest, murder, suicide, slavery, ownership? For Faulkner, they are all part of the same cultural narrative, linked parts that surface in the course of ordinary people attempting to account for extraordinary events.

For Faulkner, then, the novel is distinctly different from the repressive mechanisms of the chronicle. Every student of Faulkner's classic "The Bear," at least the long version that includes section 4, knows the dramatic events of the narrative revolve around Ike McCaslin's reading of his Uncle Buck and Buddy's account ledgers in the Commissary of their plantation. Interpreting bare facts as a novelist would, Ike uncovers the history of systematic miscegenation—the rape of African-American slave women by white masters—on which his family's wealth, power, and kinship relations are based.[5] The Christ-like Ike, by turns transcendentally good and divinely foolish, is certainly an alter ego for Faulkner, even though the author never quite makes clear what personal qualities Ike possesses that allow him to read the moral truth of the otherwise commodified accounts in those ledgers. Ike and Faulkner are above all *good* readers, in which "good" means both skilled and ethical.

In "The Bear," Faulkner sets those ledgers, which commodify human beings, against the "stories" through which people achieve their identities and social relations. The contrast is not so clear in the earlier *Absalom*, in which storytelling is not inherently good or liberatory. Faulkner knows how cultural work shapes the social fabric in which slavery and ownership are integral to its design. Rosa Coldfield and Mr. Compson tell their versions of Thomas Sutpen's tragic family history to distance themselves from what the Sutpens represent: ambitious nouveaux riches, social climbers, and iconoclasts who violate social propriety. Storytelling is for both Quentin's father and "Miss Coldfield" cathartic in the worst sense: a purgation of all they find objectionable in Thomas Sutpen and his family. In telling the story of the Sutpens, however, they cover up their own complicity in that tragedy and yet allow us to see their responsibility for it. That *difference* is what distinguishes Faulkner (and his moral characters, like Ike McCaslin) from the mystification of the Old South, its rationalization of plantation life and the slavocracy, and its insistent projection of evil onto other social forces, usually coming from outside the South: Sutpen's Haiti, the carpetbagger's North, even Shreve McCannon's Canada, one major destination for the Underground Railroad.

Rosa Coldfield tells her story to Quentin because she thinks he might "'enter the literary profession as so many Southern gentlemen and gentlewomen too are doing now and maybe some day you will remember this and write about it. You will get married then I expect and perhaps your wife will want a new gown or a new chair for the house and you can write this and submit it to the magazines'" (9–10). Quentin thinks, "*Only she dont mean that. . . . It's because she wants it told*" (10). Quentin doesn't specify what Rosa "dont mean," but he's probably referring to her suggestion of a profit motive, because Rosa elsewhere does imagine that Quentin might bear his Southern legacy, wherever he might live, by taking over the storytelling responsibilities for his family. The "literary profession" is indeed proper work for "Southern gentlemen and gentlewomen too," Rosa believes, because it contributes to the veneer of respectable culture that covers the ugly history of the white South. Quentin thinks that Rosa herself might well have told publicly the Sutpens' story, because "if she had merely wanted it told, written and even printed, she would not have needed to call in anybody—a woman who even in his (Quentin's) father's youth had already established herself as the town's and the county's poetess laureate by issuing to the stern and meager subscription list of the county newspaper poems, ode, eulogy and epitaph, out of some bitter and implacable reserve of undefeat" (11). Faulkner satirizes women authors, especially those like Rosa who write occasional poetry for the local newspapers, but he also has in mind his own pretensions to authorship. Anxious to distinguish his authority from Rosa's and yet well aware of how deeply indebted he is to this Southern legacy of storytelling, Faulkner struggles through *Absalom, Absalom!* to find a proper literary ethics.

In mocking Rosa's dilettantism, Faulkner recalls Mark Twain's notorious parodies of Julia A. Moore's maudlin verse and thus indulges a familiar, if tiresome, sexism.[6] Yet in the context of the novel his trivialization of Rosa as "poetess laureate" repeats Thomas Sutpen's more devastating insult of her. What causes Rosa to break her engagement to Thomas Sutpen is his proposal "that they breed together for test and sample and if it was a boy they would marry" (177). Just as Toni Morrison's Sethe is infuriated by schoolteacher's treatment of his slaves as livestock, so is Rosa horrified to be reminded that Sutpen considers women primarily means of reproduction.[7] When Sutpen comes to town in search of a wife, "the women merely said . . . that he had now come to . . . find a wife exactly as he would have gone to the Memphis market to buy livestock or slaves" (42). Unlike the Compsons and De Spains, Sutpen makes no effort to disguise his treatment of women (or slaves). In defending his marriage to the Octoroon wife who gives birth to their son (Charles Etienne de Saint Velery Bon), Charles Bon lectures Henry Sutpen on the close relationship between the courtesans of New Orleans and the Southern belle:

"No: not whores. Not even courtesans—creatures taken at childhood, culled, and chosen and raised more carefully than any white girl, any nun, than any blooded mare even. . . . For a price, of course, but a price offered and accepted or declined through a system more formal than any that white girls are sold under since they are more valuable as commodities than white girls, raised and trained to fulfill a woman's sole end and purpose: to love, to be beautiful, to divert; never to see a man's face hardly until brought to the ball and offered to and chosen by some man who in return, not can and not will but *must*, supply her with the surroundings proper in which to love and be beautiful and divert, and who must usually risk his life or at least his blood for that privilege. No, not whores." (117)

In this remarkable passage, Charles Bon raises the Octoroon prostitutes of New Orleans above "white girls," but he stylistically links the two, equating the courtship rituals of plantation society with those of the urban bordello. Following the complex motifs of doubling whereby Faulkner demonstrates how white aristocratic appearances are sustained by repressing African American realities, the Octoroon courtesans reveal the unconscious of the white Southern belle.[8]

Just what Thomas Sutpen proposes to Rosa is what he enacts with Milly Jones just one year after Rosa flees Sutpen's Hundred in 1866. Born in 1853, Milly is only thirteen or fourteen when in 1867 "Sutpen takes up with Milly Jones" (380). Milly's mother Melicent was "rumored to have died in a Memphis brothel," and we know that the Jones family represents the poor whites marginalized by the slave economy who thus become active participants in the racial hatred essential to the caste system of the Old South. As Thomas Sutpen's abuse of the child Milly suggests, women are not only treated as children by this paternalistic society, they are abused as children even before they have become adults. Sutpen is a "demon" in Rosa's estimation, because he exposes the elaborate fictions that maintain all of these distinctions: white Southern belle, prostitute, African-American woman, child, poor white woman. Yet in recognizing her identity with all of these other oppressed people in the South, Rosa feels neither compassion for nor solidarity with them. She is horrified and flees Sutpen's Hundred, only to return again and again to re-enact the repetition-compulsion that results from profound repression.[9]

Why, then, would Faulkner implicate himself in this process by insulting Rosa with his mockery of her modest literary talents? To be sure, we could attribute the remark to Quentin—it occurs in indirect discourse—or even to the paternalism of Jefferson at large, where Rosa is gently mocked for her literary pretensions. But Faulkner *does tell the story* of the Sutpens, which Rosa, Mr. Compson, Quentin, even Shreve and Charles Bon, tell only in part and from particular perspectives. As contemporary readers of *Absalom* know, Quentin cannot claim authorship because he is already dead at the end of *The Sound and the Fury* (1929). Quentin is spectral in *Absalom*, already fictionally dead, so that Faulkner himself must be Rosa's principal competitor for the "true story."

At first glance, Faulkner's insult of Rosa seems hardly comparable with Sutpen's, which dehumanizes her as fundamentally as the slavocracy does African Americans. Faulkner's gentle mockery of Rosa's poetic talents in "ode, eulogy and epitaph," however, suggests that she deals primarily in idealizing verse or laments for the dead. Her "poetry" does little to renew or revitalize the social order, but instead merely expresses the Old South's "bitter and implacable reserve of undefeat" (11). Thomas Sutpen wants a male heir to replace Henry Sutpen and restore the honor of the Sutpen name. He seeks to revitalize his family name and presumably his claim to aristocratic privilege by using Rosa as a biological means, but his insult also encompasses his disregard for what Rosa Coldfield and her family represent in the society of Jefferson: some claim to cultural authority. It would be unthinkable, of course, for the blunt and uncultivated Thomas Sutpen even to consider the value of Rosa's poetic contributions to the local newspaper in his marriage proposal, but Rosa knows that Thomas Sutpen's "insult" goes beyond his immodest proposal to her and encompasses his desire to use her respectable name to restore his family's tarnished reputation. Most readers recognize that one of Thomas Sutpen's major failures is his inability to *love* other people, including his children, his slaves, his two wives (Eulalia Bon and Ellen Coldfield), his fiancée (Rosa), and his mistress (Milly Jones).

Quentin concludes that Rosa tells him her part of the story to encourage him to carry on the legacy of Southern storytelling on which the social status of the Coldfields, Compsons, and De Spains depends. To be sure, these white class pretensions are merely foolish daydreams by 1909–10, the years Quentin attends Harvard and attempts to retell the story to Shreve McCannon. Quentin's suicide in Cambridge, Massachusetts, in

1910 ought to announce the end of a storytelling tradition that preserves the lies of the white ruling class from the antebellum to the post–Civil War era. Faulkner, then, competes not with Rosa, but with Thomas Sutpen, which is perhaps why both "insult" Rosa Coldfield.

In the tradition of avant-garde modernism in which William Faulkner certainly figures importantly, albeit eccentrically given his insistent Southern regionalism, the struggle between genealogical and cultural authority is central. T. S. Eliot's insistent trivialization of sexual reproduction in *The Waste Land* depends on his efforts to revitalize cultural values and claim his own authority. The sad, dirty liaison between the "typist" and "the young man carbuncular" in "The Fire Sermon" is "witnessed" by Tiresias only to remind us of the decadence of the modern age, but the episode is the prelude to Eliot's eulogy for Queen Elizabeth I, the Virgin Queen who represents for him the cultural vitality of England in the Elizabethan Age.[10] In the same section, St. Augustine (helped along by Eliot's version of Buddhism) "burns" through his youthful lust in Alexandria to achieve the sort of ascetic transcendence central to Christianity's divine love.[11] In response to what Eliot considers the sexual decadence of the modern age, he counsels literary sublimation and its more enduring "procreation" of cultural values. Ezra Pound metaphorized the brain as a "great clot of seminal fluid," and his *Cantos* work to create a complex genealogy, even kinship system, among the political and cultural "thrones" he identifies throughout history and around the globe.[12] William Faulkner is neither a version of Eliot's Christian poet nor Pound's fascist artist, but he resembles both of his contemporaries in his insistence upon the role of aesthetics in cultural revival and thus in social rule.

Thomas Sutpen fails in the end, killed by Wash Jones, the squatter occasionally employed by Sutpen and whose "honor" is quixotically threatened when Sutpen gets Jones's granddaughter Milly pregnant. Faulkner wants us to conclude that Sutpen meets the sordid end that he himself deserves for the lies he told and the secrets he tried futilely to keep. Thomas Sutpen fulfills the prophecy of the De Spains, Compsons, and Coldfields about a "new" South, even though he establishes his plantation in Yoknapatawpha County, Mississippi in 1833, twenty-eight years before the beginning of the Civil War. To the heirs of the ruined Southern aristocracy, like Rosa Coldfield and Mr. Compson, Thomas Sutpen is a prophetic version of the later, hated "carpet-bagger," who arrived to profit from the postbellum anarchy and socioeconomic reorganization of the South after Emancipation. But "carpet-baggers" were from the North, not the West Virginia mountains, where Sutpen was born in 1807 (or 1808) before West Virginia was in fact a state, certainly not from Haiti, where Sutpen emigrated and married the "only child of Haitian sugar planter of French descent" in 1827 (381).[13]

For Faulkner, Thomas Sutpen is not a Northern carpetbagger; he is the ghostly embodiment of everything behind the Southern romance of graceful plantation life and culture. What the Compsons and De Spains despise about Thomas Sutpen is the way he reveals their own lies, so that they work desperately to control his family "tragedy" in hopes of renovating their own social authority. Yet in distancing themselves from what Thomas Sutpen represents, they trivialize themselves and reduce their stories to mere gossip. In exposing the elemental truth Sutpen expresses, Faulkner tries to avoid the faded gentility that captures Miss Coldfield and Mr. Compson and drives Quentin to an early end. Yet in equating Sutpen's truth with the authority of the South, Faulkner cannot help himself from desiring, even emulating, that terrible power.

Thomas Sutpen's authority depends on the inextricable relationship he establishes between his identity and his ability to kill. Although state laws throughout the antebellum South varied considerably with respect to the authority they gave slave-owners over the lives and deaths of their slaves, actual practices of slaveholders seem to confirm the godlike authority over life and death exercised by so many white masters. Sutpen is not an ordinary slave-owner, but a philosophical abstraction of slave-owning—in short, a literary representation of its social psychology. He represents the terrifying reality of an individuality possessing philosophical being possible only as a consequence of another's lack of identity. He represents the beneficiary of that system in which the slave experiences "social death." As Orlando Patterson points out, the "slaveholder class" generally denied the violence of this situation by genuinely believing "that they cared and provided for their slaves and that it was the slaves who . . . had 'been raised to depend on others.'"[14] Condemning both this mystification and the power behind it, critics of the slavocracy focus understandably on the terrible consequences for the African Americans who suffered its material, psychological, and sociological terrorism. But the other side of the system is just as important for us to understand,

Faulkner argues, if we are ever to overcome the inherent power dynamics of such a caste system in which some people possess spiritual "being" and others are reduced legally to "chattel."

The moral center of *Absalom, Absalom!* is the story Thomas Sutpen tells General Compson about his origins in West Virginia and then Tidewater Virginia. I want to stress the fact that *Sutpen* tells his story, even if it is Rosa who will retell it in her letter and Quentin and Shreve retell it to each other in that cold Harvard dormitory room. Usually taken to be the antithesis of the Southern art of storytelling, Thomas Sutpen nevertheless spins a yarn that is perhaps the most riveting one in the entire novel, even if we never read precisely his version but instead a mediated account. Sutpen tells the story while hunting down his French architect, in an episode that reminds us that the enslavement of African Americans was shared by many other peoples, albeit usually to lesser degrees. The story Sutpen tells is Faulkner's great mythic parable of the psychological origins of slavery and its complementary class and gender distinctions. Whereas the title of the novel refers us to the Biblical parable of King David and his rebellious son Absalom, Sutpen's story offers its own version of a will-to-power that virtually "invents" slavery as an institution and legitimates the authority of the white master.

Born in the frontier wilderness that was not yet West Virginia in 1807–8, raised in a pre-agrarian hunting and gathering economy that seems tribal and communal, the young Thomas Sutpen appears to lack any sort of being or identity. As an adolescent—"he was eleven or twelve or thirteen now because this was where he realized that he had irrevocably lost count of his age" (228)—he moves with his family to Tidewater Virginia, identifiable with Jamestown, site of the early colony, where he confronts the true meaning of ownership and its complement, colonialism.[15] Sutpen's (or Faulkner's or Rosa's or Quentin's) account is aptly dream-like and vague with regard to details, and it thus has the qualities of some mythic origin story:

> He was just there, surrounded by the faces, almost all the faces which he had ever known . . . living in a cabin that was almost a replica of the mountain one except that it didn't sit up in the bright wind but sat instead beside a big flat river that sometimes showed no current at all and even sometimes ran backward, where his sisters and brothers seemed to take sick after sup-

> per and die before the next meal, where regiments of niggers with white men watching them planted and raised things he had never heard of. (227)

Sutpen's family seems to repeat the famine and illness suffered by the settlers of the early Jamestown colony, which was poorly situated along a peninsula (now an island) formed by the slow-moving and marshy James River as it empties into the Atlantic. As important to the American origin story as Plymouth Plantation, Jamestown usually invokes the redemptive myth of Pocahontas (*Matoaka* in the Pamunkey language), whose salvation of Captain John Smith and marriage to John Rolfe are used as mythic justifications of the European colonization of the South and as curious testaments to the aristocratic authority of those "First Families of Virginia," who can trace their genealogy back to this symbolic marriage of native and European Americans.[16] The adolescent Thomas Sutpen does not, however, witness these American mythemes; instead, he spies American "civilization" in the form of a master-slave tableau:

> And the white man was there who owned all the land and the niggers and apparently the white men who superintended the work, and who lived in the biggest house he had ever seen and who spent most of the afternoon (he told how he would creep up among the tangled shrubbery of the lawn and lie hidden and watch the man) in a barrel stave hammock between two trees, with his shoes off, and a nigger who wore every day better clothes than he or his father and sisters had ever owned and ever expected to, who did nothing else but fan him and bring him drinks. (227–28)

Faulkner carefully sets up this moment as a critical threshold in Thomas Sutpen's transition from childish innocence to adult experience: "Because he had not only not lost the innocence yet, he had not yet discovered that he possessed it" (228). Yet in working at the mystery posed by the man in the hammock, who owns everything and yet does not have to labor, Sutpen comes to adult consciousness at the cost of his innocence.

Faulkner creates a scene of literary self-consciousness in which Sutpen virtually recognizes himself in his power to kill. Descartes's *cogito ergo sum* is effectively replaced by Sutpen's *cogito ergo neco*, even if Faulkner's backwoods character never utters these Latin words. "I think, therefore I can kill" does seem to be Sutpen's motto from the moment he witnesses the twinned relationship of chattel slavery and land ownership. Drawing on his limited experience, the young Sutpen tries to explain the man in the hammock who owns everything by analogy with a "mountain man who happened to own a fine rifle" (228), but he cannot comprehend how the chance of such possession would allow "another . . . to say to other men: *Because I own this rifle, my arms and legs and blood and bones are superior to yours* except as the victorious outcome of a fight with rifles" (229). Faulkner is masterful at conveying two messages at the same time: the boy's incredulity before the owner's authority and the ineluctable truth of that mastery. Faulkner achieves this effect by the rhetorical use of double negatives and a variety of other negative constructions, most of which follow the logic of psychic repression, anticipating the more famous concluding lines of the novel, in which Quentin answers Shreve's question, "Why do you hate the South?" with his terrible cry: " 'I don't hate it,' he said. *I don't hate it* he thought panting in the cold air, the iron New England dark; *I don't. I don't! I don't hate it! I don't hate it!*" (378).

Sutpen thinks by association from possession of that rifle to the possibility he can kill the white master, especially after the young man has been humiliated by the white owner's slave who tells the boy to deliver his message to the back, not the front, door of the plantation house: "*But I can shoot him*" (234). Although the young Sutpen's grandfather rejects this option, Faulkner repeats it as if to keep it open: "*But I can shoot him*: he argued with himself and the other: *No. That wouldn't do no good*: and the first: *But I can shoot him. I could slip right up there through them bushes and lay there until he come out to lay in the hammock and shoot him*: and the other: *No. That wouldn't do no good*: and the first: *Then what shall we do?* and the other: *I don't know*" (235). Although Sutpen is speaking with his grandfather, the dialogue also has the qualities of a mental debate by a single person, sorting out the ethical dimensions of some profound problem.

"*Because I own this rifle*" and "*But I can shoot him*" are the twin claims the young Sutpen makes in this stunning "awakening," even if he and his grandfather both repudiate the effectiveness of these means to power. We should not forget that the young Sutpen turns to this murderous alternative to compensate for his inability to deliver his father's message to the slave-owner:

> *He never give me a chance to say it and Pap never asked me if I told him or not and so he can't even know that Pap sent him any message and so*

> *whether he got it or not cant even matter, not even to Pap; I went up to that front door again and I not only wasn't doing any good to him by telling it or any harm to him by not telling it, there aint any good or harm either in the living world that I can do to him.* (238–39)

Communication of any sort, whether a simple message or a complex story, seems to be of no consequence in the social order glimpsed by the young Sutpen. Faulkner here seems to anticipate the more postmodern sentiments of Don DeLillo, who understands the terrorist or political assassin to have perversely assumed the social authority of the novelist.[17] Long before Lee Harvey Oswald, Timothy McVeigh, and al-Qa'eda, the slavocracy refined its terrorist techniques from the Middle Passage to the colonial subjection of bodies and psyches forcibly displaced to a foreign land. With its ban against African-American literacy, its efforts to deprive poor whites, like the Sutpens, of education and economic opportunity, the Southern slave system relied on the breakdown of communication and the commodification of human relations.

Abandoning the device of the grandfather as interlocutor, Faulkner turns subsequent conversation into Thomas Sutpen's internal dialogue as he lies in bed at night:

> He thought "If you were fixing to combat them that had the fine rifles, the first thing you would do would be to get yourself the nearest thing to a fine rifle you could borrow or steal or make, wouldn't it?" and he said Yes. "But this aint a question of rifles. So to combat them you have got to have what they have that made them do what the man did. You got to have land and niggers and a fine house to combat them with. You see?" and he said Yes again. He left that night. . . . He never saw any of his family again. He went to the West Indies." (238)

Rifle, *shoot*, *property*: these are the different names Faulkner gives to the stages by which ownership of land and people becomes imaginable. They are rhetorical metonymies (literally: "changes of name") for the same activity, all of them describing in almost syntactically correct form—*I will shoot this rifle to seize what my neighbor has*—the historical process of the primitive accumulation of capital. Slavery and land ownership, both of which are impossible according to any basic conception of the human and the natural, are the consequences of the usual violence. For those things that cannot be properly owned, the owner cannot trace his rights to anything other than theft or piracy. So just how "childish" is the adolescent Thomas Sutpen in his peep at Southern white "civilization"?

"He went to the West Indies" (238). *Rifle*, *kill*, *ownership*, *slavery*, *colony*. The names proliferate, but the message is the same. From seventeenth-century Jamestown, Sutpen travels back in time to Columbus's fifteenth-century Hispaniola, retracing the violent genealogy of the European colonization of the Americas and its slave economy. Faulkner's ability to tell this story, which implicates not just Southern slaveholders but all descendants of those European conquerors and slave traders, is uncanny. Of course, the terrible origin story Faulkner offers us is a testament to his rhetorical and imaginative talents, but it is also an expression of Faulkner's bewildered admiration for Sutpen. Faulkner cannot even control the racial slurs that spill across the page in his account of Sutpen's fantasy. The angry adolescent Sutpen is responsible for "the monkey nigger" and "the nigger [who] was just another balloon face slick and distended with that mellow loud and terrible laughing so that he did not dare burst it" (234), but Faulkner writes with a certain enthusiasm, understanding how the ugliness of these racial epithets derives from a superiority integral to the caste system of the Old and the New South.

The only African American who gets a "speaking part" in *Absalom, Absalom!* is Charles Bon, who is killed again and again in a narrative designed to expose the culture of death produced by an economy of ownership. In killing Charles Bon, Faulkner silences him, allowing his dialogue to recirculate only in the memories of his white narrators and, of course, through the author himself.[18] Sacrificial, certainly Christological, Bon figures emblematically in the narrative and thus cannot by any means be trivialized, but his symbolic power is primarily identifiable with the "tragedy" of the Sutpen family. Charles Bon is certainly a member of that family in Faulkner's narrative, even if he cannot claim a proper genealogical or even legal relationship with the white ruling class of the South. African-American social inclusion, then, is ambivalently treated in Faulkner's narrative: recognition of African-American identity can redeem the tragic action of *Absalom, Absalom!* by lifting the repression of the family ties (and thus community relations) that connect black and white Southerners indissolubly, but this social psychological therapy is achieved in and through white cultural mechanisms.

In sum, Faulkner does not align himself with Charles Bon or even with his son, Charles Etienne de Saint Velery Bon, who "married a full-blood negress, name unknown, 1879," and thus returns his father's and mother's ("an octoroon mistress whose name is not recorded" [383]) racial hybridity to "full-blood" blackness and the anonymity, in virtual spite of the aristocratic grandeur of his given names, achieved by his own son, the "Jim Bond," whom Shreve McCannon predicts will constitute a group—"the Jim Bonds"—that will "conquer the western hemisphere" (378). Faulkner does not align himself with the dilettantish Rosa Coldfield, the vanished De Spains, or the powerless Compsons—the gentility of the Old South in Yoknapatawpha—but instead with Thomas Sutpen, the parvenu and social climber who lacks utterly the "culture" and thus manners Rosa expects and yet who tells the only story in the novel to challenge Faulkner's literary authority. Even Charles Bon's comparison of the Southern (white) belles with the African-American prostitutes of New Orleans is subordinate finally to Sutpen's story of a will-to-power that encompasses human and territorial conquest not only of the South but also of the legacy of European contact with the Western Hemisphere. What Shreve McCannon predicts for the destiny of those "Jim Bonds" follows that logic: *another* "conquest," even if it is troublingly identified with sexual procreation: "of course as they spread toward the poles they will bleach out again like the rabbits and birds do, so they won't show up so sharp against the snow" (378). But let there be no mistake about it, McCannon insists, "it will still be Jim Bond; and so in a few thousand years, I who regard you will also have sprung from the loins of African kings" (378).

Faulkner's alternative to Sutpen's militarism—"Because I own this rifle . . ."—is certainly his more humane literary story, wherein author and reader *imagine* others in order to understand them. Much has been written about how Quentin and Shreve share the story of the South in the cold dormitory room at Harvard in ways that substitute communication, imagination, and finally compassion for the racial divisions and class hatreds of the slavocracy. Anyone would prefer, of course, their conversation as the metaphor for Faulkner's relationship with the reader either to Rosa's mystification or, much worse, Sutpen's "wrestling" with his slaves to demonstrate ritually his physical (and psychological) superiority. Yet there is still some residual element in Faulkner's version of the story that is intended to be too encompassing, too white, too tragic, and too universal to allow him escape from the ghost of Thomas Sutpen. Literature's power is not always humane, does not inevitably redeem us, and can reveal only some truths by hiding others. Like Quentin, Faulkner has good reasons to hate the South and its storytelling traditions.

If we take seriously Shreve's prediction, then one of those reasons is profoundly racial and indicates how Sutpen's will-to-power enthralls Faulkner to the end of the novel. The "Jim Bonds" are taking over, not by virtue of their abilities to tell their stories, not through their powers to recognize their complicity in the symbolic story of the Sutpens, but by some perverse natural selection, "like the rabbits and the birds" that adapt in order to survive. Cultural work without economic, political, and psychological power, Faulkner argues, is mere dilettantism, a dying art, like Rosa's odes and epitaphs. The history of the South Faulkner represents in *Absalom, Absalom!* will repeat itself, now as a revenge cycle in which those oppressed will assume power by what appears to be a law of nature. Of course, such repetitions repudiate human history as we understand it, so that the stories told in *Absalom* will be eventually forgotten, their figured pages whitened to silence in the long view Shreve offers at the end.

In *Playing in the Dark*, Toni Morrison analyzes six "linguistic strategies employed in fiction to engage the serious consequences of blacks."[19] It is worth noting that Morrison explicitly adapts her categories from James Snead's analysis of "the characteristic features of racial division" in literary language in his book, *Figures of Division: William Faulkner's Major Novels*.[20] Two of Morrison's "linguistic strategies" are particularly apt to the mode of literary mystification that works so powerfully in Faulkner's *Absalom, Absalom!* "Metaphysical condensation," Morrison writes, "allows the writer to transform social and historical differences into universal differences."[21] "Dehistoricizing allegory" seems to be its proper complement, because such allegory "produces foreclosure rather than disclosure" by postponing social change to such "an unspecified infinite amount of time" that "history, as a process of becoming, is excluded from the literary encounter."[22] In his effort to implicate all of us in the story told by Quentin and Shreve in New England, Faulkner uses the South as a specific region to create an allegory for a tragic human condition. By concluding with the Canadian Shreve McCannon's prediction "that in time the Jim Bonds are going to conquer the western hemisphere," Faulkner metaphysicalizes and dehistoricizes the specific class, gender, and racial problems of the New South. By situating the complementary cultural work of storytelling (or more generally communal representation) in a white imaginary and excluding African Americans from their own self-representation, Faulkner perpetuates the Southern arts of mystification in his very effort to reveal their perversity.

Faulkner's modernist style and form contribute to the reader's identification with white Southern tragic heroes like Thomas Sutpen and his heir, Quentin Compson. The sins of slaveholding and subsequent racism are passed on to the United States in general, which is in many respects appropriate and just. In her recent novel, *A Mercy* (2008), Toni Morrison reminds us that Southern slavery was not restricted to the South in seventeenth-century colonial America and included native Americans and indentured Europeans, as well as African Americans.[23] Morrison encourages us to identify with the African-American slave, Florens, and the Native American slave, Lina, both of whom have been displaced radically from their homes. Their tragic fates are our own, but Faulkner focuses instead on the tragic histories of white Southerners and by extension what Morrison's characters refer to as the "Europes," whose colonial ambitions have created the conditions of slavery, classism, and sexism in the first place in the Western Hemisphere. Morrison's characters represent themselves over and above the semiotics of the dominant Euroamerican culture, but Faulkner's African Americans are occluded and primitivized, their white masters rendered in the complicated histories that still resonate in the present. Indeed, the stream-of-consciousness narrations suggest an eternal present in which the responsible reader participates, as Shreve does in his conversation with Quentin in that chilly dorm room in Cambridge, even trying out his own version of Quentin's story, despite being unfamiliar with the American South.

Of course, Faulkner wants us to be shriven in reading *Absalom, Absalom!*, and his intentions are probably good as far as the liberal imagination is concerned. We must accept responsibility for white Euroamerican imperialism, especially slavery. We must acknowledge America's (including colonial America's) original sin. We must recognize what suffering it has brought *our* posterity. Reading any of Faulkner's novels performs this sort of catharsis and revival of our democratic aspirations, but it leaves African Americans in the dead-zone of those victimized by such a will-to-power, zombies dependent on the social psychology of "tragic" America and its "original sin." All of this means that we are dependent primarily on a problematic "civilization" that we must somehow redeem, but that is still traceable to Europe, not to Africa, Asia, or the indigenous peoples of the Western Hemisphere. Where is Charles Bon's story? Indeed, Shreve attempts to tell it while taking over Quentin's narration at one point in their conversation, but the experiment cannot succeed for this Canadian who has never visited the South and has little contact with African Americans. The point is not simply that African Americans must tell their own stories, although Morrison and Snead are making just that important point, but that the African American and Native American—and Chinese American, Mexican American, Japanese American, Korean American, et al.—contributions to U.S. national identity need to be acknowledged. In wrestling with his slaves, Thomas Sutpen imagines he can win and Faulkner's readers that they can understand. But they are all mistaken; they need to be thrown and pinned, surprised by the victims, who have fought them to turn the tide.

Notes

1. Aristotle, *Aristotle's Theory of Poetry and Fine Art*, 4th ed., trans. S. H. Butcher (New York: Dover Publications, Inc., 1955), pp. 15–16.

2. John Carlos Rowe, "Mark Twain's Critique of Globalization (Old and New) in *Following the Equator: A Voyage around the World*," *Arizona Quarterly* 61:1 (Spring 2005), pp. 109–35.

3. Frederick Douglass, *Narrative of the Life of Frederick Douglass, an American Slave, Written by Himself* (New York: Penguin Books, 1982), p. 103. Of course, one of Douglass's purposes in his 1845 *Narrative* is to provide some means of overturning the symbolic power of the slavocracy. See John Carlos Rowe, *At Emerson's Tomb: The Politics of American Literature* (New York: Columbia University Press, 1997), pp. 96–123.

4. William Faulkner, *Absalom, Absalom!* (New York: Random House, 1964), pp. 379–83, includes a "Chronology" and "Genealogy" for the characters, but it is clear that the factual references in this section are utterly overwritten by the narrative itself, in which these mere personal details are overwhelmed by the entanglements of the characters' lives and fates represented in the novel. Faulkner thus uses the "Chronology" and "Genealogy" not simply as mnemonic devices for readers, but also as indications of the superiority of the novel over chronicle as the proper mode of historical representation for complex human events.

5. William Faulkner, *Go Down, Moses* (New York: Random House, 1942), pp. 243–301.

6. Twain's best known parody of Julia A. Moore's "Sweet Singer of Michigan," is

"Ode to Stephen Dowling Bots, Dec'd.," in chapter 17 of *Adventures of Huckleberry Finn*, ed. Thomas Cooley (New York: W. W. Norton, 1999), pp. 122–23.

7. Toni Morrison, *Beloved* (New York: Random House, 1987), p. 125: "It was schoolteacher who taught them otherwise. . . . Watchdogs without teeth; steer bulls without horns; gelded workhorses whose neigh and whinny could not be translated into a language responsible humans spoke."

8. John Irwin, *Doubling and Incest / Repetition and Revenge: A Speculative Reading of Faulkner* (Baltimore: Johns Hopkins University Press, 1975), p. 9.

9. Sigmund Freud, "The 'Uncanny,'" in *On Creativity and the Unconscious: Papers on the Psychology of Art, Literature, Love, Religion*, ed. Benjamin Nelson, trans. under the supervision of Joan Riviere (New York: Harper and Row, 1958), p. 145.

10. T. S. Eliot, *The Waste Land* in *The Waste Land and Other Poems* (New York: Harcourt Brace Jovanovich, Inc., 1962), pp. 36–41.

11. Ibid., p. 41.

12. John Carlos Rowe, *The New American Studies* (Minneapolis: University of Minnesota Press, 2002), pp. 124–30. Pound's reference to the brain as a "great clot of seminal fluid" comes from his "Preface" to Remy de Gourmont, *Des Amours*.

13. Shreve points out to Quentin that "there wasn't any West Virginia in 1808 because . . . West Virginia wasn't admitted . . ." (220). Shreve's historical pedantry irritates Quentin—"'All right,' Quentin said. . . . 'All right all right,'" but Faulkner wants us to know that Sutpen is born on the frontier of Virginia (220).

14. Orlando Patterson, *Slavery and Social Death: A Comparative Study* (Cambridge, MA: Harvard University Press, 1982), p. 338.

15. In the "Chronology," Faulkner is more specific about Thomas Sutpen's age at the time of the family's move: "1817 Sutpen family moved down into Tidewater Virginia, Sutpen ten years old" (379).

16. The curiosity in the myth of the First Families of Virginia that they are "descended" from Rolfe and Pocahontas is, of course, that it validates the ethnic hybridity and miscegenation that in all other respects Southern white aristocrats treated as a social taboo. On the Pocahontas myth, see Robert S. Tilton, *Pocahontas: The Evolution of an American Narrative* (New York: Cambridge University Press, 1994).

17. See John Carlos Rowe, "The Dramatization of *Mao II* and the War on Terrorism," *South Atlantic Quarterly* 103:1 (Fall 2003), pp. 21–43.

18. See my discussion of the problem of "the African-American voice" in Faulkner's fiction in *At Emerson's Tomb*, pp. 222–46.

19. Toni Morrison, *Playing in the Dark: Whiteness and the Literary Imagination* (New York: Random House, 1992), pp. 67–69. The six categories are: economy of stereotype, metonymic displacement, metaphysical condensation, fetishization, dehistoricizing allegory, and patterns of explosive, disjointed, repetitive language.

20. James A. Snead, *Figures of Division: William Faulkner's Major Novels* (New York: Methuen, 1986), pp. x–xi.

21. Morrison, *Playing in the Dark*, p. 68.

22. Ibid.

23. Toni Morrison, *A Mercy* (New York: Alfred A. Knopf, 2008).

[4]

OUR *INVISIBLE MAN*: THE AESTHETIC GENEALOGY OF U.S. DIVERSITY

No, I am not a spook like those who haunted Edgar Allan Poe; nor am I one of your Hollywood-movie ectoplasms. I am a man of substance, of flesh and bone, fiber and liquids—and I might even be said to possess a mind.

—Ralph Ellison, *Invisible Man* (1952)

They're only shadows, Bliss, Daddy Hickman whispered. They're fun if you keep that in mind. They're only dangerous if you try to believe in them the way you believe in the sunlight or the Word. —Ralph Ellison, *Juneteenth* (1999)

RALPH ELLISON'S *Invisible Man* predicts with extraordinary accuracy how postmodern politics will depend upon symbolic action, charismatic celebrity, and rhetorical exhortation. Fifty-eight years after the novel's publication, we speak commonly of *aesthetic* politics and refer thereby to the rhetorical and symbolic means through which the sublime diversity of the United States is rendered meaningful or *representable*. Today these political issues are profoundly entangled with hermeneutic concerns exemplified by the mass media of film, television, and the Internet (and digital technologies), but on the publication of *Invisible Man* it was still imaginable that the aesthetic aspects of politics might be theorized in the imaginative space of the novel. In his efforts to write the unfinished novel posthumously published as *Juneteenth*, Ellison acknowledges that the novel is no longer (and perhaps never was) the appropriate abstraction of the aesthetic aspect of politics. In *Juneteenth*, African-American religion and Hollywood film struggle for authority over the aesthetic politics practiced variously by Senator Adam Sunraider, a.k.a. Bliss, and Reverend A. Z. Hickman, a.k.a. "God's Trombone."[1] To be sure, Ellison's *Juneteenth* incorporates all of these different media, but it does not claim the integrative, even transcendent function *Invisible Man* could propose in 1952: an aesthetic meditation on politics that is one of the few modern American fictions to deserve the title of a "political novel."

Juneteenth is organized around a singular event of confession and recollection: Senator Sunraider's deathbed conversation with Hickman, the African-American preacher who raised him. Storytelling is certainly thematized, and we might even say that such cathartic acts are often considered essential to the novel as a literary form, but *Juneteenth* does not represent its own narrative medium as an effective challenge either to Sunraider's political power or Hickman's religious authority. In contrast, *Invisible Man* offers the novel itself as a counter-force to the misguided politics of the Communist Party (the Brotherhood), Black Nationalism (Ras, the Exhorter), and Black Accommodation (Bledsoe and his historical mentor, Booker T. Washington). When these and other political parties, philosophies, and historical accounts fail, Ellison and his narrator turn to literature. Contemplating his friend Tod Clifton's unexpected departure from the Brotherhood and sudden murder by the police, the narrator wonders: "And I, the only witness for the defense, knew neither the extent of his guilt nor the nature of his crime. Where were the historians today? And how would they put it down?"[2] These questions are meant rhetorically, because the reader knows that Tod Clifton's murder is not a likely topic for "historians today." Paradoxically, the narrator is by virtue of his ignorance of Tod's guilt or crime thereby enabled to tell his story, which will otherwise be deliberately forgotten. In this fictional moment, Ellison pits white history against minority literature, and it results in one of the most extraordinary tours de force in the modern novel:

> What did they ever think of us transitory ones? . . . birds of passage who were too obscure for learned classification, too silent for the most sensitive recorders of sound; of natures too ambiguous for the most ambiguous words, and too distant from the centers of historical decision to sign or even to applaud the signers of historical documents? We who write no novels, histories, or other books. What about us, I thought, seeing Clifton again in my mind. (*Invisible Man*, 332)

In this moment, the narrator paradoxically discovers literature as a means of representing a collective minority, specified in the "we who write no novels, histories, or other books" and who are *not* specified by race, ethnicity, class, or any other identifying feature other than their shared exclusion from one crucial part of conventional definitions of *literacy*: writing. Unfortunately, this transracial vision is rare, perhaps unique to this vision in the novel. As I shall argue in the second half of this chapter, Ellison's reliance on a black-white binary to criticize racism and on African Americans as the representative minority limits the political potential of this transracial ideal.

In the moment of his greatest despair and confusion regarding the possibility of political action—confused by Tod Clifton's departure from the Brotherhood and his murder by the police—the narrator proceeds to *represent* and then *identify with* the young men he observes on the subway platform. Ellison's aim in this crucial moment seems to be to comment on how his own novelistic process departs from that of the traditional Euroamerican "novels, histories, or other books" from which these young men have been excluded. In Ellison's prose, in the modernist weave of the narrator's urban confusion, the three young men in their zoot suits turn out to be "black" and by no means illiterate, because they "speak a jived-up transitional language full of country glamour, think transitional thoughts," and read "magazines" that turn out to be "comic books" (333–35). They are clearly not "natural western men" and thus prompt the narrator to identify with them in one of his recurrent moments of social alienation: "These fellows whose bodies seemed—what had one of my teachers said of me?—'You're like one of these African sculptures, distorted in the interest of a design.' Well, what design and whose?" (333).

These three hipsters are "outside history," beyond the "science" of the Brotherhood's Marxism and certainly "invisible" to the racist ideology of white America, and for that very reason they suggest symbolically for the narrator an alternative "literacy" and thus a different form for the African-American novel. In the aesthetic genealogy of African-American culture, they draw on the archetypal features of the "Black Christ," reinforced perhaps by their collective figuration of the Christian trinity (father–son–holy ghost) or the classical Fates:[3]

> But who knew (and now I began to tremble so violently I had to lean against a refuse can)—who knew but that they were the saviors, the true leaders, the bearers of something precious? The stewards of something uncomfort-

> able, burdensome, which they hated because, living outside the realm of history, there was no one to applaud their value and they themselves failed to understand it? (333)

Ellison uses these young black men to represent the contingency of history, its eccentricity and refusal to fit the "science" of Marxism or the "reason" of white bourgeois capitalism:

> What if Brother Jack were wrong? What if history was a gambler, instead of a force in a laboratory experiment, and the boys his ace in the hole? What if history was not a reasonable citizen, but a madman full of paranoid guile and these boys his agents, his big surprise! (333)

The narrator's identification with these three young men is intended to be powerful and profound, reinforced by Ellison's use of appositive pronouns: "What was I in relation to the boys, I wondered. Perhaps an accident, like Douglass. Perhaps each hundred years or so men like them, like me, appeared in society, drifting through; and yet by all historical logic we, I, should have disappeared around the first part of the nineteenth century, rationalized out of existence. Perhaps like them, I was a throwback" (334). The narrator's comparison of himself to Frederick Douglass in the moment he is trying to figure out his relationship to these three young men, cast off by history, has two important connotations. First, Ellison reminds us that slavery has not been successfully abolished, that many people are still living under conditions analogous to those of the antebellum slaves Douglass represented in his writings, speeches, journalism, and political activism. Ellison refers in this moment not only to the economic racism that segregated African Americans; he also includes the cultural racism that excludes them from the official histories and accounts of civilization's achievements. Second, the narrator's responsibility now depends more on the legacy of African-American abolition and rights struggles than on the Marxist "science" of the Brotherhood.

In 1952, Ellison's identification with these black youth is radical, even a forecast of the Beat counterculture that would challenge the dominant right-wing ideology of Cold War America. But Ellison's method of literary identification more closely resembles Lionel Trilling's "liberal imagination," in which cultural differences are recognized and then critically understood by an author. Ellison does not imitate the argot of these young men, the style of their zoot suits, or the visual rhetoric of those comic books in their pockets. Instead, Ellison writes a great American novel that draws extensively on U.S. literary traditions and avoids African-American dialect, except when he represents the speech of a rural or uneducated African American. Scholars have responded in various ways to Ellison's high-cultural style, but his avoidance of African-American dialect is understandable given the fierce arguments on this topic among the writers of the Harlem Renaissance. Richard Wright's criticism of Zora Neale Hurston's use of dialect in *Their Eyes Were Watching God* is just one example of this debate, and Ellison chooses to follow a high-cultural path, risking thereby charges that he is merely imitating Euroamerican sources.[4]

Ellison's liberal identification is hardly as one-sided as Faulkner's in *Absalom, Absalom!*. Ellison begins both with African-American subjectivity as central to his narrative perspective and as the basis of his plot, whereas Faulkner competes with the Southern white masters, like Sutpen, for rhetorical authority, effectively silencing his African-American subjects, reducing them to mere victims. Ellison's narrator faces countless frustrations as a consequence of racism and remains unnamed in part as a consequence of his social invisibility, but he also chooses strategic anonymity as a cover to launch his critical account of the social damage caused by racism. Yet the subject position of the narrator resembles Ellison's author-function: both speak in the language understood by the ruling class. The jive of those zoot suiters, like the mad speech of the World War I veteran in the "Golden Day" episode in the novel, will never communicate to those subscribing to the dominant ideology. Ellison and his narrator must write and speak in high-cultural, rational discourse, thereby constituting a particular audience that would exclude those zoot suiters. In this regard, Ellison must end up writing *for them*, thus representing their interests in contexts that are not accessible to them, including cultural, economic, and political venues. Ellison's claim as an author to serve as such a representative or go-between differs significantly from Faulkner's "liberal guilt," but it is nonetheless a version of the "liberal imagination" Trilling codified in 1950, even if Trilling's *Liberal Imagination* has little to say about African Americans and the central racial issues of the era.

The origin of the narrator's transformation can be traced back to the moment in the headquarters of the Harlem office of the Brotherhood, when Brother Tarp hangs a portrait of Douglass on the narrator's office wall. When the narrator tries to thank him, Tarp answers: "Don't thank me, son. . . . He belongs to all of us" (286). Tarp teaches the narrator a political and literary lesson, which has much to do with the narrator's ultimate decision to leave the Brotherhood and to go "underground" into that liminal space most critics have considered analogous to the imaginative world of Ellison's novel. Whether writing his "autobiography" over and over again, writing his former "master" to declare his liberty in the *Liberator*, or purchasing his own freedom with money lent him by English abolitionists, Douglass used his personal identity in countless symbolic ways to represent other African Americans.[5] Throughout *Invisible Man*, the narrator struggles to find his own individuality, and the novel has often been criticized because scholars have confused the narrator's desire for bourgeois individualism with Ellison's political and aesthetic views. But Ellison clearly sets in opposition Marxist collectivism, bourgeois individualism, and a third term: African-American representivity, whereby one person speaks "for" others who are dispossessed, illiterate, enslaved, disenfranchised, or otherwise radically cast outside of history. Just as Trilling distinguishes his version of the "liberal imagination" from postwar middle-class liberalism, so Ellison creates a middle term between the extremes of left and right politics in the 1950s.

The portrait of Frederick Douglass on the narrator's office wall acts with the power of a talisman as the narrator throws himself into his work of organizing the African-American community. He succeeds brilliantly in Harlem because he draws on African-American traditions of representivity or "symbolic action" traceable to Frederick Douglass, Marcus Garvey, and W. E. B. Du Bois. Like Du Bois incorporating African-American traditions and historical leaders from Alexander Crummell to Booker T. Washington into his own authorial identity in *The Souls of Black Folk* (1903), the narrator imitates and adapts political practices that have worked before in the organization and representation of African Americans. Like Garvey, the narrator relies on parades and symbolic displays to play upon the community's need for spectacle and theatricality: "Our work went so well that a few Sundays later we threw a parade that clinched our hold on the community" (286) and "I organized a drill team of six-footers whose duty it was to march through the streets striking up sparks with their hobnailed shoes. On the day of the parade they drew crowds faster than a dogfight on a country road. The People's Hot Foot Squad, we called them" (287). Like Douglass, the narrator plays on his celebrity, less for its own sake and more for its political functionality: "My name spread like smoke in an airless room. . . . Speeches here, there, everywhere, uptown and down. I wrote newspaper articles, led parades and relief delegations, and so on. . . . Articles, telegrams and many mailings went out over my signature, some of which I'd written, but most not. I was publicized, identified with the organization both by word and image in the press" (287).

What the narrator refers to as "the sheer corn" of his reliance on symbolic actions and political celebrity to give coherence and focus to the Harlem community is another way of describing his ingenious reliance on sentiment as well as reason, on experience together with historical knowledge, on personal feelings and philosophical truth. These lessons are explicitly linked by the narrator to Frederick Douglass—his grandfather's hero—with whom he identifies not only as an historical figure but as a rhetorician. During the narrator's greatest success in organizing the Harlem district, he observes: "For now I had begun to believe, despite all the talk of science around me, that there was a magic in spoken words. Sometimes I sat watching the watery play of light upon Douglass's portrait, thinking how magical it was that he had talked his way from slavery to a government ministry, and so swiftly. Perhaps, I thought, something of the kind is happening to me" (288). Understood exclusively as the narrator's expression of his unbridled ambition, his identification with Douglass anticipates his condemnation by the Brotherhood and his marginalization; interpreted as the moment in which he self-consciously recognizes his reliance on the African-American heritage of political activism, his "reflection" in the "watery" glass of Douglass's portrait constitutes his own political mirror-stage, a moment that transforms both his aspirations for individualism and Ellison's efforts to write the Great American Novel into different political and aesthetic ambitions.

Of course, Brother Wrestrum's condemnation of the narrator to the Brotherhood as a "petty individualist" (apparently misquoting Brother Jack's "petit bourgeoisie") is based on the narrator's interview with a popular magazine, the accompanying photograph of him as a celebrity, and Wrestrum's conclusion that the narrator "aims to control the movement uptown. He wants to be a *dictator*!" (302). In this regard, Ellison is both historically and prophetically accurate; virtually every charismatic

African-American leader from Marcus Garvey and W. E. B. Du Bois to Martin Luther King Jr. and Malcolm X has been criticized for being *too* powerful and exiled or murdered as a consequence. The fact that these four leaders were perceived as too powerful by such different groups as the federal government (Garvey's deportation and Du Bois's harassment by the State Department and FBI), white Southern racists (King's assassination), and black nationalists (Malcolm X's assassination) indicates not only the pervasiveness of this view but Ellison's prophetic power, insofar as he had only the benefit of Garvey's deportation as an historical example when he wrote *Invisible Man*.

Ellison's clairvoyance, however, is not supernatural but the result of his understanding of the double bind facing African-American political leaders struggling to participate in the wider "representative democracy." On the one hand, many different kinds of "representation" in the modern United States depend on literacy, whether the mediating texts are novels, newspapers, congressional bills, or voters' ballots. On the other hand, nineteenth-century African Americans relied on a wide range of non-print media for communication, in part as a consequence of the racist taboo forbidding literacy among Southern slaves and in part respecting the heritage of orality, music, and performance as communicative modes in African and Afro-Caribbean cultures.[6] "White folks seemed always to expect you to know those things which they'd done everything they could think of to prevent you from knowing," the narrator observes at one point, but Ellison makes it clear that African Americans have responded to this system of racialized knowledge by developing alternative epistemologies (239). Yet how are African-American political leaders to negotiate these two worlds, where success in one realm virtually guarantees failure in the other?

The narrator's unexpectedly successful speech at a Harlem meeting of the Brotherhood is a consequence of his reliance on African-American preaching traditions and the "call-and-response" he prompts in the audience, especially "a man's far-carrying voice" that counterpoints the narrator's speech with metaphors from baseball: "We with you, Brother. You pitch 'em we catch 'em!" (258). Members of the Brotherhood are deeply divided over the appropriateness of the narrator's speech, even though its success with the audience cannot be denied. Concluding that his rhetoric needs to be disciplined, they assign him the conscientious study of books.

For four months, the narrator is re-educated by Brother Hambro, a "tall, friendly man, a lawyer and the Brotherhood's chief theoretician," and "a fanatic teacher" (270). Such "training" is supposed to prepare the narrator to become "chief spokesman of the Harlem District," but as soon as he returns to Harlem he resumes his successful reliance on oratory, symbolic action, and public spectacle. Although this return to African-American popular media is the chief cause for the Brotherhood's criticism of the narrator's conduct in Harlem (in addition to Brother Wrestrum's jealousy of his success), Ellison suggests that the oratorical tradition of "call-and-response" might be a way out of the double bind of African American political leadership and the one-sided dogmatism of white leaders, such as those in charge of the Brotherhood.

John Callahan and Gregory Stephens have argued in different contexts that the call-and-response techniques Ellison incorporates into the novel invoke the centrality of the form in African-American culture and its adaptability "to the vernacular culture of an experimental democratic society."[7] As a way of describing the discursive "dissensus" and the multiple forms required to negotiate the different interests of a multiethnic, multicultural United States, "call-and-response" is merely a metaphor for a much more complicated process of how such political debate is conducted in diverse media. But the central premise of such a trope is for Ellison the inevitable duality of *every* American, who is pulled between identification with a specific, often historic, community and the wider American democracy. As Ellison famously wrote about himself: "My cultural background, like that of most Americans, is dual."[8] The narrator of *Invisible Man* concludes: "Now I know men are different and that all life is divided and that only in division is there true health . . . diversity is the word. Let man keep his many parts and you'll have no tyrant states" (435).

Ellison tries to extend what Du Bois interpreted as the characteristic "double consciousness" of African Americans to democratic experience itself, suggesting that multicultural democracy is unthinkable without recognizing the human duality evident in African-American social and cultural history. Hortense Spillers interprets this duality as one of the distinctive features of "black culture," especially as it criticizes and aims to reform the dominant ideology.[9] To be sure, "America is woven of many strands," so that Ellison does not advocate the specific elements of African-American communities as "models" for other peoples, as white

Euroamericans have done for too long with their own cultural values (435). Instead, Ellison relies on the symbolic value of African-American duality, suggesting how it provides an analogy for other political and cultural differences, including a reformed "whiteness," if such "colorlessness" is still imaginable in place of the more specific community identifications of Irish-American, German-American, Italian-American, et al.[10]

Invisible Man is thus neither a "protest novel" nor the "Great American Novel," but instead political theory that departs from the books in Marxist orthodoxy assigned and taught to the narrator by Brother Hambro. Ellison's novel incorporates many of the political forces, each amenable to good and evil purposes, we may guess are missing from the Brotherhood's reading list: popular cultural practices and institutions, including those like music, dance, performance, and religion that often operate outside the archivable "history" of print culture; the comic books, street argot, and hip fashion of the three young men he witnesses on the subway platform; the gaudy display and sentimental appeals of marches, parades, funerals, and sport (if we take seriously the man in the audience who calls out the narrator's rhetorical "pitches"); sexual desire; consumer culture, if we can imagine Tod Clifton's hawking of those "Sambo dolls" serving a critical purpose (why else does the narrator save one of those dolls until nearly the end of his narrative?). One may either play cynically with these different media for multicultural representation and negotiation, as Reverend Bliss Proteus Rinehart does (or at least the narrator's imaginary performance of Rinehart), or one can begin to mobilize them on political and social stages as the constitutive forces of democratic "representivity"—the means through which different peoples, many of them otherwise barred from political or cultural representation in the official History, may construct their own alternative histories that collectively challenge, perhaps even revise, History as it has been written. John S. Wright traces the possibility of such a "counter-history" to the narrator's recognition in the three young African American men on the subway platform that "They are not anomalies but part of a whole uptown populace of 'surreal variations' on downtown styles. The narrator now no longer sees that populace as a fixed mass to be led, but as a mysteriously fluid configuration of personalities and motives in terms of which his own capacities for leading must be recalculated and his ideal of leadership and its genesis reexamined."[11]

In order to achieve this end, Ellison must deconstruct the Euroamerican novel, especially its reliance on the devices of *Bildung* and their construction of a bourgeois subject in the protagonist or hero: the "representative man" of romanticism and realism. Structured around the mythological patterns favored by the Euroamerican *Bildungsroman* and its nonfictional complement, the autobiography, *Invisible Man* substitutes disillusionment for education, recovery of African-American history rather than modernist progress, descent into the underworld—Ellison's equivalent of the political unconscious—as a destiny rather than an origin, a nameless and "invisible" protagonist for the conventional hero, and political relevance in place of aesthetic achievement ("meaning," for example, over "style"). Formally jagged, tonally contrapuntal, stylistically repetitive and digressive, rhetorically mock-heroic and bathetic, *Invisible Man* successfully represents the "duality" the narrator identifies as the prerequisite for citizenship in Ellison's ideal democracy. In accomplishing this cultural work, Ellison places African-American cultural practices at the center, rather than the margin, of the U.S. symbology and develops a protagonist whose racialized "identity"—what he terms his "invisibility"—opens the entire question of what we mean by "democratic representation" by implicating the conventional paths of *Bildung*, together with its agents and heroes (those "representative" men), in a history of "illusionment" based on the crucial fantasy of racial difference.[12]

If my analysis of what Ellison was attempting to represent in *Invisible Man* is even partially correct, then the novel deserves its reputation as one of those rare literary works that transcends its specific genre and continues to influence different fields of knowledge: an "epoch-making" book in Kenneth Burke's judgment in the 1980s.[13] Yet the limitations of this novel are at least as noteworthy and deserve attention precisely because they are prompted by Ellison's challenge that his readers reconsider their fundamental modes of social, national, ethnic, and personal identification and representation. As many previous scholars have pointed out, Ellison criticizes the *Bildungsroman* only to end up substituting the major features of the modernist novel, which also relies on disillusion in the place of enlightenment, an "anti-hero" whose beginning is in his end, anti-formal rhetorical organization and aleatory style, the incorporation of popular culture, gestures toward the political rather than simply the aesthetic avant-garde, and a pervasive ironic mood drawn from the shifting and unstable appearances of modern life. Even Ellison's argument that the African American understands this modern predicament, this existentialist dilemma, better than most other people and thus may have some unique solutions for the reader has numerous precedents in the texts of both high modernism and the Harlem Renaissance.[14] Ellison bases his claim that there is "no dichotomy between art and protest" on the evidence of modern literature by Dostoevsky, Malraux, and Kafka and their precursors Sophocles, Cervantes, Dickens, and Twain.[15]

Ellison's democratic duality also relies on a limited black-white binary, which cannot be dispelled however faithfully the critic traces Ellison's attention to the different kinds of African Americans and Euroamericans who struggle for political and cultural representation in the dramatic action of the novel. It is also a duality that depends crucially on an ideal of American exceptionalism that Ellison ends up affirming even against the decisively transnational characteristics of his "invisible man." Of course, the narrator is constructed of many different parts from literatures and cultures around the world: West African and African-American folktales of the trickster, Dostoevsky's unnamed narrator in *Notes from Underground*, Melville's Ishmael and the confidence men, Douglass's autobiographical "I," Joyce's Stephen Dedalus, Louis Armstrong, blues singers, and jazzmen like John Coltrane and Charlie Parker. Yet where are the Native Americans, Asian Americans, Latinos, and other ethnic minorities missing from the novel's settings in the rural South and New York City? What are we to conclude from Ellison's sexist representations of white and black women, as well as his singular characterization of the gay white male, Mr. Emerson? And in this same vein, we might ask legitimately why Ellison's criticism of U.S. imperialism seems so ambivalent, even muted, in a narrative otherwise full of references to African-American slavery and racial oppression as instances of internal colonization.

Like Richard Wright, Ellison stereotypes women in his feminine characters. Mary Rambo, the maternal African-American woman who runs the boarding house where the narrator lives on his arrival in New York City, offers nurture and domestic comfort in the place of political activism and social reform. She is the only developed African-American woman in the novel; Hester and Edna at "The Golden Day" make very brief appearances and reinforce stereotypes of the jook-joint prostitute.[16] Mary's symbolic significance is unmistakable and thus especially troubling in its singularity. Thirty years after Du Bois would write in *Darkwater* that "All womanhood is hampered today because the world on which it is emerging is a world that tries to worship both virgins and mothers and in the end despises motherhood and despoils virgins," fifteen years after Zora Neale Hurston would shatter the illusion of African-American feminine domesticity and abjection with characters like Big Sweet in *Mules and Men* (1935) and Janie Crawford in *Their Eyes Were Watching God* (1937), Ellison's cartoon of Mary Rambo seems anachronistic and certainly politically incorrect.[17] Fleeing the anarchy of the riot, the narrator is running to Mary Rambo before he falls into the sewer. Running away from Sybil, the white "nymphomaniac" banker's wife, who begs the narrator to "rape" her, the narrator rushes into the riot. Sybil is merely a more extreme variation on his first white seductress, the nameless wife of Hubert; this progressive couple accepts each other's sexual adventures as equivalent to their financial contributions to the Brotherhood, both of these interests assuaging their white urban guilt. Explicitly endorsing the narrator's "new assignment" to "the Woman question," this woman makes her feminism part of her seduction: "'Something has to give women an opportunity to come to close grips with life. Please go on, tell me your ideas,' she said, pressing forward, her hand light upon my arm" (313). Ellison tries to avoid criticism for his own marginalization of feminism by redirecting our attention to the relative trivialization of women's rights in the platform of the CPUSA. When the narrator is reassigned from Harlem to "lecture downtown on the Woman Question," the narrator searches "their faces for signs of amusement," thinking he has "just been made the butt of an outrageous joke" (306–7). But it is Ellison who will work out the details of this "joke" in the scenes in which he casts the narrator with Hubert's seductive wife and the drunken Sybil pursuing him from his apartment into Harlem, cooing "Boo-ful!" like the equally misogynistic portrayals of the sirens and false prophets in T. S. Eliot's *The Waste Land*.

In a similar fashion, Mr. Emerson, son of the addressee of the narrator's seventh and final letter of recommendation from Bledsoe, weirdly condenses his homosexuality with the artifacts of his father's importing firm and the neoprimitivism Ellison attributes to white advocates of the Harlem Renaissance, like Carl Van Vechten. Like the modernist art "decorating" Hubert and his wife's apartment, the office of the importing firm is "beautifully arranged" with "paintings, bronzes, tapestries" from around the world (137). From the open copy of Freud's *Totem and Taboo* to the "aviary of tropical birds set near one of the broad windows" through which the narrator can see "two ships plying far out upon the greenish bay," the scene entangles modern commerce with the "internationalism" of the slave trade (137). Although the gay Mr. Emerson has clearly rebelled against his father, he also still enjoys the life his father's commerce provides, and this seems to be a curious commentary on his homosexuality. Riffing on Leslie Fiedler's famous interpretation of the homoerotic relationship between Huck and Jim in "Come on Back to the Raft, Huck Honey," Ellison has the young Mr. Emerson compare himself to Huck and the narrator to Jim (143). To be sure, Mr. Emerson completes his ambivalent relationship to his father and the dominant white ideology by revealing the contents of Bledsoe's letter to the narrator, but this rebellion, much like that of Mr. Emerson's nineteenth-century namesake's participation in Abolition, is deeply ambivalent, laced with his own homoerotic desire. And, of course, the job the narrator "earns" in this exchange is neither as Mr. Emerson's companion at a party at the Calamus Club nor work as his "valet," but his final offer of "a possible job at Liberty Paints" (146). Sidestepping the possible alignment of women's and gay rights with African-American rights, ambivalently linking his own trivialization of both political issues and their personal identifications with the sexism of the CPUSA and how corporate capitalism's homosociality depends on profound homophobia, Ellison utters the word *diversity* on numerous occasions prior to the epilogue primarily to focus it narrowly on the model of black-white relations in the United States.

Lawrence Jackson identifies several personal and historical factors influencing Ellison to revise *Invisible Man* to be a less radical book. The original manuscript of the novel included substantial sections from the journal of Leroy, a "dead merchant marine" who had boarded at Mary Rambo's before the narrator arrived. Jackson points out that "Leroy's journal of philosophical guerilla warfare was the Invisible Man's prized possession" in the original manuscript, and it is the one paper "text" the Invisible Man cannot bring himself to burn when he symbolically (and practically) burns the contents of his briefcase to "light" his way through the sewer into which he has fallen while fleeing the Harlem Riot.[18] Jackson considers Leroy another example of the novel's "heroic black male characters," ranging from Trueblood to Clifton and Rinehart, each of whom teaches the narrator a lesson before being rejected, in the manner Pound would cast off "masks" or personae in *Hugh Selwyn Mauberley*. Writing "like a criminal," Leroy prefers Nat Turner to Frederick Douglass, thus qualifying the highly symbolic moments in the novel when Brother Tarp hangs Douglass's portrait on the narrator's office wall in Harlem and the narrator's identification with his grandfather (family lineage) through Douglass.[19] At the urging of his friend Harry Ford and later his editor at Random House, Albert Erskine, Ellison deleted all of Leroy's journal from the novel, except for a few surviving lines in the epilogue. Leroy's journal appears to have been inspired in part by the sort of African-American transnationalism in Du Bois's contributions to *Crisis* and in Langston Hughes's *Big Sea*. The character Leroy certainly drew on Ellison's own experiences in the merchant marine; indeed, he specifically traces the gestation of the novel to "the summer of 1945, in a barn in Waitsfield, Vermont, where I was on sick leave from service in the merchant marine."[20] Jackson concludes that "the decision to eliminate Leroy's journal removed chunks of the novel that would have reflected the international scope of Ellison's earliest intentions. It was difficult for him to shave his global perspective, in the era of decolonization movements and formidable anticolonial analyses, like Franz Fanon's. . . . Some of these early sections [of the unrevised manuscript of *Invisible Man*] . . . reflected an international political consciousness that made the hero decidedly less naive."[21]

Jackson argues that Ellison chose to represent the narrator's "internationalism" primarily through modernist cosmopolitanism (Eliot, Joyce, et al.) in part to align his work with the aesthetic values of the New Critics and in part to dissociate himself from the radical internationalism of black nationalists, like the Nation of Islam, and of the Communist Party. It is more likely, I think, that Ellison's white literary advisors were urging Ellison to follow the aesthetic values of their colleagues among the New York intellectuals, including Trilling. The New Critics were skeptical of avant-garde modernism, especially its anti-formalism, but Trilling and other New York intellectuals defended the modernists for employing radical styles and experimental forms that challenged conventional social discourse. And as I noted in the Introduction, Trilling's *Liberal Imagination* champions an aesthetic cosmopolitanism that was an alternative to leftist internationalism. Jackson contends that Ellison was adapting to the political climate in the United States at the outbreak of the Korean War, when patriotic and anti-communist feelings were especially strong.[22] Whatever Ellison's reasons for eliminating Leroy's journal, the final novel collapses transnational interests into national, multicultural questions, so that when the narrator insists "diversity is the word" the reader knows he is referring primarily to its representation in U.S. rather than global democracy. Ellison uses the character Ras not only to parody Marcus Garvey's unsuccessful Back to Africa movement, but also to allude more obliquely to such advocates of pan-African, anti-colonial struggle as W. E. B. Du Bois and black nationalists like Carlos Cook.

The distinction Ellison makes between his narrator's cultural interests, especially in his references to modernist and African-American art and literature, and the dogmatic politics of the Brotherhood seems forced. Ellison knew members of the CPUSA in the mid-1930s, which was the era of the Popular Front's more inclusive appeal to peoples from many different ethnic and class backgrounds and its reliance on a wide variety of different cultural media.[23] In addition, Ellison makes only the barest references to World War II in *Invisible Man*, despite his claim in his 1981 Introduction to the thirtieth anniversary edition of the novel that it "had been conceived as a war novel."[24] The only major character to address war as an issue is the World War I veteran in the "Golden Day" episode, who represents eccentrically the African-American serviceman's protest of the customary racism in the postwar United States.[25] Admittedly, the veteran's speech to the narrator expresses African-American anger about the nation's failure to reward their service, but his "madness"—a schizophrenia clearly attributable to U.S. racism rather than to shell-shock (or PTSS)—together with the chaotic scene at the Golden Day leave the authority for this critique in serious doubt. When the veteran turns to Mr. Norton and criticizes the narrator as "a walking zombie! . . . a walking personification of the Negative. . . . The mechanical man!" he not only foreshadows the narrator's experiences in New York City but Tod Clifton's curious end hawking "Sambo Dolls" on the streets of the city. But this roundabout, elliptical linkage of a World War I veteran, the narrator, and Tod Clifton can only be considered a highly stylized *literary* treatment of the explicitly political and historical issues facing African Americans returning home during and after World War II.

Ellison reported the Harlem Riot of 1943 for the *New York Post*, so he was familiar with the event that triggered African-American urban rage: the police shooting of an unarmed African-American serviceman attempting to protect his mother and wife from police arrest.[26] When he incorporates his experiences of the riot into *Invisible Man*, however, he substitutes Tod Clifton for the African-American serviceman, suppressing thereby the contemporary issue of how the international lessons of anti-racism brought home by war veterans were in direct conflict with domestic policies. In "Harlem Is Nowhere" (1948), Ellison refers to "the spontaneous outbreaks called the 'Harlem riots' of 1935 and 1943" as "explosive matters—which are now a problem of our foreign policy," by which he probably means the racial issues in the news as a consequence of the U.S. occupation of Japan and the more general failure of the postwar United States to have dealt with what Du Bois so prophetically termed in 1903 the "problem of the Twentieth Century"—"the color-line."[27]

Ellison's neglect, perhaps repression, of the international perspectives on race earned by African Americans and other minorities as a consequence of their military service in World War II reflects his eagerness to identify racial problems with the domestic policies of the United States and thus find solutions to such problems within the nation. This historical defect in Ellison's fictional representation of the Harlem Riot of 1943 is also symptomatic of his desire to link international issues with his own literary cosmopolitanism, as if he were competing with the CPUSA, black nationalists, Harlem rioters, and returning African-American servicemen. The narrator of the epilogue insists he is ready to end his "hibernation," to shake "off the old skin and . . . leave it here in the hole," to come out from the underground where his memoir has been written (438–39). Ellison's political theory of diverse representivity demands this sort of re-emergence and reincarnation of his "disembodied voice" as practical politics and social reform. In a positive vein, I contend that many of the political values and practical politics advocated by Ellison's narrator inform the civil rights movement, the anti-war movement, and the women's movement—national and multiethnic movements that relied on symbolic actions, popular media, and cultural recovery work that "embody" the "diversity" Ellison's Invisible Man calls for in the epilogue.

Yet in a more critical sense, I conclude that in his zeal to distance himself from the CPUSA and black nationalists, including those who might resemble the fictional Leroy, Ellison located his own internationalism primarily in the aesthetic domain of his own fictional composition. To be sure, Ellison broadened the cosmopolitanism of T. S. Eliot, James Joyce, William Butler Yeats, André Malraux, and other European modernists whose works echo in his novel to include African-American rural and urban experiences in his own criticism of the modernization process. Recalling on the eve of his "re-education" by Brother Hambro the words of Woodridge, the professor of his "literature class back at college," the narrator remembers Woodridge's adaptation of Joyce's response to the Irish problem (in *Portrait of the Artist as a Young Man*) to the task of African-American cultural construction: "Stephen's problem, like ours, was not actually one of creating the uncreated conscience of his race, but of creating the *uncreated features of his face*. Our task is that of making ourselves individuals. The conscience of a race is the gift of its individuals who see, evaluate, record. . . . We create the race by creating ourselves and then to our great astonishment we will have created something far more important: We will have created a culture" (268). The narrator remembers and then rejects this advice—"But no, it wasn't Woodridge" (268)—before he has learned the lesson of Douglass, whose "individualism" was actually the iconic representation of nineteenth-century African-American cultural unity, as Tarp reminds him: "He belongs to all of us." With respect to what Ellison achieved aesthetically, we must also recognize how Douglass emerges in the novel from a wide range of references to the African presence in U.S. culture, including Ellison's weave of African-American folklore, jazz, blues, dance, bodily movement, and street argot. Indeed, the figure of Douglass is constructed microcosmically in imitation of what Ellison himself described as the hybrid form of the entire novel, which drew upon "the rich culture of the folk tale as well as that of the novel" and the "jazz" that appears in the "wild star-burst of metamorphosis."[28]

Yet in the 1950s, such politically powerful representation, whether we call it Douglass's historical identity or the narrator's fictional "invisibility," remains ineluctably *American*, bound up with a nationalism that many of Ellison's predecessors and contemporaries knew depended on racial hierarchies and ethnic division. Because they largely accepted the national framework for civil rights, anti-war protest, and women's rights, the great rights movements of the post–World War II era also missed the transnational opportunities and complications of today's so-called global era. Like Ellison, many imagined that a reformed and improved U.S. democracy that recognized "diversity" might set an example for the rest of the world. In his 1984 epilogue to his *Atlantic Monthly* article, "Indivisible Man" (1970), James Alan McPherson draws a curious conclusion, intended to praise Ellison but oddly apposite to my criticism of him: "He has very painstakingly cultivated the psychological habits that could make his countrymen more than mere expressions of this group or that. His work has been involved in exploring the cultural foundations of a nation-state. Perhaps it is ironic that the implications of his work are just beginning to be realized, at a time when the institution of the nation-state is becoming obsolete."[29] Of course, Ellison reminds us repeatedly that the "duality" of African-American identity, the power of its double-consciousness, calls attention to how American society should be imagined in relation to, rather than apart from, the global peoples, cultures, and languages of which it is composed.

Yet in the postwar era of formal decolonization and the anticipation by many African-American intellectuals, including Ellison's friends and mentors Langston Hughes and Richard Wright, of the *recolonization* and *neocolonialism* likely to be directed by the United States, Ellison's aesthetic cosmopolitanism in the service of American diversity contributed to the problem, rather than the solution. Relying on the black-white binary, trivializing women's rights and gay identity, cutting Leroy's journal, choosing Douglass over Nat Turner, satirizing black nationalists in the reductive "Africanism" of Ras, the Destroyer—replete with spear, shield, and African dress in the Harlem Riot scenes—and international socialism in the dogmatic "science" of the Brotherhood's Marxism, Ellison invites the criticism directed in recent years at modernist cosmopolitanism for its cultural contributions to the "new" colonial formations we see today in the American empire. Ellison's efforts to theorize a new multicultural politics that would take us beyond the bitter hatreds of racialized identities and to coordinate African-American cultural practices (and their media) with Euroamerican modernism still deserve our admiration. In its own time, *Invisible Man* was "epochal," but in part because it marked the limitations of an epoch still governed by the nation-state and its ideal model, the United States. It is little wonder that Ellison could not finish his second novel, the fragments of which attempt vainly to engage the changing political climate of the United States as it moved through the civil rights period toward the global challenges of our present era.

In *Juneteenth*, Ellison tries to transcode the themes and politics of 1952 to the culture of spectacle and theatricality of our postmodern era, but they will not work. The black-white binary remains; the stereotyping of African-American and white women, despite more varied and psychologically complex characters, persists; and the Freudian psychology of the 1940s and 1950s offers even less adequate explanations of the cultural symbology. Watching his first motion picture with his foster father, the Reverend "Daddy" Hickman, the child who will grow up to make his fortune as a motion-picture director and then wield political power as a race-baiting U.S. senator, wounded by an African-American assassin firing from the Congressional gallery, recognizes his "mother" in the movie-star shadowed voicelessly on the screen: "Goodehugh-cudworth, she called me Goodehugh. If not my mother, who moves in the shadows? And again as I look through the beam of pulsing light into the close-up looming wide across the distant yet intimate screen, I'm enthralled and sweetly disintegrated like motes in sunlight and I listen . . . straining to hear some sound from her moving lips, . . . some faint intonation of her voice above the printed word which Daddy Hickman reads softly to me, explaining the action" (*Juneteenth*, 244–45). This is an allegory of sorts, perhaps unintended by Ellison, of his plight as an American novelist at the end of the democratic promise of the nation-state, after the novel's "printed word" has been displaced by the shadows of film and other electronic media in their global flows. Ellison believed too much in these shadows, invested too much in his invisibility or his "theory," and as a consequence he never really found his way underground.

Notes

1. Ralph Ellison, *Juneteenth: A Novel*, ed. John F. Callahan (New York: Random House, 1999), p. 3.

2. Ralph Ellison, *Invisible Man* (New York: Random House, 1972), p. 332.

3. For the tradition of the "Black Christ" from Nat Turner to W. E. B. Du Bois, see Eric Sundquist, *To Wake the Nations: Race in the Making of American Literature* (Cambridge, MA: Harvard University Press, 1993), pp. 592–623, and John Carlos Rowe, *Literary Culture and U.S. Imperialism: From the Revolution to World War II* (New York: Oxford University Press, 2000), pp. 208–14.

4. Richard Wright, "Between Laughter and Tears," *New Masses* (October 5, 1937).

5. For a more developed account of Douglass's rhetorical construction of his political representivity, see my *At Emerson's Tomb: The Politics of Classic American Literature* (New York: Columbia University Press, 1997), pp. 96–123.

6. See Lindon Barrett, *Blackness and Value: Seeing Double* (New York: Cambridge University Press, 1999), pp. 55–93.

7. John Callahan, *In the African-American Grain: The Pursuit of Voice in Twentieth-Century Black Fiction* (Urbana: University of Illinois Press, 1988), p. 15; Gregory Stephens, *On Racial Frontiers: The New Culture of Frederick Douglass, Ralph Ellison, and Bob Marley* (New York: Cambridge University Press, 1999), p. 125.

8. Ellison, "Change the Joke and Slip the Yoke," *Shadow and Act* (New York: Random House, 1964), p. 58.

9. Hortense J. Spillers, "The Idea of Black Culture," public lecture sponsored by African-American Studies and the University of California Humanities Research Institute, March 31, 2003.

10. Echoing Melville's interpretation of "whiteness" as "the visible absence of color" in *Moby-Dick*, eds. Harrison Hayford and Hershel Parker, Norton Critical Edition (New York: W. W. Norton and Co., 1967), p. 169, Ellison's narrator concludes that "white . . . is not a color but the lack of one" and suggests that striving to become white is thus a desire for "colorlessness," in explicit opposition to America's multicultural ideals.

11. John S. Wright, "The Conscious Hero and the Rites of Man: Ellison's War," *New Essays on "Invisible Man,"* ed. Robert O'Meally (New York: Cambridge University Press, 1988), p. 173.

12. My argument appears to contradict Kenneth Burke's "Ralph Ellison's Trueblooded *Bildungsroman*," in *Speaking for You: The Vision of Ralph Ellison*, ed. Kimberly W. Benston (Washington, DC: Howard University Press, 1987), pp. 349–59. In "Shadowing Ellison" in this same collection, p. 67, John S. Wright points out how "Ellison appropriated . . . [Kenneth Burke's] theories of symbolic action after first hearing Burke's critique of Adolph Hitler's *Mein Kampf* in 1937," so Burke's influence on *Invisible Man* and arguably his *understanding* of the novel should not be ignored. But Burke finally confesses that his "comparison and contrast" of *Invisible Man* with Goethe's *Wilhelm Meister* is an "ironic 'matching' of Wilhelm Meister's all-white involvements with your narrator's black-white tension" (355).

13. Ibid., p. 357.

14. Notably in Jean-Paul Sartre's discussion of Richard Wright in "For Whom Does One Write?," in *What Is Literature?*, trans. Bernard Frechtman (New York: Harper and Row, 1965), pp. 71–74. The essays collected in *What Is Literature?* were originally published in *Les Temps Modernes* and in book form in 1947.

15. Ellison, "The Art of Fiction: An Interview," *Shadow and Act*, p. 169.

16. Hester is the "brown-skinned woman with red hair" who flirts with Mr. Norton in an upstairs room while the narrator scrambles to get this white college trustee out of the bar (*Invisible Man*, 71). Her name ironically recalls Douglass's Aunt Hester, whose whipping by the overseer is witnessed by the young Douglass early in *Narrative of the Life of Fredrick Douglass, an American Slave, Written by Himself*, ed. Houston Baker, Jr. (New York: Penguin Books, 1982) and constitutes for the young man and the

reader "the blood-stained gate, the entrance to the hell of slavery" (51). This episode in Douglass's 1845 *Narrative* has led to considerable interpretive controversy over the years, because it has divided readers over the issue of whether Douglass is indulging our voyeuristic interest in Aunt Hester's naked body being whipped or challenging the plantation romance's, and by extension antebellum slavery's, ideology of the sexually exotic African-American woman. By naming the jook-joint prostitute after Douglass's mythologized Aunt Hester, Ellison follows the line of T. S. Eliot in *The Waste Land* regarding the degradation of our cultural myths in the modern age (often through feminine agency, which is a mark of Eliot's misogyny) and pushes the interpretation of Aunt Hester in Douglass's *Narrative* in the direction of the voyeuristic. By giving his Hester "red hair," he also uses her to foreshadow the white wife of Hubert, who drops her "red robe" to seduce the narrator.

17. W. E. B. Du Bois, *Darkwater*, in *The Oxford W. E. B. Du Bois Reader*, ed. Eric J. Sundquist (New York: Oxford University Press, 1996), p. 565. See my discussion of Du Bois's feminism in *Darkwater* in *Literary Culture and U.S. Imperialism*, pp. 210–16.

18. Lawrence Jackson, *Ralph Ellison: Emergence of Genius* (New York: John Wiley and Sons, Inc., 2002), p. 415.

19. Ibid.

20. Ralph Ellison, introduction to *Invisible Man* (New York: Random House, Inc., 1980), p. vii.

21. Jackson, *Ralph Ellison*, p. 427.

22. Ibid., p. 416.

23. Ibid., p. 172.

24. Ralph Ellison, introduction to *Invisible Man* (1980), p. vii. Two thirds of Ellison's introduction (pp. xi–xxiii) focus on World War II, as if thirty years later Ellison feels compelled to explain why he shifted his focus from the setting of his original plans for the novel to the "narrative that was upstaged by the voice which spoke so knowingly of invisibility" to him (xi). The use of an inspiring muse or genius to explain literary decisions has, of course, a long literary heritage, to which Ellison appeals in other respects in this introduction, but it is also a notoriously unconvincing way to account for such changes.

25. The only explicit reference to World War II in the novel I can recall occurs in the epilogue in the middle of a long series of historical examples used as metaphors for the irrational guilt experienced by African Americans for their own oppression: "the trip to the chamber with the deadly gas that ends in the oven so hygienically clean" (*Invisible Man*, 434).

26. Ralph Ellison, "Eyewitness Story of Riot: False Rumors Spurred by Mob," *New York Post* (August 2, 1943), p. 4.

27. Ralph Ellison, "Harlem Is Nowhere," *Shadow and Act*, p. 301. This essay was written in 1948 for *Magazine of the Year*, which failed before the essay was published. It was subsequently included in Ellison's *Shadow and Act*. W. E. B. Du Bois, *The Souls of Black Folk* (New York: Penguin Books, 1989), p. 1.

28. Ralph Ellison, introduction to *Invisible Man* (1980), pp. xxii–xxiii.

29. James Alan McPherson, "Indivisible Man," in *Speaking for You: The Vision of Ralph Ellison*, p. 29.

[II]

POSTWAR LIBERALISM AND THE NEW COSMOPOLITANISM

[5]

RACISM, FETISHISM, AND THE GIFT ECONOMY IN HARPER LEE'S *TO KILL A MOCKINGBIRD*

"Don't fool yourselves—it's all adding up and one of these days we're going to have to pay the bill for it." —Atticus Finch in Harper Lee, *To Kill a Mockingbird* (1960)

I am not concerned with gifts given in spite or fear, nor those gifts we accept out of servility or obligation; my concern is the gift we long for, the gift that, when it comes, speaks commandingly to the soul and irresistibly moves us.
—Lewis Hyde, *The Gift: Imagination and the Erotic Life of Property* (1979)

IN *TO KILL A MOCKINGBIRD*, Harper Lee represents two economic systems operating in conflict with each other in her fictional Maycomb County, Alabama. In both the African-American and white communities in the novel, barter, trade, and gift exchanges are quite common and typical of agrarian communities, in which the processes of economic production have not yet been thoroughly industrialized and reduced to equivalent values in money. In many ways, Lee sentimentalizes and idealizes this precapitalist economy and identifies it with myths of Southern hospitality, social grace, and honor. On the other hand, Lee represents the economy of Maycomb as dependent on private property and capitalist ownership, both of which have their roots not only in modern industrialism but also in the slave economy of the Old South. Lee's anti-racist argument in the novel is traditionally understood as a challenge to the inherent racism of Southern laws and legal processes of judgment. Lee also indicts the law and the less formal, but still powerful, cultural forms of Maycomb County that support an economy of property and ownership. Lee demonstrates how this economy is not only inherently racist—a legacy of slavery—but relies on unquestioned hierarchies of gender, class, and age that make Southern racism even more difficult to identify and overcome.

Lee proposes a clear economic alternative to capitalist forms of ownership, especially those traceable back to slaveholding attitudes, and to the pre-capitalist system of barter that is no longer practical in complex, urban communities. Although she does not completely reject private ownership, she modifies it by insisting that we "own" things only to the extent that we make morally responsible use of them. In order for me to define adequately this ethics of property, I will have to interpret several important episodes in the novel's dramatic action, but I want to claim in the beginning that characters' relations to their property are inextricably tied to their social and thus human connections. Lee is by no means a neo-Marxist writer or even an identifiable left intellectual of the 1950s and 1960s, but her criticism of the alienation of objects from the human labor that has produced them and the social relations in which they assume value recalls Marx's critique in *Capital* of the commodity fetishism resulting from capitalist modes of production and circulation.[1]

Lee's utopia thus does not require a proletarian revolution against capitalist owners and does not particularly demonize the bourgeoisie. In many respects, Lee locates in the professional middle class, especially as it is represented by Atticus Finch, the possibility of moral changes that will preserve Southern manners and hospitality by democratizing them and extending their value to all members of her imaginary community. Class hierarchies are also maintained, albeit in flexible ways, insofar as society follows reasonable criteria for membership in different classes. Atticus Finch tries to teach his children respect for people from all backgrounds and for the different kinds of labor necessary to maintain social order and economic health, but his very tolerance of others is an indication of his right to occupy a position of social authority as a lawyer and representative in state government. In Lee's view, Southern society needs to overcome its slaveholding past, but there are many aspects of the New South that can be incorporated into her social utopia.

Lee's vision of modest social reform is clearly liberal, which may explain the popularity of her novel in high-school English classes and its relative neglect in colleges and universities. I do not mean by this observation that higher education is interested only in literature that radically challenges social conventions, but rather that Lee's liberalism appears to many sophisticated readers to be sentimental, rather than seriously committed to major social reforms. Well written and organized as *To Kill a*

Mockingbird is, the novel is by no means avant-garde in form or style. Scout's narration is conventional in adolescent and adult literature, as is the family narrative of a single parent struggling to raise his (or her) children in a responsible manner. In my view, Lee's liberalism is more complicated and instructive than the sentimental version, which relies primarily on the observation that white Southerners should overcome their racism and respect their African-American neighbors. This moral, which the adolescent Scout knows from the outset—"I think there's just one kind of folks. Folks," she tells her older brother, Jem—cannot be taken seriously until we revise the underlying economic motives for dividing "folks" into rich and poor, black and white, men and women, odd and normal, foreign and American. Property should not determine people's identities, but their characters should be represented in what belongs to them. This social relationship between people and property is certainly a liberal concept, but in her particular interpretation of its racial connotations Harper Lee goes considerably beyond the sentimental liberalism of the 1960s.

Lee's middle-class alternative has remarkable similarities with what the anthropologist Marcel Mauss termed the "gift exchange" fundamental to many "archaic societies" and what the sociologist Jean Baudrillard would elaborate as "symbolic exchange" in his revisionary interpretations of Marx in *The Mirror of Production* and *For a Critique of the Political Economy of the Sign*.[2] I have no evidence that Lee was familiar with Mauss's work on gift exchange, which was first published in French as *Essai sur le Don* in 1950.[3] Most of the anthropological and sociological theories that relied on Mauss's research appeared well after 1960, when Lee's novel was published, and thus cannot have had any direct influence on *To Kill a Mockingbird*. My interpretation of Lee's elaboration of a gift economy in the novel will thus use the theories of Mauss and Baudrillard primarily to elucidate Lee's independent conceptualization of a utopian social and political economy with some striking resemblances to the ideas of these roughly contemporary French scholars.

Mauss's and Baudrillard's writings also help to foreground the point of contact in Lee's novel between her social analysis of racism and social hierarchy in the South and the anthropological dimension of the novel, which Lee makes explicit in her frequent references to the Mruna people of Africa. Lee appears to include Aunt Alexandra and the philanthropic interest of her "missionary circle" in "the squalid lives of the Mrunas" primarily to satirize the hypocrisy of Southern whites concerned with the welfare of people of color in Africa even as these whites continue to oppress African Americans in their own community.[4] This double standard is not limited to racial divisions; it also includes anyone who differs from the established white social order. Claudia Johnson has argued that Scout identifies with Boo Radley and with "the black people in Maycomb" because she herself is treated as "an outsider," especially when she is made "the object of brutal ridicule in the genteel ladies' missionary society."[5]

Lee's references to U.S. missionary work in Africa also add an important transnational dimension to her novel, which is generally overlooked because Lee's treatment of Maycomb's charity toward foreigners seems so satirical. Unable to treat fairly their own African Americans, the good, white citizens of Maycomb happily bear the white man's burden for their brothers and sisters in Africa. But Lee's apparently simple morality that "charity begins at home" is complicated by other transnational dimensions in the novel, which generally work to reduce the distance between U.S. civilization and foreign societies presumed to be "primitive" or at least in need of modernization.

Lee offers an insightful analysis of how kinship and other social affiliations work both positively and negatively in Maycomb, reminding us as a good anthropologist might that modern Western societies are often based on superstitions and ritualized practices as fantastic as those in so-called primitive or archaic communities. Previous interpretations of the novel have focused on the legal questions and the drama of Tom Robinson's trial to the relative neglect of the other social and economic practices represented by Lee as fundamental to the operation of a community and thus crucial for any reformer to understand. Indeed, it might be argued that Atticus Finch fails to defend Tom Robinson successfully, because Atticus does not take sufficient account of the other social and economic factors influencing the moral climate of Maycomb County and its residents. In many respects, Harper Lee has written a literary anthropology of the Old and New South as sophisticated as Hurston's *Mules and Men*, Faulkner's *Absalom, Absalom!*, and James Agee and Walker Evans's *Let Us Now Praise Famous Men*.

At first, gifts in the novel appear to be merely signs of genteel society and its sentimental attachment to conventions of Southern hospitality. The Finches' neighbor, Aunt Maudie, bakes cakes for her friends, especially Scout, Jem, and Atticus, and these gestures are tokens of the kindness behind her otherwise fierce self-reliance. Sharing food, however, can mean much more than merely conventional hospitality, as Scout learns when Jem invites Walter Cunningham home for dinner. Proud and poor, the Cunninghams "are country folks, farmers," who were hit hard by the 1929 "crash" (*To Kill a Mockingbird*, 27; hereafter *M*). When the new schoolteacher, Miss Caroline, tries to help Scout's classmate, Walter Cunningham, by offering to lend him a quarter to buy his lunch, Scout tries to explain, "You're shamin' him, Miss Caroline," only to be punished by the teacher for her interference (*M*, 28). As these events unfold in the classroom, Scout reflects in indirect discourse on the Cunninghams' use of gift exchange as a way to compensate for their poverty. When Mr. Cunningham hires Atticus to help him with the legal problems of an entailment on his farm, he pays the lawyer with "a load of stovewood in the back yard," "a sack of hickory nuts" that "appeared on the back steps," "a crate of smilax and holly" at Christmas, and "a croker-sack full of turnip greens" in the spring (*M*, 27). These seasonal payments suggest both that the Cunninghams are close to nature as farmers and rely on a more "natural" law than that of the modern economy of money, which includes such abstractions as mortgages and entailments.

Atticus understands the social ecology that ties him closely to the farmers' fortunes, and he accepts graciously the Cunninghams' barter economy, even if he knows it is a residual form that cannot survive in complex, urbanized communities: "Atticus said professional people were poor because the farmers were poor. As Maycomb County was farm country, nickels and dimes were hard to come by for doctors and dentists and lawyers" (*M*, 27). He also understands that the modernization of farming comes with political as well as economic consequences: "Entailment was only a part of Mr. Cunningham's vexations. The acres not entailed were mortgaged to the hilt, and the little cash he made went to interest. If he held his mouth right, Mr. Cunningham could get a WPA job, but his land would go to ruin if he left it, and he was willing to go hungry to keep his land and vote as he pleased" (*M*, 27). Like the Vanderbilt Fugitives and other neo-agrarian groups in the 1920s and 1930s, Mr. Cunningham clings to the dream of the yeoman farmer capable of maintaining his family and rejecting government interference. Atticus Finch may respect this ideal, but he certainly doesn't view it as a practical solution to

Depression-era economic and social problems. Atticus serves in the state legislature and during the action of the novel spends two weeks in Montgomery when "the state legislature was called into emergency session" to respond to "sit-down strikes in Birmingham," "bread lines in the cities," and as "people in the country grew poorer" (*M*, 126). According to Jem, Atticus tackles as a state legislator "reorganizing the tax systems of the counties and things" (*M*, 126). Lee gives us few other details about his political work, but Atticus Finch is clearly committed to government's role in economic revitalization.

Mr. Cunningham imagines that he owns his farm in an absolute sense and this self-reliance is the basis of his honor; he belongs to what Atticus terms "a set breed of men" (*M*, 27), in which the modifier *set* means resolute, obstinate, or unyielding, as in the idiom "set in one's ways." Thus he will be beholden to no one and must repay every service or gift with whatever means he has or else refuse such a gift, as his son Walter does. Atticus Finch understands what the gift teaches us about ownership in a completely different fashion. What we own belongs to us in trust only for the benefit of our social relations; everything belongs to the community. Property is not, however, held in common but by individuals, who for a variety of reasons (inheritance, earning power, opportunity, frugality) own more or less than each other. The value of what we own depends crucially on how we use it, so that by hoarding goods we degrade their value and by sharing goods we increase their social value. When Jem invites Walter Cunningham home for dinner, he is attempting to solve two problems: reconcile Scout and Walter, who have fought after being disciplined by Miss Caroline, and feed Walter without "shamin' him" by offering him outright charity (*M*, 28).

Jem has learned well his father's lessons, and he makes certain Walter will come to dinner by arguing "Our daddy's a friend of your daddy's" (*M*, 29). When they are all at the dinner table, "Atticus greeted Walter and began a discussion about crops" that not only makes the young man feel at home but also gives him a sense of sharing with Atticus some of his expertise as a farmer: "While Walter piled food on his plate, he and Atticus talked together like two men, to the wonderment of Jem and me" (*M*, 30). Of course, it is at this very moment that Walter, feeling comfortable at last in the Finches' home, asks for molasses, swamps his dinner with it, and provokes Scout's contempt. The African-American cook and housekeeper, Calpurnia, calls Scout into the kitchen and corrects her: "Don't matter who they are, anybody sets foot in this house's yo' comp'ny, and don't you let me catch you remarkin' on their ways like you was so high and mighty!" (*M*, 31). Named for Julius Caesar's third wife, who had a prophetic dream of his assassination, Calpurnia is far more than just a housekeeper and cook in the Finch household; she is clearly a surrogate mother for Jem and Scout and generally anticipates the growing social authority of African Americans in modern Alabama.[6] Cal also helps directly link the economic issue of property ownership with the legacies of slavery at this early stage in the novel. Humiliated by Cal, Scout recommends that her father "lose no time in packing her off," but Atticus coolly replies: "I've no intention of getting rid of her, now or ever. We couldn't operate a single day without Cal, have you ever thought of that? You think about how much Cal does for you, and you mind her, you hear?" (*M*, 31).

The Finches' hospitality involves far more than simply feeding Walter Cunningham's body; dinner involves conversation and consideration for his person and family, even though Walter is only eight or nine years old.[7] Of course, people have offered food as a sign of courtesy and hospitality throughout history and in virtually every society; the self-evident use-value of food makes it one of the primary goods in a gift economy. Referring to the practice among Brahmins of personifying food in the goddess Anna, Marcel Mauss concludes: "It is in the nature of food to be shared out. Not to share with others is 'to kill its essence,' it is to destroy it both for oneself and for others" (*The Gift: The Form and Reason for Exchange in Archaic Societies*, 57; hereafter *G*). Food offers an especially interesting mediation between humans and their property, because food is an exchangeable and valuable commodity precisely for its use by humans. Unused food spoils; used food is consumed and transformed into another state. It thus reminds us that within the social system everything is "owned" only to the extent it is used and its true value based on this social performativity.

Mauss's interpretation of the gift's function in "archaic societies" is that it provides a fundamental reciprocity in both giver and receiver (*G*, 13–14). To accept a gift involves as much responsibility as to give the gift, so that Walter Cunningham's willingness to feel at home in the Finches' house is his part in the gift of their hospitality. As Lewis Hyde points out: "The bonds that gifts establish are not simply social, they may be spiritual and psychological as well. There are interior economies and invisible economies."[8] Not all gifts should be accepted, so the decision to accept a gift involves the recognition of a social bond: "Gifts from evil people must also be refused lest we be bound to evil. In folk tales the hero is well advised to refuse the food and drink offered him by a witch" (Hyde, 73). Although Mauss is quite specific about the different ways gifts function in different societies, many social and political theorists influenced by the gift economy have concluded that the "gift" in fact symbolizes the social bond in itself. Some gifts are, of course, more symbolically significant than others. The North Pacific tribes, such as the Kwakiutl, who practice "potlatch" or the ceremonial giving away of possessions to mark significant social events (weddings or promotions in rank, for example), endow the practice with special prestige (Hyde, 28–29). Whether foundational or merely occasional, the gift is understood by anthropologists and sociologists to be performative and symbolic, originating or renewing the social bond in ways that may become habitual but still carry traces of the purpose of sharing a community. Hyde understands religious ritual, myth, literature, and other expressive forms to serve these ends, insofar as the cultural text relies on a semiotic code understood primarily by those belonging to its interpretive community. What Hyde terms "gift aesthetics" includes a wide range of cultural practices and is well illustrated in his study by the poetry of Walt Whitman and Ezra Pound (Hyde, 143–59).

The social bond established by gift exchanges can thus be found in many different societies and has much to do with the symbolic character of the gift. What is given and received is never the discrete object itself, but the symbolic significance acknowledged by both parties in the transaction. I will argue, then, that the real "gift" is language, especially when it is genuinely reciprocal, so that giver and receiver enter into a social contract primarily as a consequence of their agreement to communicate with each other. This idea could be taken quite literally, that a community depends on a shared language or languages (the community need not be monolingual); or it could be understood more figuratively, that what holds a society together is the semiotic code that defines it as distinct and even unique. Every object in a community has a symbolic value that may be quite explicit, such as the cross in Christianity, or may be merely tacit, such as the boss's large office, but objects have social significance only insofar as they are recognizable within a symbolic system.

When applied to the dinner invitation extended by the Finches to young Walter Cunningham, the symbolic, semiotic, economic, and ethical consequences of the gift explain how Lee uses a conventional example of Southern hospitality early in the novel to set up several major themes related to property, ownership, social responsibility, slavery, and racism. Scout mistakenly assumes that their housekeeper Calpurnia should be fired for criticizing her rudeness toward Walter, but Atticus makes it clear that Cal is a crucial member of the family who is not subject to such arbitrary authority. The reader is reminded that slavery relied on the legal definition of people as chattel owned and absolutely controlled, and Lee suggests that in the New South, racial and economic attitudes are still deeply entangled. The moral goal of the novel is not simply to argue that people should not be treated as things or as property, but that people *and* objects constitute dynamic social relations.

Much later in the novel, when Atticus spends the night in front of the Maycomb jail to keep Tom Robinson from being lynched, Scout will defuse the anger of the lynch mob by appealing to "a familiar face, . . . at the center" of the group: "Hey, Mr. Cunningham. How's your entailment gettin' along?" (*M*, 164). Scout still may not understand exactly what a legal entailment involves, but she knows that it establishes a human relationship between her father and Mr. Cunningham. Reminding Mr. Cunningham of her father's kindness, even though Mr. Cunningham "paid" his legal bill in full with firewood, nuts, and flowers, Scout points out how property rights have significance primarily as symbols of social relations. Once again, I want to stress that Lee is not developing a socialist argument, because she emphasizes the importance of individual rights to property throughout the novel, but she does argue consistently that ownership is conditional and subject to the appropriate regulation of the social purpose of the property in question. If we understand the human uses of commodities, then it is much more difficult to commodify people either as slaves, children, women, or other racially or socially inferior subjects.

Even though she defends individual property rights when they are exercised in socially responsible ways, Lee understands that Maycomb County is itself based on what Marx termed "the primitive accumulation of capital" or outright theft (Marx 1:874). The county is named for Colonel Maycomb, whom "Andrew Jackson appointed . . . to a position of authority" during "the Creek Indian Wars" of 1813–14 and who promptly got lost and had to be "rescued by settlers moving inland" (*M*, 272). Earlier in the novel, Lee attributes the location of the town of Maycomb as a consequence of the "nimblewittedness of one Sinkfield, who in the dawn of history operated an inn where two pig-trails met [. . .] and supplied ammunition to Indians and settlers alike, neither knowing or caring whether he was a part of the Alabama Territory or the Creek Nation so long as business was good" (*M*, 140). Andrew Jackson added to his reputation as an Indian fighter and hater with his successful campaign against the Creeks, who like the Cherokee were forced west to Oklahoma Territory by the 1840s. Like Faulkner, Lee uses the history of Indian removal to remind her reader that the property rights so fiercely defended by the Southern gentry are in fact based on military conquest, genocide, and slavery.

Most of the characters in the novel defend their property as Mr. Cunningham does: by forgetting its origins, insisting upon their absolute right to it, and demonizing anyone who threatens to take it from them. Atticus Finch, of course, is the exception, and he frequently teaches Jem and Scout not only that what you own is to be shared with others but also that the model for social property is not a valuable commodity but a linguistic or semiotic act. As a good father, he reads regularly to his children and sets an example of daily reading imitated by Jem. The stories and plays Scout, Jem, and Dill act out in the yard during their summer vacations are part of a distinctive Finch household culture of storytelling, reading, and performance.

Miss Maudie is another exception to the rule of personal property rights in Maycomb. She shares her home with Mr. Avery, much as she cooks for friends and neighbors, but her real love is her garden. When her house accidentally burns to the ground, she seems almost pleased, claiming that she "always wanted a smaller house. . . . Gives me more yard" and "more room for my azaleas" (*M*, 80). Gardening, as well as reading and writing, are modes of tending rather than owning nature and language respectively; such practices are represented by Lee as viable alternatives to the property ownership derived from colonialism and slavery.

Marx argues that the capitalist commodity represents the alienation of the worker from his own labor in a fetishized manner that substitutes "the fantastic form of a relation between things" in place of "the definite social relation between men themselves," which the humanly produced object ought to symbolize (Marx 1:165). Well before Freud, Marx develops the idea of the fetish as a psychological substitute for the real object of desire; in Marx's interpretation, "the fetishism of the world of commodities arises from the peculiar social character of the labour which produces them" (Marx 1: 165). Instead of recognizing a common bond with other workers by way of the labor common to all humans, the individual sees only his or her "private labour" in the work he or she has produced. Once commodities are exchanged, individuals have an opportunity to "equate their different kinds of labour as human labour," which results in the valuation of such labor as it is embodied in different commodities as "a social hieroglyphic" (Marx 1:166–67). Interestingly, Marx considers the human task of deciphering this "hieroglyphic" to be both essential to the social bond and like a language: "Later on, men try to decipher the hieroglyphic, to get behind the secret of their own social product: for the characteristic which objects of utility have of being values is as much men's social product as is their language" (Marx 1:167). Capitalist exploitation, of course, works to alienate the commodity from this social significance and to substitute instead a magical or mysterious independence. The task of Marxian demystification is thus to restore to the commodity its status as both socially valuable (or in some cases valueless) and the materialization of human labor, which is to say socially constructed.

The plot of *To Kill a Mockingbird* turns on several crucial objects with both fetishistic and symbolic significance: the gifts Boo Radley leaves in the tree for Jem and Scout to find on their way home from school (*M*, 40–41, 67–68), the "chiffarobe" Mayella Ewell asks Tom Robinson to break up for firewood (*M*, 191), and Scout's costume as a "ham" she wears to the Halloween pageant at the school (*M*, 266). In the remainder of this essay, I will interpret these different objects as Lee's tokens of a revisionary conception of property and ownership, following a logic that has certain resemblances with Marx's analysis of the ideal commodity and his critique of the alienated, capitalist commodity. Indeed, most previous critical accounts of the novel have paid little attention not only to these specific objects, with the possible exception of Boo Radley's gifts, but also to the symbolic economy they help constitute. Because the legal questions in the novel have attracted so much attention, few critics have paid enough attention to the political, economic, and semiotic levels. Claudia Johnson understands that the law fails to protect Scout, Boo Radley, and Tom Robinson because "hidden social codes contradict their stated legal and religious principles," but the social problems addressed by Lee go beyond Johnson's claim of mere hypocrisy or a double standard (Johnson, 3). Here it is worth recalling my earlier thesis that Lee focuses on the institution and rhetoric of the law precisely to demonstrate the failure of the law alone to overcome the problems of racism, sexism, ageism, and classism that have plagued the South from slavery to the post–World War II era in which she wrote the novel.

The mysterious gifts Boo Radley leaves for Jem and Scout in "a knothole just above . . . eye level" in the live oak "at the edge of the Radley lot" are excellent examples of primitive fetishes, which substitute their own forms for Boo's expression of interest and affection in the two children (*M*, 40). Until Mr. Radley fills up the knot-hole with concrete, Boo leaves four different presents: Wrigley's Double-Mint gum in its silvery wrapper (*M*, 40); "a small box patchworked with bits of tinfoil collected from chewing gum wrappers," containing "two scrubbed and polished" Indian-head pennies, dated "nineteen-six and nineteen-hundred" (*M*, 41); "a tarnished medal" awarded in "spelling contests" in the Maycomb County schools (*M*, 68); "a pocket watch that wouldn't run, on a chain with an aluminum knife" (*M*, 68). Adolescent readers of the novel have long prized these episodes in which gifts magically appear in the Radleys' tree, and it is probable that they understand implicitly the magic of the gift economy that is at work. All of the presents are clearly symbolic, from the elementary exchange of food with the chewing gum to the more sophisticated artwork of the decorated box containing the Indian-head pennies. The spelling medal not only allows Boo to identify with Jem and Scout's education, but it also explicitly connects his other symbolic acts with language. In a figurative way, Boo is a prize-winning speller, because he is able to communicate with the children without being present. The Indian-head pennies are explicitly interpreted by Jem as talismanic: "They come from the Indians. They're real strong magic, they make you have good luck" (*M*, 42).[9] They are also specifically dated 1906 and 1900, linking them with the watch, which even though it is broken represents symbolically the temporality of social and human relations. At a basic level, these gifts are ways for Boo Radley to tell obliquely some of his private history to Jem and Scout; in a more sophisticated sense, they constitute a mysterious bond between the children and Boo Radley that must be interpreted and acted out. Jem, Scout, and Dill understand the communicative aspect of these gifts and decide "to give a note to Boo Radley" (*M*, 53), which Dill paraphrases: "We're askin' him real politely to come out sometimes and tell us what he does in there—we said we wouldn't hurt him and we'd buy him an ice cream" (*M*, 54).

Atticus criticizes the children for invading Boo Radley's privacy, and his lecture, which Scout summarizes, precisely follows U.S. legal precedents regarding individual rights to privacy (*M*, 56–57). Challenging the eldest child, Jem, with "You want to be a lawyer, don't you?," Atticus clearly identifies his position with legal authority (*M*, 57). Yet when Atticus is "out of earshot," Jem yells after him: "I thought I wanted to be a lawyer but I ain't so sure now!" (*M*, 57). Jem's doubt will increase after Atticus's failure to defend Tom Robinson, and this early incident seems to express Lee's conviction that the law is insufficient to solve profound social problems. In the case of Boo Radley, the problem is never fully clarified but has something to do with dysfunctional family relations. Whether Boo is psychologically unstable and thus stabs his father or the father's authoritarian rule drives Boo to violent rebellion, the Radley family is a constant reminder to Atticus Finch that the law has limited authority to govern social and personal relations. Atticus tries to prevent the children from treating Boo Radley as an object of their own entertainment when he forbids them to "give a note" to Boo, because he has already witnessed the play about Boo Radley that Jem, Scout, and Dill staged in the yard. As Claudia Johnson has pointed out, play is the children's best means of coping with their "fear and desire" of the Other.[10] They understand more profoundly than Atticus that Boo for a long time has been crying out for attention and communication, not protection. As the rest of the plot will demonstrate, Boo Radley's sense of *family* obligation to the children, especially Scout, begins with the symbolic gifts he offers them and the communicative bond they represent.

A similar logic of relations between humans and objects helps organize the main plot of the novel, in which Tom Robinson is falsely accused of rape by Mayella, Bob (Robert E. Lee) Ewell's daughter. The Boo Radley subplot and Tom Robinson's trial do not appear to be fully related, except insofar as the Finch children and their cousin, Dill, find themselves treated as social outcasts, not unlike Boo Radley, as a consequence of

Atticus's decision to defend the African-American Robinson. When the children create the black-and-white snowman, "Morphodite," during a rare snowstorm in Maycomb, Lee's effort to link racism to more general discrimination against children, liberal lawyers, the aged, and other social categories does become clearer, but it also seems a little contrived (*M*, 74). But even before Boo Radley defends Scout and Jem from Bob Ewell's vindictive attack, Lee relates both plots in terms of individuals' different attitudes toward objects. The poor white Ewells live in a rundown place behind the Maycomb dump, where family members scavenge the waste products of this society until "the plot of ground around [their] cabin" looks "like the playhouse of an insane child," including "a dirty yard containing the remains of a Model-T Ford (on blocks), a discarded dentist's chair, an ancient icebox, . . . old shoes, worn-out table radios, picture frames, and fruit jars, under which scrawny orange chickens pecked hopefully" (*M*, 181–82).

Even in the midst of this monument to waste, "one corner of the yard . . . bewildered Maycomb," because it is decorated with "six chipped-enamel slop jars holding brilliant red geraniums, cared for as tenderly as if they belonged to Miss Maudie Atkinson" and said to be Mayella Ewell's (*M*, 182). At just over nineteen years old (*M*, 191), Mayella still has some ties to the childhood world in which objects can be magical by expressing our relation to nature, even though she will falsely accuse Tom Robinson of rape to cover up her father's alcoholic abuse. Maycomb is "bewildered" by these little spots of floral beauty because they contradict so obviously the rest of the Ewells' property, which represents their poverty and parasitism. For Lee, the property also represents the more general decadence of a society governed by alienated commodities, which no longer perform their proper work of social bonding but instead express the disconnection of people. It is no surprise that this neglected part of town is also an African-American neighborhood, where those marginalized by slavery and then racism have been sequestered in a ghetto.

Bob Ewell complains that the African-American neighborhood devalues "my property" (*M*, 186), but the truth is that he resents how his proximity to his neighbors signifies that poor whites and African Americans are similarly marginalized. The specific act that triggers the series of events leading to Tom Robinson's arrest and trial is Mayella Ewell's request that Tom come into the house "and bust up this chiffarobe for me" for firewood (*M*, 191). The idiomatic combination of the French terms *chiffonier* (chest of drawers) and *garderobe* (wardrobe) in the regional term "chiffarobe" calls attention to the Ewells' vulgar slang and their comic pretensions.[11] Mayella's testimony under oath that her specific request provoked a sexual assault is, of course, a complete lie. Tom testifies that he had broken up that specific item of furniture, at Mayella's request, two years before the events in question.

The Ewells are obviously not cultivated or well educated, and these defects are evident in both their living conditions and their use of language. Several times, Judge Taylor must ask Bob Ewell to "keep your testimony within the confines of Christian English usage, if that is possible" (*M*, 185). Mayella's lie that she asked Tom to break up that "chiffarobe" on this occasion covers up the fact she invited him into the house to express her sexual desire for him, threatening the Southern white taboo against miscegenation. Mayella lies on the stand under oath about that "chiffarobe," and then Lee uses that lie to create an imaginative link between objects and human relations. Indeed, the "chiffarobe" originally represented Mayella's desire for companionship or human warmth as much as the utility of a cooking fire when she first asked Tom to break it up for her. But when Mayella uses the task of breaking it up to *repress* her sexual and human desire for an African-American male, Lee's readers should understand Mayella's perversion of the gift exchange in ways that encompass the history of racial discrimination and abuse in the South. The fact that Mayella wants a useful object destroyed to serve another, more pressing need—firewood for cooking—emphasizes how the Ewells define their social relations by way of destroying objects. Behind the fetishized commodity is the secret truth of stolen labor and shattered lives. In such an economy, certain individuals and groups must serve as ritual scapegoats, as Tom Robinson and other African Americans clearly do throughout the novel. Long before Mayella lies on the witness stand in court, then, her family has systematically lied to their African-American and white neighbors by destroying the social bonds represented in part by our relations to objects. Not only have they dehumanized African Americans during and after Southern slavery, but they have also destroyed the social environment for themselves and others, whether white or black.

There is another episode in the novel involving furniture that seems remote from the central plot, but which provides a subtle commentary on the broken promise of the gift exchange in Mayella's relationship with Tom Robinson. That "chiffarobe" represents domesticity and family relations, both of which are perverted in the dysfunctional Ewell family. Just before the climactic event in the novel, when Boo Radley will save Scout and Jem from Bob Ewell, Scout tells the story of a Halloween prank played against the maiden ladies, "Misses Tutti and Frutti Barber," in which "some wicked children . . . stealthily made away with every stick of furniture" in the Barbers' house "and hid it in the cellar." Although Scout denies "having taken part in such a thing," the reader assumes she knows more than she is telling about this event. The two sisters insist that the furniture was stolen by "those traveling fur sellers who came through town two days ago. . . . 'Dark they were, . . . Syrians' " (*M*, 265).

The theft of African Americans' rights to their own labor and property under slavery and then under the systematic economic and political racism of the post–Civil War South was rationalized by the common white Southern fantasy of the "thieving" African American. In fact, the African-American community of Maycomb is represented as being extremely self-sufficient and as independent as possible from the white community it knows to be a persistent threat. When Atticus is out of town in Montgomery, Calpurnia takes Jem and Scout to her church, the "First Purchase African M. E. Church . . . in the Quarters outside the southern town limits, across the old sawmill tracks" (*M*, 128). Although they are initially confronted by the reverse racism of Lula, who tells Cal "you ain't got no business bringin' white chillun here—they got their church, we got our'n" (*M*, 129), other members of Cal's church give the children a warm welcome and teach them much about the gift economy of the African-American community of Maycomb. Lee is careful to explain that the church is named "First Purchase" (like many other African-American churches in the South), "because it was paid for from the first earnings of freed slaves" (*M*, 128). Reverend Sykes formally welcomes the children, announces the meeting of "The Missionary Society . . . in the home of Sister Annette Reeves next Tuesday" (*M*, 130–31), and urges the congregation to contribute to a "collection taken up today and for the next three Sundays" to help Tom Robinson's wife Helen (*M*, 131). When the collection doesn't add up to enough, Reverend Sykes calls out individuals to contribute more (*M*, 132). And when "Zeebo, the garbage collector" (*M*, 129) leads the congregation in hymns, Jem and Scout learn about "lining" or the oral tradition by which an illiterate congregation participates in the singing of hymns by repeating a lyric sung by the minister or choir (*M*, 134).

Zeebo is Calpurnia's eldest son, and his mother taught him to read using "Blackstone's *Commentaries*" (*M*, 135), suggesting not only the importance of the law for African Americans but revealing to Scout the "modest double life" (*M*, 136)—Lee's variation on Du Bois's famous "double-consciousness"—that Calpurnia must lead in the racially divided South. The church anchors the African-American community, but "white men gambled in it on weekdays" (*M*, 128). The space of the church is finally less important than the communal activities it helps organize, ranging from an African-American missionary society to charity for Tom and Helen Robinson and even the inadvertent education of two white children. Cal's son Zeebo is a leader in the church, thanks to his literacy, even though his job as garbage collector links him with the waste culture associated with the Ewells. Unlike them, Zeebo performs honorable, even if modest labor—he carts off the mad dog Atticus shoots in chapter 10 (*M*, 106)—and draws his dignity and status from his responsibilities to the African-American community. Of course, the lining method by which the congregation sings hymns reminds the reader of the call-and-response participation of the worshipers in many African-American churches, in which the minister and the deacon are considered merely organizers of the congregation's self-representation, rather than absolute authorities.

Tom Robinson's initial attitude toward Mayella Ewell, even though she is a white woman, seems to reflect the communal spirit of the African-American church, and parallels Calpurnia's generosity toward Jem and Scout. When asked on the witness stand by Atticus about his relationship with Mayella, Tom answers that he helped Mayella out of kindness: "Seemed like every time I passed by yonder she'd have some little somethin' for me to do, choppin' kindlin', totin' water for her. . . . I was glad to do it, Mr. Ewell didn't seem to help her none, and neither did the chillun, and I knowed she didn't have no nickels to spare" (*M*, 203). Scout draws the conclusion that Mayella asks Tom to help her primarily for the conversation and the company, because Mayella "must have been the loneliest person in the world" (*M*, 204). Cut off from the ruling white society, abused regularly by her father, and socially banned from communication with other marginalized people, such as African Americans,

Mayella typifies the social outcast. Yet at the moment her alienation prompts her to recognize in the African-American *other* a common bond of victimization, she is forced by her father to reaffirm white supremacy and racially demonize Tom Robinson (Johnson, *Casebook*, 85–88). Unlike Mayella Ewell, Jem and Scout will identify with marginalized *others* in the novel, including Boo Radley and Tom Robinson, so that they realize the symbolic prophecy of their "black and white" snowman, "Morphodite." Indeed, when Jem's arm is broken in the struggle to fight off Scout's attacker, we are reminded of Tom Robinson's useless arm, which was injured in a cotton gin (*M*, 198–99).[12]

Lee orchestrates the object-relations in the novel to culminate in the climactic events that bring together the Boo Radley subplot and the main plot of Tom Robinson's persecution by the Ewells. When Scout goes to the Maycomb School Halloween pageant dressed as a ham, she gives comic materiality to the processes of commodification and objectification variously treated by Lee throughout the novel. Scout's costume appears to be merely a comic device, ironically commenting on pork as an important agricultural product in Alabama while making it difficult for Scout to see her way through the dark to and from the school. Indeed, the humor of the costume is part of the plot; when Scout appears late on stage during Mrs. Merriweather's parade of the state flag, "Judge Taylor went out behind the auditorium and stood there slapping his knees so hard Mrs. Taylor brought him a glass of water and one of his pills" (*M*, 272). Yet the ham costume reminds us that children, like African Americans and the elderly and Boo Radley, are routinely commodified and treated according to stereotypes, rather than as individuals. On the other hand, Scout's costume reminds us that agriculture defines this community—the Halloween pageant celebrates the harvest after all—and that social relations are defined to a great extent by the uses and abuses of a society's products. As a communal icon, Scout dressed as a ham reconstitutes that social bond, recalling the episodes in the novel when in chapter 3 Walter Cunningham is invited to the Finches' house for dinner (*M*, 29); in chapter 22 the African-American community thanks Atticus Finch for defending Tom Robinson with "hunks of salt pork, tomatoes, beans, even scuppernongs," and "a jar of pickled pigs' knuckles" (*M*, 226); and of course the "two pig-trails" where "Sinkfield" established the inn that grew into the town (*M*, 140).

When Bob Ewell follows the children home from the school to take his promised revenge on Atticus Finch for defending Tom Robinson, he repeats the same pattern he used when he falsely accused Tom of raping Mayella. Scapegoating children as he did an African American and his own daughter Mayella, Ewell displays his cowardly character. Interestingly, Mayella's request for Tom to smash up that "chiffarobe" is paralleled by Bob Ewell's efforts to "mash" the ham costume Scout wears and the more general imagery of broken objects with which the Ewells are associated (*M*, 283). In his effort to destroy the talismanic power of socially significant objects, however, Bob Ewell actually helps revitalize their original purposes. Ritually sacrificing Bob Ewell with his own murderous knife, either accidentally or deliberately, Boo Radley performs a restorative act that enables him to re-enter the public sphere and achieve formal recognition first by the children and then by the adults, including the lawyer (and father) Atticus Finch and the sheriff Heck Tate, who covers up Boo's actual role in Bob Ewell's death (*M*, 287). The mythical dimensions of the narrative have often drawn comment from scholars, so that when "Boo" is transformed by his heroic act from a local "haint" into "Arthur Radley," as Atticus formally introduces him to Scout, we know that there is some aura of Arthurian legend surrounding this Southern knight-errant (*M*, 285).[13]

Atticus Finch recognizes Arthur Radley by speaking his full, proper name, offering him the hospitality of his home, and by thanking him formally for his gift: "Thank you for my children, Arthur" (*M*, 291). The sacrificial actions concluding the novel not only bring together the subplot and main plot; they also serve to restore the social bond by reaffirming its symbolic significance. Cultural rituals from everyday hospitality to school pageants, plays, and literature help renew the social order by way of communicative acts that maintain the human contract and permit some outsiders to be exorcised from the community and others to be reincorporated. The anthropological and mythopoetic dimensions of Lee's novel thus comment not only on her fictional community in Alabama of the mid-1930s but also on the novel form itself. In these respects, Lee anticipates Lewis Hyde's elaboration of Mauss's ideas into the aesthetic theories of *The Gift* and Jacques Derrida's conception in *Given Time* of language as what gives humans the time and space of their social contexts.[14]

As theoretically sophisticated, even postmodern, as Harper Lee's *To Kill a Mockingbird* appears when interpreted in terms of its explicit gift economy, its critique of modern commodity culture, and its insights about how racism works in conjunction with other modes of social exclusion, there is an inevitable horizon or limitation to Lee's view in this remarkable novel. Having linked racism with other social processes that cannot be changed exclusively by formal legislative means or legal justice, Lee proceeds to drop Tom Robinson from the dramatic action, riveting our attention on the psychodrama of Arthur Radley, Bob Ewell, and the Finches in the final movement of the novel. At one level, we may admire Lee for reminding her readers in 1960 that Southern racism is the responsibility of the white people who continue to subscribe to it at the expense of their social health and moral integrity. On the other hand, the primarily white denouement, even when we recognize the important role played by the African-American community in the education of Scout and Jem, leaves us with a conclusion that replaces African-American agency with the white liberal paternalism of Atticus Finch, who at times resembles too closely Faulkner's Ike McCaslin or Roth Edmonds in *Go Down, Moses.*[15] Our sentiments are also drawn primarily to the heroic Arthur Radley, whose actual crime—the killing of Bob Ewell would after all be prosecuted as such in most states—is excused, even as the innocent Tom Robinson is shot when he tries to escape from prison (*M*, 248).

Such limitations deserve our attention and should not be merely wished away in our admiration of Harper Lee's achievement. Lee's liberalism is not the same as Faulkner's liberal guilt in *Absalom, Absalom!*, because she acknowledges the different social reality of African Americans, even their agency in characters such as Calpurnia, but she still subordinates them to what she understands as the more central and urgent criticism of the dominant white culture. What would have happened had Tom Robinson saved Scout and been thereby exonerated of the false crime of which he is convicted? Why must Boo Radley be saved, even renamed, and not Tom? What prevented Lee from developing more fully Calpurnia's social and personal powers to bring together people of different racial backgrounds? And finally why is the transnational dimension in the novel so fully domesticated, incorporated into a story of U.S. social progress at that critical historical interval between the stalemate in Korea, the ongoing Cold War against the Soviet Union, and our covert support of the

French in Indochina after Dienbienphu that would lead us disastrously into the Vietnam War only five years later? Dangerous as it is for the scholar to ask literary texts to be written differently, my rhetorical questions suggest the extent to which Harper Lee's liberal imagination limits the transracial and transnational possibilities of her literary argument.

Notes

1. Karl Marx, *Capital: A Critique of Political Economy*, trans. Ben Fowkes, 2 vols. (New York: Random House, 1977), vol. 1, pp. 163–77.

2. Marcel Mauss, *The Gift: The Form and Reason for Exchange in Archaic Societies*, trans. W. D. Halls (London: Routledge, 1990), p. 5. Jean Baudrillard, *Selected Writings*, ed. Mark Poster (Stanford: Stanford University Press, 1988), pp. 57–63.

3. Marcel Mauss, *Essai sur le Don* (Paris: Presses Universitaires de France, 1950).

4. Harper Lee, *To Kill a Mockingbird* (Philadelphia: J. B. Lippincott Co., 1960), p. 241.

5. Claudia Durst Johnson, *"To Kill a Mockingbird": Threatening Boundaries* (New York: Twayne Publishers, 1994), pp. 2–3.

6. Her august name also recalls ironically the slave names of the Old South. On slave names in the Old South, see Genovese, *Roll, Jordan, Roll: The World the Slaves Made* (New York: Random House, 1974), p. 447.

7. I am guessing at Walter's age. He is Scout's classmate in school, and Scout is "nearly nine years old" somewhat later in the novel (167).

8. Lewis Hyde, *The Gift: Imagination and the Erotic Life of Property* (New York: Random House, 1979), p. 57.

9. Boo Radley's given nickname and his status as mysterious neighbor link him directly with local stories about "haints" or ghosts who haunt the area of Maycomb. Of course, the climactic action of the novel takes place on Halloween, when Bob Ewell attacks Scout on her walk home from school at night and Boo Radley saves her and kills her attacker. Local spirits and ghosts are complementary aspects of the talismanic powers of the fetish and often associated in archaic societies with the magic of such objects.

10. Claudia Durst Johnson, *"To Kill a Mockingbird": A Student Casebook of Issues, Sources, and Historic Documents* (Westport, CT: Greenwood Press, 1994), p. 77.

11. It may well be that "chiffarobe" is a regional expression in Alabama and does refer to a specific item of furniture, so my conclusion here about the Ewells' specific vulgarization of the French is just a speculation.

12. Carolyn Jones, "Atticus Finch and the Mad Dog: Harper Lee's *To Kill a Mockingbird*," *Modern Critical Interpretations of "To Kill a Mockingbird,"* ed. Harold Bloom (Philadelphia: Chelsea House Publishers, 1999), p. 110.

13. Johnson, *"To Kill a Mockingbird": Threatening Boundaries*, p. 79, makes helpful connections between D. W. Winnicott's theories of children's use of play to adapt to reality and anthropological theories of social myths and legends. Winnicott's *Playing*

and Reality (London: Tavistock, 1971) is also considered one of the key works to develop the importance of object-relations in modern psychoanalysis.

14. Derrida's argument in *Given Time: I. Counterfeit Money*, trans. Peggy Kamuf (Chicago: University of Chicago Press, 1992), treats language as an alternative "economy" to capitalism and is thus an appropriate gloss on my argument in this essay.

15. I am thinking here of my criticism of Faulkner in chapter 3.

[6]

ALIEN ENCOUNTER: THOMAS BERGER'S *NEIGHBORS* AS A CRITIQUE OF EXISTENTIAL HUMANISM

Those encounters which counteract themselves because they are organized, those encounters to which good will, busy-body behavior and canny desire for power tirelessly exhort us, are simply covers for spontaneous actions that have become impossible. —Theodor Adorno, *The Jargon of Authenticity* (1964)

What Berger has done . . . is to commence where liberalism ends, in the world of ideas. —Harvey Swados, "An American in Berlin" [Review of *Crazy in Berlin*] (1958)

THOMAS BERGER is a prolific and complex writer, who has published two dozen novels, a collection of stories, and several other volumes in a career that did not really begin until 1958, when Berger in his mid-thirties published the positively reviewed *Crazy in Berlin*, first in the tetralogy recounting the adventures of the Ohio-born German-American Carlo Reinhart, U.S. Corporal of the Occupation Army in post–World War II Berlin when first introduced to the reader in this novel. In his review of *Crazy in Berlin*, Harvey Swados recognized Berger as a postwar U.S. author interested in going beyond "the traditional liberal American novel" about World War II "in which the well-intentioned writer sighs over the pity of it all and invites us as readers to sigh with him while he hates the Nazis as his enemy and loves the Jew as his brother. That we can do for ourselves."[1]

Swados contends that Berger's fiction begins where "liberalism ends," but in the late 1950s such "liberalism" means the sentimental platitudes the "well-intentioned writer" merely echoes without analyzing in the effort to create new ideas. What does the evil of the Nazis teach us in 1958? What are the lessons to be learned from the Holocaust so that it will not be repeated? Such questions were crucial in 1958 as the Cold War threatened people with a nuclear holocaust in the continuing legacy of violence from World War II, now enacted by the United States and Soviet Union, key partners in the Allied victory. Although neither Swados nor Berger invokes Lionel Trilling's "liberal imagination" in the former's review or the latter's *Crazy in Berlin*, both endorse positions distinct from the naïve liberalism Trilling condemns and close to his own idea of a middle path.[2] Swados and Berger's version of this critical liberalism in the 1950s was the American existentialism they would share with such postwar writers as Ralph Ellison, Saul Bellow, Norman Mailer, Joseph Heller, and Thomas Pynchon. In his review of *Vital Parts* (1970), the third novel in the Crazy in Berlin series, Brom Weber identifies Berger as a "comic allegorist of the worthwhile Middle American" who "promises a continued development of the tragicomic mode of vision, something American literature badly needs to compensate for the overextended silence of such formerly active writers as Ralph Ellison, Joseph Heller, and Thomas Pynchon."[3] Sometimes termed "black humor" and sometimes "absurdist," Berger's "tragicomic mode of vision" is deeply existentialist. Poor Carlo Reinhart stumbles and struggles—in Yiddish culture he would be the classic "schlemiel"—with his overweight body, his poor education, his cognitive limits, the split between his mind and body, but in the end of all four novels he represents a "simple humanism" that disguises the more complex existential humanism of Camus and Sartre.[4]

Berger's protagonist in his tetralogy borrows many qualities from Berger himself: German-American background, Midwestern upbringing, and military service in postwar Berlin. Prototype of the white male of the 1980s complaining of his "beset manhood," satirized in the same period as the "DWM" (Dead White Male) whose time has passed, Carlo Reinhart redeems the stereotype by embodying humane qualities the other characters generally lack—specifically those of the black nationalist, Splendor Mainwaring, and the Jewish Communist, Nathan Schild, in *Crazy in Berlin*; the erotic, counter-cultural Eunice in *Vital Parts*; and the predatory Genevieve Raven whom Reinhart marries in *Reinhart in Love*.[5] Even the anti-Nazi survivors, Bach and Otto Knebel, whom Carlo meets in *Crazy in Berlin*, challenge and test his humanism with intellectual arguments he struggles to understand but which finally change Carlo more than they do Bach and Knebel.

Without offering a thorough psychobiographical interpretation, I want merely to suggest that Berger is himself working through the problematic situation of the postwar white American male, who is already beset on several sides by changing social, economic, and cultural conditions. Given the insistent scapegoating of German Americans in this period, Berger's anxieties are understandable and his efforts to think imaginatively through these cultural problems in the Crazy in Berlin series follow the critical function of Trilling's liberal imagination. In similar ways, Theodore Geisel, "Dr. Seuss," struggled with his own German background, especially after the rise of the Nazis to power and subsequent revelations of the Holocaust. As Donald Pease argues, Geisel worked through these anxieties in his famous children's books, incorporating themes of racial and religious tolerance, anti-war messages, and universal human values he believed might overcome such hatred and redeem his own heritage.[6]

In yet other ways, however, Berger's Carlo Reinhart suggests a certain defensiveness regarding the attention paid to other groups, such as victims of the Holocaust, German displaced persons, "liberated" women, youth culture, African Americans and other minorities, and intellectuals. Berger solves fictionally the problem of his ordinary hero, Reinhart, by embodying in him a more humane understanding of these others' problems. Reinhart thus possesses certain powers of sympathetic identification that allow him both to experience others' sufferings and recognize their self-centered limits. Reinhart concludes each of the four novels with "a mild triumph," in part because he comprehends, dimly at times, the entire human tragicomedy.[7] Much as Swados and Berger himself wish to believe that Berger's Crazy in Berlin series takes us beyond postwar liberalism, Carlo Reinhart exemplifies a certain existentialist version of liberalism that could be adapted easily to neoliberalism in the 1990s.

As Berger continued to write installments of the Crazy in Berlin tetralogy from 1958 to 1981, when *Reinhart's Women* was published, he responded in his own ways to the changes in fashion of U.S. fiction, especially the growing interest in postmodern forms and styles from approximately 1965 to 1975.[8] Like other postmodern experimentalists, Berger relied on irony, pastiche, and parody of established literary forms and stylistic conventions. His best-known novel, *Little Big Man* (1964) parodies the western; the Crazy in Berlin tetralogy and *Arthur Rex: A Legendary Novel* (1978) modernize the Arthurian quest motif; *Who Is Teddy Villanova?* (1977) parodies the "noir" detective genre; and *Neighbors* (1980) and *The Feud* (1983) satirize the suburban melodrama. Postmodern U.S.

fiction has a strong foundation of philosophical existentialism, depending as the fiction does on historical contingency, social construction, and the central role of social and linguistic conventions in lived reality. Within these social and historical constraints, the individual has a limited means of expressive possibilities, but the chief mode of asserting one's identity is by recognizing the fictionality of all such constructions. Parody, irony, pastiche are thus key means of liberating the self-conscious individual.[9] Given the existentialist tenor of his first novel, *Crazy in Berlin*, Berger readily adapted his new novels to the growing popularity of postmodern fiction while retaining most of his philosophical foundations. This pattern is by no means unusual for U.S. writers who established themselves in the 1950s and then responded to changes in the prevailing literary realism in the postmodern era. Norman Mailer, Philip Roth, Saul Bellow, Bernard Malamud, John Updike, and many others made similar formal shifts while maintaining their existentialist foundations intact.

In the late 1960s, it appeared that the existentialist no-exit of postwar literary realism prompted the literary experimentalism pioneered by John Barth, Robert Coover, Thomas Pynchon, John Hawkes, William H. Gass, William Gaddis, Raymond Federman, and Don DeLillo. The "surfictionists" and "fabulists" created their own self-referential worlds and repudiated the traditional claims of the novelist to represent reality. As different as this literary avant-garde seemed to be from the literary realists of the 1950s, both shared the outmoded values of what we would term today *existential humanism*. The imaginative freedom of the fabulist or surfictionist was claimed as a consequence of a reality constructed principally in the mind in response to the arbitrariness and contingency of the empirical world. Confronted with the "lie" of another man's truth, the avant-garde writer romantically bid for his own palace of thought and art. Where the existential realist found contemporary man alienated, impotent, subordinate to powers he rarely understood, and thus condemned to an identity and life that were inauthentic, the fabulist transformed such failure into self-conscious knowledge, dependence into playful rebellion, and alienation into the bravura of the isolated individual, the iconoclasm of the avant-garde genius.

Both existential realism and surfiction inclined to similar moral homilies, often repeating popular clichés they had hoped to condemn or at least transform; art, love, care, communication, self-awareness were various and yet strangely equivalent "cures" for the contemporary malaise. Such solutions all had one common feature: the honest confrontation of man's essential predicament as an alienated, mortal, conscious creature driven by his elementary desire for being. Whether self-consciously playful or ruthlessly realistic, such existentialist art claimed the visionary ability to see such truths as the rest of the culture labored to bury this terrifying knowledge beneath the facades of order, respectability, and stable meaning.[10] Despite the strong historicist assumptions of postmodern fiction, it also tended to universalize these human conditions. However differently they might be deployed throughout history and in different cultures, human behaviors followed a certain mythic deep-structure: all men are subject to their irrepressible sexual desires; all men suffer delusions of grandeur; all men are inherently violent. Georg Luckács argues in "The Ideology of Modernism" that many moderns universalized the very specific socio-economic conditions of second-stage modernization in a "metaphysics" of alienation, contingency, and human absurdity, effectively neutralizing efforts at specific political reforms.[11]

Contemptuous of all philosophical generalities and universals, Thomas Berger recognizes that his skepticism belongs to the existentialist's valorization of particularity over generality and that before one knows it, his readers are muttering, "Existence precedes essence." Of course, such a conclusion itself stands as a universal. The variety of Berger's formal experiments between 1958 and 1983 belongs with the sort of imaginative and metamorphic powers Norman Mailer's Rojack considers sanity: "the ability to hold the maximum of impossible combinations in one's mind."[12] In this regard, the Reinhart series of novels is a good measure of the problem confronting Berger, because it consists of four novels written over nearly a quarter of a century (1958–81) during which the existential literary mode I have been describing was transformed from a rebellious rejection of bourgeois America to part of the middle-class's very equipment for living in the late 1970s and early 1980s. The political name for this existentialist temper is liberalism, especially in the United States in this period.

Carlo Reinhart is at once a schlemiel and survivor. His ability to endure postwar absurdity in Berlin and Ohio has much to do with his gradual recognition of his anti-heroic humanity—a recognition that assumes positive value by the time he achieves the relatively confident and stable maturity of *Reinhart's Women* (1981). The young Reinhart of *Crazy in Berlin* barely survives the psychic warfare governing human and political relations in a world where the sheer banality of existence seems defined by its unpredictability.[13] As the title suggests, Reinhart goes briefly "crazy" in a literal sense in the novel. The mature Reinhart may not be able to transcend such contingency, but he has seen enough of an arbitrary world to have acquired a certain hard-won stoicism and pragmatic orderliness. Taken together, the four novels in the series educate Carlo out of the naiveté of his youth through the disillusionment and cynicism of early adulthood and the repeated failures of his early middle age to the wise, even charitable skepticism of his role in *Reinhart's Women*, where he can reflect calmly: "How strange could be the most banal of life's sequences."[14] The culmination of such an existentialist education is Carlo's discovery that the cultivation of a genuine skill, such as cooking, provides the sort of tangible defense against the arbitrariness of existence he had missed in his previous ventures, such as real estate (*Reinhart in Love*) and cryogenics (*Vital Parts*). Cooking, like writing, requires a certain stylization of the material (food or words) that provides the cook or author with some validation of his existence in an otherwise arbitrary and contingent world. The sensuous qualities of both words and food help overcome a sense of deep alienation.

Berger defends his conception of artistic representation as a response to existential contingency in his interview with Richard Schickel on the occasion of the publication of *Neighbors*: "I need some rest between novels, but I never take much, because real life is unbearable to me unless I can escape from it into fiction. An exception might be made if I could experience something remarkable in actuality, but I find that the older I get the less fecund becomes my non-literary fancy: I've either done or don't want to."[15] Russel Wren, Berger's version of the Hammett-Chandler detective, employs deliberately mixed or florid metaphors "as a willed ruse to lure me away from panic—the fundamental purpose of most caprices of language, hence the American wisecrack."[16] Like other existential humanists, Berger imagines his fictions to be defenses against those deceptions and distortions in our experience that are effected either by the sheer perversity of nature or the willful act of some other, more powerful author: convention, culture, commerce. In his apparent deathbed letter to his son Blaine in *Vital Parts*, Carlo writes: "The whole of life, as we know it, is a construct of mind, perhaps of language."[17] In context, Carlo's wisdom sounds treacherously like Harry's banal philosophizing in *Neighbors* or Bob Sweet's glib counsel in *Vital Parts*. Carlo's appositive clause, "as we know it," makes his equation of life with "mind" or "language" a virtual tautology. Staring into the void that he has himself chosen, the existential hero, Carlo, counsels his alienated (and jaded) son. The comedy of Berger's parody requires only that we recall Carlo's "living-in-the-face-of-death" is his "choice" (for $10,000!) to have himself frozen by Bob Sweet and Dr. Streckfuss to publicize their Cryon Foundation. Despite the brilliance of such parodies, Berger's novels do seem to lead us relentlessly to the very existential platitudes for which so many of the characters are mercilessly condemned. The artist's understanding of the essential ideality of the world—its fabrication by minds and in words—seems best used in Berger's terms to construct an interpersonal space, in which a particular self and a concrete other may confront each other in terms of need as basic and human as the hunger served by an exquisite meal, the desire for sexual intercourse, or the appeal for communication. Like Ford Madox Ford, Berger imagines satisfaction of hunger or the desire for being to be measured more in terms of pleasure than use. Indeed, for his own philosophical purposes Berger deliberately confuses or conflates the Kantian distinction between appetitive and artistic desires, if only to argue that in modern consumer societies most biological functions have been subordinated to psychic needs.

The defense art provides against the intrusions of a world of chance is an existential recourse that relies on the ordering function of the imagination, thus giving the literary author a certain privilege in an otherwise dysfunctional world. Describing his own writing as a form of creative dreaming and thus invoking Freud's famous essay "On the Relation of the Poet to Day-Dreaming," Berger tells Schickel: "I write each novel in a trance that is peculiar to each book alone. Hence when I am forced to awaken from it I am thrown into a horror of actuality from which I find no relief until I can enter another fantasy. Has not recent research into sleep established that if a mortal is inhibited from dreaming he will go mad? Perhaps written fiction has some similar efficacy in broad daylight. But I am much more interested in the treat than the treatment."[18] In his two chapters on Freudian psychoanalysis in *The Liberal Imagination*, "Freud and Literature" and "Art and Neurosis," Trilling distinguishes similarly between the aesthetic "treat" and the psychoanalytic "cure," although Trilling is by no means as ironic as Berger three decades later. "Forced to awaken," "thrown into a horror of actuality," "no relief": Berger's descriptive phrases are typical of the modernist's and existential humanist's response to an unsatisfying reality, prompting the defensive gesture toward simulated, artistic control. Even Freud agrees: the daydreamer cannot control or understand his dreams; the poet generalizes and universalizes his fantasies, sharing them with other dreamers.[19]

Berger's literary order and coherence are not explained simply by observing that his style—diction, grammar, narrative tone—contrast sharply with the clichés and idle chatter of his characters. Berger is not merely protecting his own narrative order (and authority); he is actively *purging* those forces of disorder by using the techniques of the satirist: parody, bombast, bathos, hyperbole, caricature. Satire achieves its end by *estranging* familiar, and thus often unrecognized, social ills. Such estrangement is rarely, however, the dispassionate work of the cultural anatomist; more often, it betrays a fundamental fear on the part of the writer that he himself is prone to the sins he condemns. Like Ezra Pound in *Hugh Selwyn Mauberley*, James Joyce in *Portrait of the Artist as a Young Man*, and T. S. Eliot in *The Waste Land*, Berger follows a venerable modernist tradition when he attempts to define his own artistic order and identity in terms of his *denial* or *refusal* of all that so persistently and absurdly *is*. This sort of denial—often associated with the discipline, even asceticism, of the modern artist—is an active negation, a will to obliterate the actual and replace it with one's own fiction, even as the artist recognizes the impossibility of sustaining such a beautiful illusion in the face of so many competing lies. Such aesthetic will-to-power re-enacts the very willful, narcissistic world Berger satirizes in his fiction.

Nowhere is this aesthetic double bind more evident than in Berger's treatment of "liberal culture" in his fiction. Swados considers Berger an author capable of taking us beyond liberal sentimentalism, but others view Berger as a fundamentally conservative author, mocking liberalism as utter folly and embracing the conservatism of many satirists. Berger often seems to be struggling to deny the hip psychology and popular existentialisms that by the 1960s sounded uncannily like his own harder won understanding of the world. In *Crazy in Berlin*, Carlo begins to take control of his existence when he recognizes his elementary relation to another human being, the Jewish double agent, Nathan Schild; it is a recognition Carlo makes only after Schild has been killed and after Carlo has killed in the vain effort to save Schild. Carlo's knowledge lends itself all too easily to the jargon of the existential psychoanalysis popularized in the 1960s: "Existential thinking . . . finds its validation when, across the gulf of our idioms and styles, our mistakes, errings and perversities, we find in the other's communication an experience of the relationship established, lost, destroyed, or regained. We hope to share the experience of relationship established, but the only honest beginning, or even end, may be to share the experience of its absence."[20] This quotation from R. D. Laing's *The Politics of Experience* might serve as an adequate commentary on the moral lesson of *Crazy in Berlin*, even as it does an injustice to the complexity of Berger's vision in that novel, to say nothing of his technical virtuosity. Nevertheless, by the late 1960s, it is fair to say that such jargon threatened the basic philosophical and aesthetic values of many writers like Berger, whose work had first appeared with the bravura of the postwar avant-garde.

In *Neighbors*, Berger addresses these very problems and attempts to demonstrate how the internal logic of existentialism encourages such popularization. Stanley Trachtenberg argues that one of the consequences of Berger's comedy is that "the loss of coherence between various aspects of self comically fragments the notion of identity and thus fictionalizes the existential concept of authenticity as a shaping condition of it."[21] If the self is multiple, if existence precedes and informs essence, if "I" am nothing more than the sum of my actions and choices, then the very ideal of existential authenticity is already a function of inauthenticity. The customary existential response to this charge is that the recognition or "self-consciousness" of such inauthenticity is the highest form of honesty. Yet the Marxist critique of modernism generally indicts this claim for existential self-consciousness as one more way in which the dominant ideology rationalizes its contradictions.[22] By transforming the inauthenticity of a specific historical moment into a metaphysical condition, the existentialist claims a transcendent knowledge that unwittingly conserves and perpetuates the existing order. In traditional Marxism, this universalizing of specific historical conditions is one aspect of "false consciousness," which Theodor Adorno extends to existentialism in *The Jargon of Authenticity*. As Trent Schroyer summarizes Adorno's argument: "His basic thesis is that after World War II [existentialism] became an ideological mystification of human domination—while pretending to be a critique of alienation."[23] Indeed, the methodological procedures of phenomenology are transformed in the work of Karl Jaspers and Martin Heidegger into reified abstractions by subsequent existentialist philosophers, like Albert Camus and Jean-Paul Sartre. Rather than making possible new and transvaluing approaches to existing socioeconomic problems, phenomenology became a "philosophy" with its own stable concepts. For Adorno, the "jargon" of this philosophy achieves the same end as advertising slogans, popular clichés, and other commodified phrases in contemporary life: "Whoever is versed in the jargon does not have to say what he thinks, does not even have to think it properly. The jargon takes over this task and devaluates thought."[24]

In Berger's *Neighbors*, such jargon is embodied in Harry and Ramona, who change personalities with the same ease that they slip into different sets of verbal conventions. They are nothing but surfaces, shaped only of the clichés and verbal chicanery of "high-tech" media culture, already taking shape before the dawn of the digital age. Harry and Ramona simulate the spontaneity, vitality, and metamorphic qualities often associated with the existential anti-hero. "Harry apparently never did the expected," Berger tells us in a narrative aside.[25] This inconsistency, even contradictoriness, is finally what lures Earl Keese into the apparent adventure of the open road together with Harry and Ramona. Earl's "fatal stroke" cuts this journey short and seems to mark symbolically the difference between the Keeses' middle-class respectability and the shape-shifting lives—the pure "becoming"—of Harry and Ramona. Yet, the interest of Berger's narrative derives not from the tired scenario of the suburbanite waking to the nightmare of existential truth; rather, *Neighbors* holds the reader by means of the uncanny relationship between bourgeois stability and the contrived unpredictability of Harry and Ramona. In my view, this uncanny relation is analogous to the relation Berger finds between his own aesthetic values and the existential jargon that was so popular in the 1970s.

Although John G. Avildsen's film, *Neighbors* (1981), departs significantly from Berger's novel, it demonstrates the effects of such a popularization overtaking Berger's effort to reflect more seriously on philosophical issues that by the early 1980s had been thoroughly commodified in popular culture. Cast as the square suburbanite Earl Keese, John Belushi is joined by his comedic partner, Dan Aykroyd, playing the subversive shaper-shifter Harry, in the film only one year after Belushi and Aykroyd took their *Saturday Night Live* parody musical sketch, "The Blues Brothers" to the big screen in the blockbuster film *The Blues Brothers* (1980).[26] It is virtually impossible to watch Belushi and Aykroyd in the film *Neighbors* without seeing them imaginatively as Jake and Elwood Blues from *The Blues Brothers*, doing their parody of two white boys with black soul. The series of parodies that Belushi and Aykroyd perform in the two films extends back to *Saturday Night Live* clips running in the viewer's brain, so that Earl and Harry—Harry is renamed "Vic" in Landis's film—in Berger's novel become mere tag names for the dizzying set of changeable identities that Berger set out to criticize. The novel is thus rapidly consumed by a popular cultural production that Fredric Jameson considers typical of postmodernity's irreducible "pastiche" and "surface without depth."[27] Berger's novel becomes a crucial part of the very "jargon of authenticity" he hoped to criticize and so rapidly as to dazzle the historical observer.

In the novel, Harry and Ramona's relationship with the Keeses is properly "uncanny," in the technical Freudian sense of the term. The very title and situation of the novel—*Neighbors*, and how we live as neighbors with each other—encourage psychoanalytic reflection on Freud's German terms, *heimlich* ("homely") and *unheimlich* ("unhomely," thus "uncanny"). The English translation of "*das Unheimliche*" allows us to forget how intimately Freud associates the notion with its opposites, home and hearth: "Among its different shades of meaning the word *heimlich* exhibits one which is identical with its opposite, unheimlich. . . . In general we are reminded that the word *heimlich* is not unambiguous, but belongs to two sets of ideas, which without being contradictory are yet very different: on the one hand, it means that which is familiar and congenial, and on the other, that which is concealed and kept out of sight."[28] Freud explains this apparent paradox in terms that are basic to his understanding of the psychic and literary Double; the "uncanny" is, in fact, "nothing new or foreign, but something familiar and old-established in the mind that has been estranged only by the process of repression."[29] Throughout *Neighbors*, Harry and Ramona evoke a certain familiarity from the Keeses that seems to suggest their strangeness may be a consequence of the Keeses' repression as much as it is a function of Harry and Ramona's "alternative" lifestyle.

Up to a certain point, an existentialist reading of *Neighbors* accounts quite nicely for the "uncanny" relation Harry and Ramona have with the Keeses. Earl and Enid have taken "control" (one of Earl's favorite words) of their lives only by disguising their essential alienation and the sheer contingency of their human situation. At home neither in the suburbs nor the city, the Keeses share the homelessness of Harry and Ramona. Like Twain's middle class, the Keeses labor principally to disguise from themselves the fact of their own powerlessness and insignificance. In the midst of the farce that dominates the drama of *Neighbors*, there is a familiar narrative development: the progressive exposure of all the Keeses' values as elaborate fictions with intricate genealogies disguising their imaginative origins. Halfway through the novel, Earl suddenly realizes that "he had no idea of what [Enid] did all day" (*Neighbors*, 118; hereafter *N*); early in the novel, Berger notes: "For a number of years now Keese had observed his wife only by means of what she did . . . he saw the actor only through the action" (*N*, 3). Earl's memories of his daughter Elaine's childhood rarely agree with her own; in general, his relation with Elaine is more a product of his imagination than of any historical evolution. Even before she has met Harry and Ramona, Elaine mimics their curious blend of affection and domination: "I just wanted to be cruel to you for a moment. . . . Just because you're my very own dad. You're mine, you belong to me, you're my property" (*N*, 108). Given the ease with which Harry and Ramona expose the hollowness of the Keeses' values, the reader expects Berger to reveal the metaphysical truths of alienation, will-to-power as the law of human relations, and a world of unpredictable changes. Earl tries to conclude at one point, in an infamous echo: "Timing was all. A minute passes and the world is changed in every respect. The landscape out the window looks the same, but every atom is different" (*N*, 170).

In traditional existentialist fiction, the anti-hero himself or some philosophical narrator reveals bourgeois inauthenticity. In *Neighbors*, Harry and Ramona do this satiric anatomy, even though they themselves are utterly superficial, constructed from fragments of the Keeses' world, even parodic doubles of the Keeses. Harry and Ramona represent the contradictoriness of this particular suburban and capitalist world, but these characters appear strange and unfamiliar as a consequence of the Keeses' repression. What the Keeses hear in the glib, interchangeable jargon of these two latter-day hipsters is not the counter-culture, but the Keeses' own idle chatter. Harry and Ramona are "really unreal," to echo a popular teen oxymoron of the late 1970s; their reality is precisely a function of the studied, designed unreality by which they appear to others. Berger has assessed Earl's problem as his inability to "believe in his own reality."[30] Earl is introduced in terms of his "strange malady or gift": "Were Keese to accept the literal witness of his eyes, his life would have been of quite another character, perhaps catastrophic, for outlandish illusions were, if not habitual with him, then at least none too rare" (*N*, 1–2). Keese's tendency to confuse perceptual and imaginary objects is one of the sources of Berger's comedy in the novel, and this inclination helps relate that comedy to Berger's serious themes, never far removed from wit. Berger seems to be arguing that contemporary culture discourages the exercise of the imaginative faculty and encourages the sort of literalness in thought and language that is the equivalent of automation. Berger turns this conventional criticism of modern times in a new way, suggesting that the repression of our imaginative capabilities allows the imagination to escape our control, literally to "haunt" us in Freud's terms. Working with the logic of nightmare, the imagination produces strange epiphenomena that are, in fact, expressions of our own cultural schizophrenia. Harry and Ramona are in effect ghosts, spectral effects of Earl and Enid's collective unconscious. Berger takes perverse pleasure in enumerating the curious twists of imagination that are everywhere evident in advertising slogans, teen argot, and media clichés of contemporary life, but no longer belong to Earl and Enid.

One of the functions of the imagination is the mediation of inner and outer worlds, and it is the sharp distinction maintained by Earl between public and private realms that provokes many of the absurd events in the novel. Earl is outraged to learn that Harry is cooking spaghetti in his kitchen after he has conned Earl out of $32.00 to pay for take-out food. In existential terms, Earl gets what he deserves: his distrust of Harry is a form of bad faith that is simply repaid in kind. In another sense, Earl is not so much paid back as responsible for having established their relationship in terms of economic, rather than human, exchange. Earl is shocked at the idea of paying his neighbor to cook dinner, but he fails to recognize that *all* relations in his society are based on such payments. When

Earl accuses Ramona of blackmailing him to keep quiet about what he has done to Harry's car, she asks: "Wouldn't you, if you had somebody cold?" (*N*, 42). Even before he has met Harry and Ramona, Earl tells Enid: "We could probably get away with giving them no formal welcome whatever. It's scarcely a true obligation" (*N*, 1). What constitutes a "true obligation" in this society remains ambiguous, precisely because the "true" basis already involves a contradiction: a relation is determined by its exchange-value in this capitalist society, which in "human" relations is already a denial of that human element. When Earl meets Harry on the latter's lawn, Earl says ingratiatingly, even subserviently: "We're on your property now. Now you're the boss. You can make short work of me if I get out of line . . . you have the moral advantage and . . . I'm in a subordinate position . . . that gives you a tremendous edge" (*N*, 144). It is fair to say, even though we should be suspicious of all "origins" in such a novel, that Earl conceives of life and human relations in terms of basic master-servant relations and economic obligations long before Harry and Ramona arrive in the neighborhood. As early as the first page of the narrative, Earl and Enid agree that "a true obligation" would be "like giving food to a starving person," which itself is part of the economic equation on which the Keeses reflexively base their lives.

Scholars of Henry James's *The Turn of the Screw* have often observed how the Governess re-enacts each appearance of Peter Quint and Miss Jessel; this formal consistency has strengthened arguments in favor of the ghosts as objectifications of the Governess's psychic anxieties.[31] In an analogous way, most of the surprising acts by Harry and Ramona are foreshadowed by words, dreams, or acts by the Keeses, especially Earl. Ramona accuses Earl of "attempted rape," a charge later withdrawn as an apparent joke. Earl is thrilled by the brush of Ramona's breasts when she first enters his house; only minutes after Ramona's arrival, Earl is attracted by the possibility of tricking his wife into staying home while he and Ramona dine at a fancy French restaurant. Ramona certainly exaggerates Earl's idle fantasies when she accuses him of attempted rape, but her exaggeration works in the manner of every good nightmare or irrational fear. Earl is titillated by Ramona's boldness and vulgarity throughout the narrative. She may seem to be leading him on, but the sites of their near-trysts are always uncannily familiar to Earl: the bedrooms in his house, his game room, his front porch, his kitchen—homely sites.

When he does visit Harry and Ramona's house, Ramona is curiously absent—at Earl's house with Enid and Elaine, we learn later.

Earl's relations with Harry demonstrate a similar structure of *prolepsis* (the rhetorical trope of anticipation). When Earl finally sees Harry's car in the morning light, he considers how he might restore peace: "Were his car retrieved . . . and not only restored in appearance but improved—e.g., a completely new coat of paint!—he would not come away empty-handed" (*N*, 159). After Harry has looked at his damaged car, he says: "Earl, that car needs a paint job. There's no two ways about it. Now, if you want to renege, O.K., I won't sue you. I'll make it a matter of honor. I'm saying what's right" (*N*, 188). Once again, Harry calls attention to the contradictions between moral and economic values in this culture, and what he says is merely an echo of Earl's own idea of settling scores. Earl responds to Harry as if Harry were a cheap con-man trying to beat Earl out of money for the paint job. Earl is not just guilty of hypocrisy or applying a double standard; his behavior provokes, even produces, the sort of exaggerated opportunism that Harry represents. In this regard, Earl and Harry are proper "neighbors," insofar as they share this uncanny relation. When Harry says to Earl, "Has it occurred to you that we are inevitably drawn back to a kitchen table whenever we have tried to talk all evening? Maybe that does suggest we're in some basic sympathy, like members of the same family?" he may be making an observation shared by Berger (*N*, 146).

Just what causes "Harry and Ramona" (Berger represents them this way to stress their corporate qualities) to materialize in the first place takes us beyond their associations with the hidden contradictions of the Keeses' safe, middle-class existence. Their uncanniness reminds us that the bourgeoisie produces its own marginal "other," its own rebellious alternatives, in part to constrain, by means of strategic anticipation, those forces that threaten revolution. In Marxist terms, the petty master-servant contests of these suburbanites are means by which the dominant ideology displaces (and thus defuses) the political necessity of class struggle. Berger is no Marxist, of course, so his own reaction to this cultural artistry is to use his own imaginative powers to transgress the existing order's proper boundaries between order and chaos, coherence and contradiction. In *Neighbors*, Berger's own artistic values seem to undergo some sort of revaluation; rather than offering the protective space of controlled language, art seems more closely identified with the provocations and harassments of such minor criminals as Harry and Ramona. Yet Harry and Ramona are themselves part of the problem; they are merely the uncanny expressions of the incoherence, superficiality, and contradictoriness the culture has produced in its specific and historical will for truth. Berger's art differs from the derivative and reactive games of Harry and Ramona, insofar as Berger's narrative represents the entire dialectic of such banality as Harry, Ramona, Earl, Enid, and Elaine collectively express. This dialectic has an interesting consequence for the reader's relation to the artistic act. In Berger's earlier novels, especially the Crazy in Berlin tetralogy, the reader is directed toward the general skepticism of narrative tone and the ironic form. In *Neighbors*, Berger seems more interested in constructing a dramatic situation involving apparent choices, so that each reader will make a choice that will reveal his or her particular weaknesses and also subvert the formal ending of the novel. Carlo Reinhart concludes each novel in the Crazy in Berlin series with some modest triumph over life; he is a liberal existentialist who accepts the bizarre conditions of life and finds some temporary balance. In *Neighbors*, that possibility is judged to be as irrational and impossible as the rest of experience.

Berger's method in *Neighbors* is remarkably similar to Melville's in *The Confidence-Man*, a work that has also attracted many existentialist readings and yet always exceeded philosophical existentialism. Melville's novel is a labyrinth of different stories, all of which repeat the same semiotic law: character, reader, and writer unwittingly reveal their vanities and sins in the course of telling stories they imagine will shore up their identities and reputations. Writing shares with popular culture the tendency to hide much for the sake of what it would express. Berger and Melville develop complex means of turning the intentions of their characters and their readers against themselves—that is, of rendering those intentions "uncanny." The logic of such an aesthetic requires the artist to turn its method on his own identity as an author. In *Neighbors*, Berger uses Earl and Harry to parody the idea of art as a defense against a threatening world and to relate that aesthetic to glib existentialist jargon and pop psychology. In an allusion to F. Scott Fitzgerald's Jay Gatsby, Earl cries desperately: "*Everything can be put back where it belongs*" (*N*, 160). In the neighborhood of uncanny resemblances and uncontrolled acts, the very concept of ownership, as Earl understands it, has vanished. Nothing belongs anywhere. This very bourgeois cry for order is also a curious double for the modernist's claim that the form of art might redeem the waste land of the age, might give "things" proper "places"—a neighborhood of being—where they "belong." Earl insists in the best tradition of the novel: "Sequences are all-important, too, . . . and timing, in general" (*N*, 240). Yet the disturbing loss of time for Earl during his hectic weekend ("a thrill a minute") reflects how Earl's ordered time and proper sequences are only simulacra of any significant history.

In his interview with Richard Schickel, Berger notes: "Harry and Ramona would certainly seem to be outlaws in Keese's scheme of things, but perhaps, taking the wider view, it is they who protect and conserve and perpetuate. Though a larger, younger and seemingly more ruthless man, Harry can usually, when the dust settles, be identified as Keese's victim; and not even with the help of Eros can Ramona prevail for more than the odd moment."[32] On a certain level, these claims seem unproblematic; Earl himself makes the same observation more bluntly when he claims: "I've given more than I've got. I don't mind admitting I'm proud of myself" (*N*, 162). Only Berger's claim that Harry and Ramona "protect and conserve and perpetuate" seems troubling given their contempt for the middle-class world of the novel. There are two senses in which such outlaws serve such conservational ends, both of which express the transformation of Berger's aesthetic values in *Neighbors* from the liberal existentialism guiding his previous works. In one sense, their iconoclasm is borrowed from the sham spontaneity and directness of popular culture, especially the increasing visual immediacy of television and documentary film in the late 1970s, which would have us believe the sheer immediacy of all that "is" and forget the complex weave of imagination, memory, and repression governing every "event." Harry and Ramona's existential spontaneity is a kind of family-room hipsterism that transforms the contradictions of middle-class America into the "real and honest" spiritualism of pop religious or psychic gurus of the time. As Adorno points out, the "jargon" of existentialism "ends in a miserable consolation: after all, one still remains what one is."[33] Culture's "other," its eccentric margin, is often little more than the means by which it confirms its ideology and establishes its borders. In this sense, the artist may lead us to "metaphysical" visions that blind us to the contradictions of our historical and social situations. In such a case, it would seem preferable to opt for some political extreme—a deep conservatism or revolutionary radicalism—that would transform such an intolerable situation.

In another sense, Harry and Ramona may be turned ultimately to the task of artistic provocation, thus conserving those powers of the imagination, subversion, skepticism, and satire that regenerate cultural vitality. This alternative sounds much like an effort to reclaim the critical function of Trilling's "liberal imagination" for the 1980s. Berger has acknowledged his debt to Kafka as the master "who taught me that at any moment banality might turn sinister."[34] *Neighbors* demonstrates the evil of banality as much as the banality of evil in its exposure of the contradictions governing the lives of the Keeses. *Neighbors* also shows how art can share, even justify, such banality and secret contradiction when it strives to preserve itself from the corruptions of the actual and of the historical and political conditions that gave rise to it. In this sense, Berger marks the limitation of Trilling's liberal imagination and historicizes the aesthetic process, accounting perhaps for Berger's own continuing willingness to develop new forms and styles even at the risk of succumbing to the "jargon" of the contemporary moment. In a playful autobiographical aside, Berger notes: "Incidentally, this narrative may have been a bit of wish-fulfillment. I wrote the book while living in Maine, where I had no next-door neighbors of any sort. Only in such a fashion is my work ever autobiographical."[35] One is tempted to guess what sort of wish-fulfillment was involved: the desire to harass the neighbors or the need to be harassed? It is, of course, the dialectical relation of these two alternatives that constitutes the interest and novelty of Berger's novel in 1980. The reviewers quickly chose sides: Harry and Ramona *or* Earl Keese. In this case, to choose is to abuse, and one year later John Avildsen's popular film, *Neighbors*, would tangle up the plot but get the doubled relations of the characters essentially right by casting Belushi and Aykroyd as Earl and Harry ("Vic" in the film). In so doing, of course, Avildesen immediately appropriated Berger's critique of popular liberalism, rendering it too an instance of Adorno's "jargon of authenticity."

In the same year as the film *Neighbors* was released, Berger's *Reinhart's Women*, the final novel in the Crazy in Berlin series, was published, effectively reinforcing the existentialist argument of the series and bolstering the anti-hero status of the protagonist, Carlo Reinhart. Two years later, Berger published *The Feud* (1983), a sequel to *Neighbors*, as if following the cinematic practice then gaining popularity of making sequels. *The Feud* broadens the problem of interpersonal conflicts in *Neighbors* to the larger social context of the twin towns of Hornbeck and Millville. In *The Feud*, Berger demonstrates how the psychic impasses of existential humanism may be understood as sociological and the dysfunction of bourgeois individuals extended to the social organization of modern America itself. Berger's specific political positions in these three novels from the early 1980s are not particularly coherent, mixing as they do residual attitudes from the Crazy in Berlin series with his desire to overcome the impasse of liberal existentialism to which he himself has contributed. But those confusions are significant not just for Thomas Berger but for U.S. culture in general at a particularly critical juncture. With Ronald Reagan winning the presidential election in 1980, beginning in 1981 the two terms (1981–89) that would revive the Republican Party and U.S. conservatism, the United States was about to undergo a paradigm shift in which the impasses of older liberal political and cultural philosophies empowered neoconservatives and what would become neoliberalism.

Notes

1. Harvey Swados, "An American in Berlin [Review of *Crazy in Berlin*]," in *Critical Essays on Thomas Berger*, ed. David W. Madden (New York: G. K. Hall and Co., 1995), p. 29. First published in *The New Leader* (December 15, 1958).

2. Lionel Trilling, *The Liberal Imagination*, pp. 9–10.

3. Brom Weber, "[Review of *Vital Parts*]," in *Critical Essays on Thomas Berger*, p. 33. First published in *Saturday Review* (March 21, 1970), 42.

4. Douglas A. Hughes, "The Schlemiel as Humanist: Thomas Berger's Carlo Reinhart," *Critical Essays on Thomas Berger*, pp. 52–53.

5. On Berger's use of names and stereotypical characters in the Crazy in Berlin tetralogy, see Gerald Weales, "Reinhart as Hero and Clown," *Critical Essays on Thomas Berger*, pp. 82–85.

6. Donald E. Pease, *Theodore Seuss Geisel* (New York: Oxford University Press, 2010).

7. Weales, "Reinhart as Hero and Clown," p. 80.

8. On this periodization of postmodern U.S. fiction and its general characteristics, see John Carlos Rowe, *The New American Studies* (Minneapolis: University of Minnesota Press, 2002), pp. 17–49.

9. Ibid. pp. 25–26.

10. Richard Lehan, *A Dangerous Crossing: French Literary Existentialism and the Modern American Novel* (Carbondale: University of Illinois Press, 1973) provides a good overview of the influence of Continental existentialism on modern American

writers like Hemingway and Faulkner and postmodern American writers like Pynchon and Barth.

11. Georg Lukács, "The Ideology of Modernism," in *The Meaning of Contemporary Realism*, trans. John and Necke Mander (London: Merlin Press, 1962), p. 21.

12. Norman Mailer, *An American Dream* (New York: Dell Publishing Co., 1950), p. 150.

13. Brooks Landon, "The Radical Americanist," *Nation* 225 (1977), 153, argues that Berger "characteristically turns familiar means to strange ends."

14. Thomas Berger, *Reinhart's Women* (New York: Delacorte Press/Seymour Lawrence, 1981), p. 58.

15. Richard Schickel, "Interviewing Thomas Berger," *New York Times Book Review* (April 6, 1980), p. 1. Further references in Notes as "Schickel Interview."

16. Thomas Berger, *Who Is Teddy Villanova?* (New York: Delacorte Press/Seymour Lawrence, 1977), p. 21.

17. Berger, *Vital Parts* (New York: New American Library, 1970), p. 351.

18. Schickel Interview, 22.

19. Sigmund Freud, "The Relation of the Poet to Day-Dreaming," in *On Creativity and the Unconscious*, ed. Benjamin Nelson, translated under the supervision of Joan Riviere (New York: Harper and Row, 1958), pp. 53–54.

20. R. D. Laing, *The Politics of Experience* (New York: Ballantine Books, 1967), p. 56.

21. Stanley Trachtenberg, "Berger and Barth: The Comedy of Decomposition," in *Comic Relief: Humor in Contemporary American Literature*, ed. Sarah Blacher Cohen (Urbana: University of Illinois Press, 1978), p. 60.

22. Lukács, "The Ideology of Modernism," p. 21.

23. Trent Schroyer, foreword to Theodor Adorno, *The Jargon of Authenticity*, trans. Kurt Tarnowski and Frederic Will (Evanston, IL: Northwestern University Press, 1973), p. xiii. Adorno's *The Jargon of Authenticity* was first published in German in 1962.

24. Adorno, *The Jargon of Authenticity*, p. 9.

25. Thomas Berger, *Neighbors* (New York: Delacorte Press/Seymour Lawrence, 1980), p. 24.

26. *Neighbors*, directed by John G. Avildsen, screenplay by Larry Gelbart (Columbia Pictures, 1981); *The Blues Brothers*, directed by John Landis, screenplay by Dan Aykroyd and John Landis (Universal Pictures, 1980).

27. Fredric Jameson, *Postmodernism, or The Logic of Late Capitalism* (Durham, NC: Duke University Press, 1990), p. 7.

28. Freud, "The 'Uncanny,'" in *On Creativity and the Unconscious*, p. 129.

29. Ibid., p. 148.

30. Schickel Interview, 21.

31. See John Carlos Rowe, *The Theoretical Dimensions of Henry James* (Madison: University of Wisconsin Press, 1984), p. 144.

32. Schickel Interview, 21.

33. Adorno, *The Jargon of Authenticity*, pp. 115–16.

34. Schickel Interview, 21.

35. Ibid.

[7]

BURIED ALIVE: THE NATIVE AMERICAN POLITICAL UNCONSCIOUS IN LOUISE ERDRICH'S FICTION

MOST SCHOLARS UNDERSTAND postcolonial studies to be a radical methodology, academic field, and political perspective. *Postcolonial studies* is a loose term that refers to a wide variety of approaches and values, but all postcolonial work is centrally concerned with overcoming the imperial heritage in many different postcolonial contexts around the globe. Yet *how* postcolonial critics propose we should respond to the political, economic, social, and cultural legacies of imperialism varies significantly in relation to the specific postcolonial situation. More radical approaches in formerly colonized regions of Africa and Asia have argued for rejecting the national form and related institutions of civil administration inherited from Western colonizers.[1] In the Western Hemisphere and some British Commonwealth nations, like Australia and Canada and New Zealand, postcolonial theorists acknowledge the inevitability of the national form and argue instead for reforms within its boundaries, especially as such horizons are changing in this era of new immigration and other consequences of globalization.[2] Nearly four decades after the early efforts of the South Asian History Collective developed a "postcolonial" approach in India in the 1970s, we recognize a wide range of political responses to the diverse legacies of global imperialism and how postcolonial states might best address their problems.

Until quite recently, however, native peoples in the Western Hemisphere have been neglected in postcolonial studies. Thanks to work by scholars such as C. Richard King in *Postcolonial America*, Cheryl Walker in *Indian Nation*, and Walter Mignolo in *The Darker Side of the Renaissance*, Native America is becoming a more central topic in postcolonial studies, even as it poses special challenges at the theoretical and political levels.[3] I think this work has also been done by indigenous creative writers—Louise Erdrich, Gerald Vizenor, Leslie Marmon Silko, Thomas King, Sherman Alexie, James Welch, William Least Heat-Moon, Joy Harjo, and Arigon Star are just some examples—who have reflected upon many of the issues raised by postcolonial studies in relation to native peoples, even if these writers have not participated explicitly in the academic debates of the scholars above. Diverse as these native writers are, they all acknowledge the history of native peoples *negotiating* their relations to the U.S. nation. Cheryl Walker's *Indian Nation* suggests how dominant the effort has been by native writers and intellectuals to find a workable relationship to the national form in the United States, no matter how relentlessly and often violently their efforts have been rejected by Euroamericans and their governments. That history of negotiation and rejection continues today, and it is the effort of indigenous peoples to find their "home" within the U.S. state that I consider a broadly conceived "liberalism" that we need to understand better before advocating more radical views on the left or the right of how Native Americans ought to live and organize their communities.

In other words, the "liberal imagination" takes on a new historical meaning, vitality, and relevance when understood in Native American cultures. For Lionel Trilling, it would have little meaning, given his utter disregard of indigenous issues in *The Liberal Imagination*, so this chapter also serves the purpose of identifying one of those areas Trilling forecloses at a particularly urgent moment for native peoples, when the federal government's goal of "terminating" Indian sovereignty was the official postwar policy. My argument in this chapter focuses on two novels by Louise Erdrich, *The Last Report of the Miracles at Little No Horse* (2001) and *The Master Butchers Singing Club* (2003). I do not intend for Erdrich to "represent" the diversity of the native writers mentioned in the previous paragraph, but instead to respect the complex thinking and craft of a sophisticated writer in order to understand how some of the key issues in postcolonial studies are transformed when we consider Native America. I also want to point out that our best "ethnic writers," to borrow a troublesome tag, require the sort of interpretive protocols of "close reading" that are too often reserved for writers already canonized (and too often "not ethnic"). The problems of social, historical, and personal representation are particularly complex for native peoples, whose identities have been directly affected by the weird changes forced upon them by radical social attacks, historical discontinuities, and consequent psychological upheavals.

In *The Master Butchers Singing Club*, Erdrich follows a pattern from several previous works, such as *The Beet Queen* (1986) and *Tales of Burning Love* (1996), by concentrating primarily on the European immigrant communities living in her fictional Argus, North Dakota.[4] In all of these works, Ojibwe cultural history eventually influences events in Argus, Fargo, Minneapolis/St. Paul, and other Euroamerican towns Erdrich represents as either fiercely repressing or blithely unaware of this Native American presence. In all of her writings, Erdrich works self-consciously to counter this repression and overcome such ignorance, rendering Native Americans in her imaginary Upper Midwest as ineluctable characters in this landscape and thus countering the pervasive Myth of the Vanishing American.[5] It goes without saying that in the contemporary United States, Native Americans remain the repressed subjects of an imperial cultural consciousness that has only recently been addressed directly. From Edward Said's brief remarks about U.S. imperialism in *Culture and Imperialism* (1993) to my efforts in *Literary Culture and U.S. Imperialism: From the Revolution to World War II* (2000) and Amy Kaplan's arguments in *The Anarchy of Empire in United States Culture* (2002), U.S. imperialism and its cultural apparatus have become central objects of study, but too little of this scholarly attention has been devoted to the ways in which native peoples have been rendered invisible both in the material practices of U.S. genocide ("Manifest Destiny") and the complementary cultural hierarchies for proper social self-representation (the "cultural symbolic").[6] As we work toward a better understanding of the relationship between postcolonial studies and psychoanalysis, we ought to consider the processes through which native peoples are repressed to be key elements to understand, not simply for their historical significance but also in the project of recovering, reconstituting, and reaffirming native identities and presences.

My theoretical approach to this topic is informed by my understanding of postcolonial studies generally as continuing what was once termed the "critical study of colonial discourse," rather than focusing, as some have argued, on the "aftermath" of colonialism and its imperial systems. Postcolonial studies is itself always utopian and political, insofar as it attempts to formulate more equitable and liberal conditions of social belonging than were possible under colonial and national circumstances.[7] Postcolonial studies should thus be actively political and deliberately emancipatory, and it can only do so by identifying the history of those limitations and exclusions that have gone unrecognized in previous systems of social and communal organization. Implicitly or explicitly, then, all work done in the name of postcolonial studies interprets the political unconscious of the imperial practices that required the decolonizing work of independence movements and cultural reorganizations of emergent, postcolonial societies.

We should be cautious in making theoretical generalizations that go much beyond these relatively self-evident claims about an approach that necessarily encompasses the diverse history of global colonization and domination by a handful of modern nations and the very different liberation struggles and new societies overcoming such imperial rule. Scholars of Native American studies, of First Peoples in Canada, of Aborigines and Torres Straits Islanders in Australia, and of the Maori in New Zealand agree that postcolonial studies in its diversity stresses the historical and cultural particularities of different peoples' political, economic, and cultural struggles to overcome their imperial invisibility and embody themselves as visible, active, complex beings. Culture and its wide variety of symbolic instruments play crucial roles in this postcolonial work, reminding us that the details and specificities of such cultural countermemory and practice require careful, focused attention to identifiable groups and their histories, rather than sweeping, global generalizations. It is for all of these reasons, then, that I choose to focus on Louise Erdrich's contemporary contact zone in the Upper Midwest, where several communities mutually constitute each other: the Ojibwe (*Anishinaabeg* [humans] or Chippewa) people, Euroamerican immigrants (especially from Germany and Scandinavia), and the subsequent *métis* peoples of their intertwined, albeit often repressed, histories. There is a regional identity to the Upper Midwest that distinguishes it from other cultures, and thus its global character must be sought not in what it shares with other communities understood in transnational terms but as how different cultures and nationalities *enact* this region.

Fidelis Waldvogel, the Argus, North Dakota, master butcher who organizes the "singing club" of Erdrich's title, grew up in Germany hoping to become a poet and learning the butcher's trade from his father, but his first adult work is as a sniper for the German Army during World War I (*The Master Butchers Singing Club*, 1–3; hereafter *MB*). Firing from the treetops with deadly accuracy, Fidelis catches the French soldiers in their trenches, even when they "dug down deeper to escape him" and their "souls flew unerringly across the drenched slime to lodge within him" (*MB*, 5). This curious scene in which the protagonist systematically murders his enemies and then finds their souls "lodging" within him, as if they are succubi, initiates a motif of premature burial alive, violent death, and spiritual transmigration that structures *The Master Butchers Singing Club*. At first, Waldvogel's experiences in World War I seem to have nothing to do with the imperial destruction and oppression of native peoples in North America. Indeed, no reference to Native Americans is made in the text until well after Fidelis and his bride, Eva Kalb, formerly the fiancée of his best friend who is killed in the war, immigrate to America and settle in Argus, North Dakota. Yet Erdrich is perfectly aware that World War I was fought in part over shifting balances of power among the European nations, especially as far as their conflicting empires abroad were concerned. And more generally Erdrich understands that the colonization of North America followed the logic of military conflict and conquest through which European monarchies and then nations had legitimated their authorities. A kind, peaceful, loving family man, Fidelis Waldvogel nonetheless brings with him the European violence that disrupted North America centuries before his arrival there.

Of course, Fidelis and Eva believe they have left far behind the violence of the Old World, which has victimized both of them, and they devote themselves to the virtues of bourgeois work as butchers, civic responsibility as town leaders, and raising their family of four sons—Franz, Markus, Emil, and Erich—in the growing town of Argus. As in Erdrich's other novels set principally in town, Native Americans drift in and out, playing relatively small roles and often knowing little about their own family histories and identities. The political unconscious percolates beneath the surface of Argus and in *The Master Butchers Singing Club* is represented metaphorically in several incidents of burial alive. Early in the novel, Delphine, who will marry Fidelis after Eva dies of cancer, returns from a trip to discover a terrible mess and persistent smell in the house of her father, a chronic alcoholic who often passes out after long drinking binges with his friends. With the help of her bisexual, *métis* boyfriend, Cyprian, she begins the arduous task of cleaning the home where she grew up. Beneath layers of organic muck and barrels of trash, they work their way down to the door to the cellar. The noxious smell grows stronger as they open the cellar door, which reveals the decomposed bodies of Doris and Portland "Porky" Chavers and their daughter Ruthie (*MB*, 59). The grisly, apparently accidental deaths—the Chavers are trapped in the cellar and slowly starve to death as their shouts of help go unheeded by the drunken men in the house above—are investigated by Sheriff Hock throughout the rest of the narrative (at least until he is murdered by Clarisse, the diminutive undertaker, whom he has sexually assaulted), and they provide the aura of a detective plot organizing the dramatic action.

"The Cellar" (chapter 4) is followed much later by "The Room in the Earth" (chapter 9), in which three of Fidelis's sons nearly die while burrowing into a heap of dirt excavated from the cellar in the construction of a new house (*MB*, 199). Following heavy rainstorms and after the boys have dug an extensive tunnel and central room, much like that of the burial chamber for an ancient pyramid, the soggy soil collapses on them and traps Markus. Like Roy's cellar hiding the Chavers' terrible ends, the "room in the earth" that the boys carve out, and that nearly kills them, has no explicit connection with the history of violent conflict between Euroamericans and Native Americans in the Upper Midwest. Indeed, Erdrich goes to some lengths to convince us that the Chavers' deaths are merely tragic consequences of alcoholic neglect and that Markus's near death and broken arm are no more than what sometimes happens to curious little boys.

In the novel's final chapter (16), Step-and-a-Half, the strange Indian woman who wanders the town at night hears a cry coming from the Shimeks' outhouse and reaches into the rank depths to retrieve a newborn child, discarded in shame by Mrs. Shimek only moments before. Step-and-a-Half hears the child's "one cry before it sank the incremental inch that covered up its mouth," and the surrogate mother gives this salvaged life new birth by severing "the cord with nothing other than her own sharp teeth" and using her finger to clean "out the baby's mouth" (*MB*, 382). This abandoned and then miraculously saved child grows up to be Delphine, who is one of the protagonists in *The Master Butchers Singing Club*: second wife to the German-American butcher Fidelis, surrogate mother in her own right of Fidelis's and Eva's four sons, Roy's daughter and savior, and Cyprian's lover. Yet she lives most of her life unaware of her complex family genealogy. Unable to care for the baby Delphine, Step-and-a-Half gives her to her sometime lover, Roy Watzka, the alcoholic who forgets the Chavers trapped in his locked cellar, and who tells the daughter he brings up as his own that her mother, "Minnie" (Roy's nickname for Step-and-a-Half), has died.

As the reader gradually discovers, what links together all of these episodes of burial alive (and many others I haven't mentioned) is yet another burial that haunts the entire text and is rarely mentioned by the citizens of Argus: the U.S. Army's massacre of Lakota at Wounded Knee in 1890. Like a ghostly return of the repressed in Freudian psychoanalysis, Wounded Knee surfaces several times in Erdrich's novel as the unconscious of Argus, North Dakota, and by extension the entire modernization process of the United States from 1914 to 1945, the approximate dates framing this novel. We first hear at length about Wounded Knee in chapter 13, "The Snake People," when Roy tells Delphine the story of her mother's origins, but which turns out to be a fictionalized version, in which he strategically omits the story of how Step-and-a-Half/Minnie saved Delphine from Mrs. Shimek's attempted murder in the outhouse. The story Roy tells may be a fabulation intended to disguise certain facts, but it also provides a reasonably accurate version of how the Lakota were tricked into accepting the Seventh Cavalry's Major Samuel M. Whitside's notorious invitation to surrender to the Army near Wounded Knee just days before the massacre (*MB*, 324).

Step-and-a-Half is not herself Lakota, but Cree—"those Indians up north who blended with the French" (*MB*, 323)—and thus only partially based on Erdrich's mother, Rita Joanne Gourneau, who is French and Chippewa.[8] Yet the *métis* and regional identification of Step-and-a-Half with Erdrich's mother, a teacher at a BIA school when Erdrich was born, establishes a biographical connection that also has pan-Indian significance. Step-and-a-Half has accompanied her father on his journey to Wounded Knee, where he wants "to learn of this new method of dancing to bring back the dead" (*MB*, 323). Of course, the Ghost Dance religion begun by the Paiute Wovoka ("Jack Wilson") in Utah and Nevada was followed by many different tribal peoples across North America in the 1880s, especially the Lakota, and the ritual of the Ghost Dance drew many desperate and curious Native Americans to performances across the Great Plains. The famous Lakota holy man Nick Black Elk describes his own performance of the Ghost Dance and his fight with Army soldiers at Wounded Knee in the account of his life he gave to John Neihardt in *Black Elk Speaks* (1932) (*Literary Culture and U.S. Imperialism: From the Revolution to World War II*, 239–42; hereafter *LC*). For the activist members of the American Indian Movement (AIM) who fought the Federal Bureau of Investigation (FBI), Bureau of Indian Affairs (BIA), and Pine Ridge reservation police at Wounded Knee, South Dakota, in June 1975, Wounded Knee continues to represent the political rallying point for native peoples in the United States. Peter Matthiessen argues in *In the Spirit of Crazy Horse* (1992) that the FBI's pursuit and arrest of the AIM fugitives and their trials at Cedar Rapids (June–July 1976), Fargo (March–April 1977), and Los Angeles (1978) were zealously conducted not so much to bring to justice those responsible for the deaths of two FBI agents, but primarily for the political purpose of breaking up the AIM as an emerging pan-Indian movement that threatened the U.S. government's authority over the reservations and thus native peoples.[9] The invocation of Wounded Knee has, at least as far back as Nick Black Elk, constituted a symbolic initiation into Native American identity and resistance to Euroamerican colonialism. For the dominant U.S. culture, Wounded Knee has meant since 1890 the threat of Native American resistance either by military or cultural means.

Often criticized, especially by other Native American writers, for her apparent lack of political commitments, Erdrich has tended to satirize the AIM in *Love Medicine* (1984/1993) and *Tracks* (1988), notably in the politically radical, often jailed, and just as often escaped convict character Gerry Nanapush. Modeled on Leonard Peltier and other AIM activists, Gerry is profoundly sexist, incapable of functioning in the real world, and hopelessly idealistic and impractical when it comes to political efficacy. In *The Master Butchers Singing Club*, pan-Indian activism is no longer represented by Gerry, but by Step-and-a-Half, the Cree (or likely French-Cree) woman who saves Delphine from the outhouse and gradually builds a successful "notions" business in Argus, based on her salvage of the great waste of even this small Euroamerican community. Transforming the patriarchal cultural traditions of the Ojibwe, Erdrich often grants special political powers to her feminine characters, such as Fleur

Pillager and Lulu Nanapush in her other novels, but few of them can be said to claim comparable cultural authority to Step-and-a-Half, whose survival at Wounded Knee in 1890 not only connects her with the "old people" and their ways but gives her the "love medicine" that enables her to save baby Delphine. Such "love medicine"—or *Midewiwin* in Anishinaabeg—belongs traditionally only to those properly initiated into the "Medicine Society" (including men and occasionally women) in Ojibwe culture. Step-and-a-Half is obviously not a tribally recognized medicine woman, but an outcast. Perhaps for this very reason, Erdrich suggests her character is secretly descended from these powerful Ojibwe doctors of the body and soul, even as Step-and-a-Half (the name suggests transcendence) draws on her *métis* background to graft powers from other cultural sources, including Euroamerican.

Step-and-a-Half's *métis* background recalls Louis Riel (1844–1885), the leader of the Métis people who waged the Northwest Rebellion from 1872 until his execution in 1885 in both Canada and the United States.[10] Many of those who identify as Métis (the tribe, not simply the term for mixed heritage, *métis*) have Ojibwe family backgrounds. Riel plays an increasingly important historical role in Erdrich's fiction from *The Master Butchers Singing Club* to her most recently published novel, *Shadow Tag* (2010), in which the protagonist, Irene, is working on a long-delayed dissertation on Riel for her PhD in history. Painted repeatedly by her portrait artist husband, Gil, in various poses as an allegory of Native America (her surname is "America"), Irene feels "possessed" by him, trapped in these images, which are also amazingly popular and thus financially lucrative in contemporary Euroamerican society.[11] Irene's personal rebellion in the novel recalls Riel's political rebellion against the Canadian and U.S. governments, and it is clear that Erdrich prizes Riel's courage in the Northwest Rebellion as a testament to Ojibwe resistance, their affiliation with "mixed" peoples (Erdrich's own family background), the historical legacy of the rebellion as one of the last in nineteenth-century Indian resistance, and its transnational scope. Riel "crossed the line" into the United States to avoid Canadian authorities, but soon returned to Canada because he was "homesick," a common complaint among Erdrich's characters yearning for their homes, often irrevocably lost.[12]

Even though Delphine in *The Master Butchers Singing Club* is not related by blood to her surrogate mother, she obviously assumes her mother's spiritual and healing powers. She discovers the bodies of the Chavers in her father's cellar, and she eventually solves the "mystery" of their deaths as her father confesses how he sent them to look for beer, accidentally locked them in, and then left the house in a drunken stupor (*MB*, 327–328). It is Delphine's first boyfriend, Cyprian, himself part Ojibwe, who will use his aerobic talents as a gymnast to wriggle carefully through the collapsing mound of earth to save Markus Waldvogel. The simple interpretation of these acts of saving characters from burial alive is that they recall Ojibwe tales of emergence and creation, of so-called "earth-diving" motifs in Anishinaabeg identifiable with origins and resurrection. In this sense, Erdrich merely *thematizes* in her modern fiction the mythic forms of Anishinaabeg orality, reducing her references to Wounded Knee to little more than regionalist local color.

In a more sophisticated sense, Wounded Knee and the Ghost Dance religion organize pan-Indian solidarity by recalling two forgotten and related historical origins for coalitions among Native American peoples from many different tribal backgrounds. The Ghost Dance spread rapidly across the Great Plains in the 1880s, linking together many different tribal peoples and encouraging their holy men to adapt their own spiritual rites to it (*LC*, 239, 242). Ghost Dancers performed in hopes of bringing their ancestors back to life, reviving the plenty of the buffalo systematically killed by hired sharpshooters, and causing the Euroamericans to "disappear."[13] In effect, the Ghost Dance religion united different Native Americans in a coherent anti-colonial struggle, even if it was viewed by many people as merely symbolic. Many followers of the Ghost Dance religion believed that Ghost Dance shirts would protect their wearers from harm, even from soldiers' bullets, but Erdrich's Step-and-a-Half "knew the dancers were neither stupid nor deluded. They just knew something that is, from time to time, forgotten except by the wind. How close the dead are. One song away from the living" (*MB*, 387).

In Erdrich's interpretation, the Ghost Dance represents pan-Indian solidarity and an affirmation of Native Americans' interrelation of natural and spiritual forces. In contrast, Euroamericans pollute the earth and corrupt nature. From Fidelis Waldvogel merely following orders as a sniper killing his enemies in their trenches of the World War I battlefields to the daily slaughter he performs in preparing meat for sale in his butcher shop, the otherwise gentle and loving Waldvogel can never escape the history of colonial violence that he nonetheless never recognizes.[14] Similarly, the construction site where the boys play by tunneling into the dirt left from the unfinished house's basement is a reminder of those "square houses" offered to Native Americans on the reservations and considered by them to be "prisons."[15]

The violence of enclosure went far beyond such housing, of course, and included the very idea of owning the land and then polluting it with the by-products of modern progress. One of the reasons Step-and-a-Half can just reach the baby Delphine at the bottom of the outhouse is because Shimek, "a lazy man, . . . hadn't dug a deep new winter's outhouse hole and moved the outhouse according to the autumn custom" (*MB*, 382). Although on that particular night such laziness happens to be "a fortunate thing," Erdrich normally treats the general waste, both of goods and people, left by Euroamerican modernization as yet another instance of how we have failed to tend the fragile nature-culture bond. There is a strong environmentalist subtext in *The Master Butchers Singing Club*, which is yet another way Erdrich links the regional specificity of the Upper Midwest with transnational issues without collapsing the local and the global into "glocalism."[16] In fact, Erdrich's organizing theme of burial alive links the macropolitical situation of humans relentlessly polluting the globe and thus destroying themselves—in effect, burying themselves alive in a dying planet—to the circumstances of modernization organizing the imaginative history of Argus, North Dakota, that she offers in this narrative.[17]

The Master Butchers Singing Club takes the reader through World War II and the different fates of the four Waldvogel sons, some of whom fight on the German side and others for the Allies. War will continue for as long as we do not take responsibility for the sort of foundational violence that the massacre at Wounded Knee represents in the novel. At the very end of the novel, Step-and-a-Half recalls for the reader how she and her father had been buried beneath the bodies and the snow and "a roof of bullets" at Wounded Knee (*MB*, 385). When she walks out of that valley, Step-and-a-Half could never again "stay in one place" and had "ever since, . . . paced the earth" (*MB*, 385). This symbolic diaspora is Erdrich's way of reminding her readers not only of how existentially homeless we all are but also of how unsettled we must remain until true justice is offered for the crimes from which we still profit. By anachronistically constructing Wounded Knee as a sort of European original sin and the symbol of colonial violence, Erdrich reorganizes U.S. history to foreground, rather than repress, imperialism.

Erdrich's narrative also offers an alternative history in its form as well as its content. A governing assumption of all her works is that the dominant ideology's repression of imperial violence cannot be lifted by conventional historiographical means or mere demystification. Literature as an imaginative discourse can be used to challenge Euroamerican epistemologies integral to imperialism. In *The Master Butchers Singing Club*, Erdrich imitates Step-and-a-Half's diasporic experience in formal and stylistic ways that challenge not only the "property rights" of colonial inheritance but also the "proper speech" and truth that follow from such confident ownership. *The Master Butchers Singing Club*, like so many of her other books, refuses to fit the form of the novel, is filled with divergent and often conflicting languages and cultures (German, Lakota, Anishinaabeg, English, U.S.), and forces her readers thereby to encounter a political history that otherwise remains largely unconscious, unseen, unthought, and unfelt. It was what the AIM revolutionaries tried to accomplish at Wounded Knee and elsewhere from 1968 to 1975, what the Ghost Dancers tried to perform across North America in the 1880s, and what literature can occasionally achieve by forcing conventional language and history out of their tracks and making them dive below, into the depths of the lake.

In her previous novel, *The Last Report on the Miracles at Little No Horse* (2001; hereafter *LR*), Erdrich makes clear that such "magic realism" derives in large part from the contact zone of Euroamerican and Anishinaabeg cultures.[18] Characters in this novel are also "buried alive," but now often in the textuality of the postmodern age, even as its technologies reach far beyond the city to the dusty tracks of the Ojibwe reservation where most of the narrative action takes place. The problems of the information age are compounded by the different discursive and hermeneutic worlds that collide, overlap, and struggle for attention in the narrative and the region it represents. Although published two years before *The Master Butchers Singing Club*, *Last Report* extends that work's argument from late modernity into the postmodern age. In many respects, *Last Report on the Miracles at Little No Horse* is an extended meditation on the issues of cultural assimilation, hybridization, and segregation as they are worked out in Erdrich's Upper Midwest in the aftermath of modernization. This is especially explicit in the "miracles" of the Church, which are nominally the subject of this work, so that *métis* peoples, especially those converted to Catholicism, become special hosts of such miraculous events. This specifically religious problematic, traceable back to the Ghost Dance religion's hybridization of Christianity and native spiritual activities (a historical connection Erdrich does not make), can also be related more generally to the conflict between oral and print cultures in Erdrich's specific contact zone. In *Last Report*, Erdrich explicitly locates these problems in the historical period (1912–1997) and transnational circumstances—the ruralism of the reservation, the urbanization of the northern Midwest, and the global authority of the Vatican in Rome—we identify with the shift from modernity to postmodernity.

No work better illustrates the conflicted nature of this historical process than her own writing, in which oral storytelling and her efforts to represent it in print forms, as well as the conventions of print forms and culture intruding upon such oral cultures, repeatedly produce uncanny or unusual effects, some of which have the social and psychological consequences of apparent miracles. Indeed, Erdrich has been criticized by other Native American writers, notably Leslie Marmon Silko, for what appears to be her friendly negotiation of the boundaries between Native American and Euroamerican cultures. The novel form is, after all, another instance of how the "age of mechanical reproduction" transformed the "work of art," and in *Last Report* Erdrich extends such mechanics to include telematic reproduction in the final "miracle" of the book: the mysterious arrival of a fax machine on the doorstep of the Sacred Heart Mission and the Pope's letter to Father Damien appearing from out of its depths and distances the moment the machine has been correctly connected (*LR*, 353–56).

In *Last Report*, Erdrich focuses on the fortuitous consequences of the hybridization of these two cultures in ways that seem to dare her critics and to link her own identity as a writer, perhaps even as a psychological subject, to just such dangerous crossings. In her "End Notes" to the novel, which follow the epilogue in which the magical fax appears from the Pope, Erdrich offers her own "fax from the Vatican" to the fictional Father Damien, in which her own "responsibility as the author of this and my previous books" is challenged and impugned. This fax from the Vatican makes clear that the charge of possible plagiarism is even more severe because the "writer" in question who is "local to your region" is "published even in languages and places as distant as our own" (*LR*, 358). In highly self-conscious ways, Erdrich traces Christian missionary efforts on the reservations from the French Jesuits and Spanish Franciscans in North America through the period of President Ulysses S. Grant's Peace Policy, including the twentieth-century consequences of Christian dislocations of native cultures from the seventeenth through the nineteenth century.[19] The problem involves as much the globalization of local concerns as it does the theft of oral cultures in print media and the Christianizing of native spiritual practices. These conflicts exemplify Erdrich's analysis of the major antinomies of modernity of the Ojibwe people and constitute what I would term the "borders" in which her fiction is performed.[20]

It is the ethical valencing of such anomalous events in these border zones as either "miraculous" in the sense of redemptive (conventional theology), "fantasmatic" in the sense of explanatory (conventional psychoanalysis), "diabolical" (conventional theology), "hysterical" (conventional psychoanalysis) that is posed as the task for the characters in Erdrich's narratives and thus the hermeneutic model for the reader. One consequence at the ethical level is the extent to which characters are *perceived* by others to be *acting* in ways understood to be Anishinaabeg, hybrid, Catholic, or white. In *Last Report*, all of these social constructions focus on the shifting identity of Sister Agnes, who poses as "Father Damien Modeste," the (transvestite) Catholic priest serving the reservation of Little No Horse throughout the narrative's long history (1912–1997). The interesting problem is how such mobility is achieved. Can it be accomplished simply by mastering certain rhetorical and symbolic systems, in the manner of the traditional trickster, ably represented by the young Nector Kashpaw and Sister Agnes/Father Damien's drag performance in this work, or is such rhetorical manipulation always doomed to errors of the sort exemplified by Lipsha Morrissey's substitution of frozen turkey hearts for the wild goose hearts that Ojibwe tradition demands in the title story of *Love Medicine*?[21]

Like the miracles and magic realism in her previous works, the fantastic events in *Last Report* are radically ambiguous and undecidable until they are interpreted by living members of the community. In order to make an ethical judgment about such "miracles," Erdrich's ideal reader must sort out and assess the different cultural realms that meet on the reservation of Little No Horse: "pure" (Old) Anishinaabeg culture (vanishing rapidly by 1912–1916, and largely gone by 1996); *métissage*, typified by Leopolda, who vacillates between her Puyat origins, usually associated with good works, and her Catholic conversion, usually tied to personal violence; and the customary existential problems of Euroamerican culture in Argus and Fargo. Our interest in making such judgments and thereby establishing borders distinguishing different forms of community affiliation is only in part driven by conventional understanding. Erdrich suggests that the reader also desires power over the shifting, confusing, messy human relations and is thus always prone to an imperial will-to-power in the otherwise idle act of reading. As Erdrich tries to bury us in the complexities of the textual situation facing the postmodern reader, we relentlessly dig ourselves out by way of interpretive methods and reading habits that often enough plunge us deeper into historical and ethical holes. Without for a moment recalling Lionel Trilling, Louise Erdrich is calling upon her readers to employ what he called the "liberal imagination," but now operating in the much more complex and difficult area of U.S. historical relations with indigenous peoples. You must come to terms with this history, not forget it, Erdrich warns us, or you will lose your ethical foundation as a nation, a people, a community.

In *Last Report*, Erdrich uses the young Nector Kashpaw as one of her several alter egos (anticipating her use of an older Nector and the young Lipsha in *Love Medicine*) in his quest to learn print culture with the specific aim of gaining power. The interpolated story "Penmanship" in the section "The Rosary" is quite explicit in this regard, tracing Nector's education in a Bureau School and then in a Convent School, under Sister Bernadette, in the powers of rhetoric. Nector's command of written English includes the aura of authority in his impeccable penmanship, which is subsequently replaced by the typed documents he produces with a Chicago-brand typewriter while he works in the reservation's headquarters. His elegant handwriting survives in these typed documents in his impressive written signature, another form of Euroamerican power we identify with authorship. As usual in Erdrich's stories, fact and metaphor unavoidably complement each other. Erdrich's metanarrative entangles her literary authority with the legal and economic authorities legitimated by print culture and authorizing "signatures," an authority rendered problematic in the recent shift to digital media. Yet this little parable of the writer gaining the reader's attention and respect from forms as inherently empty as elegant handwriting or publisher's protocols is entangled with the details of what Nector is doing in the reservation's offices. The Commissioner of the Bureau of Indian Affairs has ordered Little No Horse to reorganize and record all of its official files, a task that Bernadette Morrissey finds so boring she assigns it to the young Nector Kashpaw. What she doesn't realize is that he is making new copies of all the files and destroying the originals, effectively granting himself primary authority for the records of the reservation—an authority that has substantial legal, economic, and social value. As Nector recognizes, the real authority he claims is historical: "He was now in charge of history, which suited him just fine, and he was only a boy" (*LR*, 173).

In traditional Anishinaabeg culture, Nector has assumed the status of tribal storyteller and member of the Midewiwin Society, or a medicine man (a role he assumes more explicitly as the tribal elder in *Love Medicine*), but he does so by way of the media and forms of Euroamerican print culture. Nector has successfully grafted the two cultures together in ways that anticipate and supersede Lipsha's disastrous efforts to do so in *Love Medicine*. Erdrich leaves it to the reader to decide the significance of this historical foreshadowing. In one sense, Nector's legal forgeries betray the proper use of Ojibwe medicine; in another sense, Nector transcodes tribal powers into a new cultural and political order, adapting oral practices to print technologies. Erdrich's ambiguity with respect to the historical meaning of any act is typical of her style and worldview, but she unequivocally represents Nector's act of appropriating the reservation's official documents as an act of revenge, initially directed against the Lazarres and Morrisseys, who have harassed Nector, his mother Margaret, and his extended family:

> During this time, and while he was getting his growth, other extreme events occurred. The Lazarres and Morrisseys became still more bold and insulting to those who did not agree with their views. Earlier they had gone so far as to kidnap, threaten, and even shave the head of Nector's mother, Margaret. The revenges that followed were distinct to the Pillagers. Fleur killed

with fear, Nanapush used piano wire, Margaret flayed her enemies to nothing with the bitter blade of her tongue.

Nector got even by the use of penmanship. (*LR*, 172)

At the end of *Tracks*, Fleur Pillager retreats to her cabin on the shore of Lake Matchimanito. The interior of the cabin is papered with the title deeds to tribal property that she hopes somehow to redeem, in order to restore the tribe by recovering its territory. Erdrich is referring, of course, to the consequences of the Dawes Act and its prevailing "Allotment and Assimilation" policies from its passage in 1887 to the Meriam Report's declaration of its failure in 1928.[22] Supernaturally powerful in traditional tribal society, Fleur gradually loses her powers as she is surrounded by Euroamerican society. Yet as her powers dwindle in the face of modern capitalism and technology, the Ojibwe mythologize her, both recalling her old powers and exaggerating their continuing influence. Knowing she must adapt her magic to counter the legal and economic power represented by the title deeds papering her cabin—she is another character buried alive by the law—she still does not know *how* to change her powers. Erdrich and her fictional delegate Nector *do* know how, even if Erdrich suggests that both are still capable of abusing such powers. It is not just *writing* that they employ to combat a society that has used this very medium to legitimate its theft of their land, personal liberties, civil rights, and the lives of many of their ancestors, but writing used to recycle the spiritual powers and magic of Anishinaabeg culture.

Nector's fatality may be that he uses white culture's worship of textuality to get even, rather than for the traditional purposes of the Midewiwin to preserve the spirit of Anishinaabeg culture. Erdrich argues clearly in *Last Report* that Euroamerican society would benefit from tribal values, especially as they are communicated in an oral culture. Erdrich places at the center of the novel's dramatic action the magical transformation of a white woman, Agnes DeWitt, first into Sister Cecilia (*LR*, 13–17), then into the German-American farmer Berndt Vogel's partner (*LR*, 17–20), then into the kidnapped victim of the bank robber Arnold "The Actor" Anderson (*LR*, 23–27), and finally into "Father Damien," the priest of the Little No Horse reservation. From a narrowly Euroamerican perspective, poor Agnes is the repeated victim of circumstances or existential contingency, tossed from place to place and driven only by her passionate and uncontrollable love of playing the piano. In Anishinaabeg terms, she is a white version of Nanabozo, or "Nanapush," the trickster god who assumes many different forms, but whom we know through some constant characteristic, which for Erdrich's Agnes seems to be her association with the spirituality of music. Nanapush recognizes the interconnectedness of all things, unlike the Euroamerican existentialist, as Erdrich suggests by including as her epigraph for the novel Nanapush's explication of the Anishinaabeg term *Nindinawemaganido*, by which is meant "everything that has existed in time, the known and the unknown, the unseen, the obvious, all that lived before or is living now in the worlds above and below" (*LR*, epigraph).

Agnes/Damien's transformations are often signaled or triggered by music or books—that is, by semiotic codes. Of course, in her role as Father Damien she repeatedly writes the Pope regarding the "miracles" she has witnessed on the reservation. Her reports are routinely ignored by the papacy throughout most of the narrative, until the very end of the novel when a fax is received from the Pope, noting that "the file of your letters and reports . . . has been inadvertently destroyed in an update and purge of the Vatican's filing system" and requesting "your assistance in reassembling the life's work," thereby giving fictive warrant for the preceding narrative and its title, *The Last Report on the Miracles at Little No Horse* (*LR*, 355–56).[23] One of the most interesting of these reported "miracles" is Sister Agnes/Father Damien's temptation by the devil in the form of a black dog. When Father Damien substitutes himself for Lulu Kashpaw, whom the Devil claims, the Devil promises to tempt him. The Devil does so when Father Wekkle arrives on the reservation, and Agnes/Damien falls in love with her fellow priest. Dividing the priests' room with a great wall of books, Sister Agnes/Father Damien still desires Father Wekkle. It is the collapse in the night of this wall of books, precipitated in part by Father Wekkle's dream-thrashing (dreaming is another non-print mode of communication, which is directly related to Anishinaabeg storytelling, including that Dog-Devil), that brings them together sexually. In dreams, gender borders, like the borders of print culture, collapse, so that Wekkle, wearing the lace-fringed moleskin sleeping outfit sewn for him by his mother, comes to Damien/Agnes in an equally ambiguous sexual identity. But it is the collapse of those *books* that brings down the conventional boundaries and, of course, fulfills the Dog-Devil's prophecy of Agnes/Damien's temptation (*LR*, 199–203).

In this episode—perhaps termed better for Erdrich, this "miracle"—print culture maintains the taboos against homosexuality, transvestism, and priests' sexual conduct in the form of a literal wall dividing the two holy "men" from each other. But sexual desire, fueled at least in part by the true holiness of both persons in their care for those living on the reservation and by the emergence of the unconscious in dreams, breaks down that barrier and encourages sexual contact. To be sure, Agnes/Damien "gives in" to temptation, so that the prophecy of the "black Dog-Devil" is fulfilled, but in so doing Agnes/Damien discovers her true sacred vocation by violating the orthodoxy of the Catholic church, its scriptural doctrines, and its mission to convert "pagans," like the Ojibwe.

Of course, this central scene of sexual intercourse between two priests buried in a heap of books brings us back to the controlling theme of these two works by Erdrich. For the French-Cree Step-and-a-Half in *The Master Butchers Singing Club*, narrative recollection of the massacre at Wounded Knee involves the recuperation of a history that has been buried for most of the residents of Argus, North Dakota. In a similar fashion, Erdrich recalls in *Last Report* Ojibwe cultural traditions otherwise buried beneath the print archive represented by the Catholic Church, its traditions of patristic interpretation, and the fetishizing of book learning in the place of human relations. Erdrich interrupts this Euroamerican archive by violating the rules governing the proper circulation of oral and print discourses in a "novel" that refuses, like all her other narratives, to be properly classified in the genre. The fax from the Vatican in her "End Notes" suggesting that Erdrich is plagiarizing her material from Father Damien's letters may be merely a *jeu d'ésprit*, but it also seriously emphasizes Erdrich's insistence that the stories she tells still belong to the oral traditions from which she has adapted them. By the same token, the monumental print archive—that wall of books Damien and Wekkle futilely build to imprison desire—of Euroamerican literature (and textuality in general) structures Erdrich's writing in ways that remind the Ojibwe reader that the oral cannot be thought or performed any longer without regard for this dominant presence. The miracle is that the old ways can recirculate in the new medium, itself undergoing changes in the course of Erdrich's novel from Nector's penmanship to the magic of the typewriter and the concluding miracle of the fax (a pun on Papal "pax"?).

Erdrich's variation on the theme of "burial alive" as a *textual* burial that also involves a resurrection and damnation suggests an interesting association with Nicolas Abraham and Maria Torok's interpretation of Freud's "Wolf Man" in *Cryptonymie*, which is prefaced by Jacques Derrida's "Fors."[24] Abraham and Torok's "cryptonymic" method of deciphering the secrets of the unconscious and the wayward paths of repression are generally associated with the linguistic turn in psychoanalysis. They offer another version of Jacques Lacan's textualization of the unconscious and one that has particular appeal to Derrida as an illustration of deconstruction. Abraham and Torok's post-Freudian method of interpreting the secret codes of the unconscious is far too complicated to summarize here, but Derrida's conclusion in "Fors" is that the unconscious is irreducibly rhetorical and must be interpreted according to its linguistic term: "The crypt then, according to the corner[s] [created out] of words. . . . 'To [en]crypt': the verb I do not believe can be properly used. 'To [en]crypt' is to code, a symbolic or semiotic operation, which consists in the manipulation of a secret code, which one is never able to do alone."[25]

In her own way, whether or not she is alluding to Abraham and Torok or Derrida, Erdrich is offering a similar interpretation of how historical layers of deceptive language and cultural misrepresentation have *produced* a "crypt," which is the unconscious of U.S. imperialist conduct toward Native American peoples. This political and historical tomb has been produced collectively by U.S. citizens and is certainly coded by U.S. ideology, whose "secret" they continue to maintain.[26] Erdrich's conclusion, like Derrida's own, is that we cannot simply lift this repression or penetrate the depth of this unconscious crypt. In and of itself, the crypt is always empty and constituted by its rhetorical "walls," like that wall of books dividing the two priests, man and woman, in the central episode of *The Last Report on the Miracles at Little No Horse*. Erdrich's task in this narrative, perhaps in all her writings, is to figure out how to turn "burial alive" into some form of cultural and personal resurrection—to perform a miracle of her own that belongs now not to the Catholic Church, not even to the Midewiwin of Ojibwe spiritual practices, but to the hybridized literary discourse she employs.

In *Literary Culture and U.S. Imperialism*, I argue that for all of its narrative problems and questions about its authority and native American legitimacy, *Black Elk Speaks* is a miraculous and heroic achievement for Nick Black Elk and his Lakota colleagues who were interviewed by John Neihardt. What is miraculous is the ability of these marginalized Lakota to speak in print culture in the first place and to do so in ways that manage to tell their "true story" even as the print threatens to cover it up, drowning them in the "sea" of *wasichus* (Lakota for "white men"). Erdrich writes in this tradition, I think, but now recognizing that the local circumstances of rural Native Americans, like the Turtle Mountain people from whom she comes and still belongs, must speak and act across the wires, through the cables, and among the languages of our rapidly globalizing world. Rather than simply adapting Euroamerican forms, Erdrich disrupts them to expose their contrived authority while recalling other ways of speaking, acting, and knowing. The miracle of her writing is its ability to dive into the violent past and emerge with new life for the multicultural peoples of the Upper Midwest—Ojibwe, *métis*, and Euroamerican.

In her novels since *The Master Butchers Singing Club*, Erdrich returns often to the theme of burial alive as a way to urge us to recover the violent history of relations between indigenous and Euroamerican peoples. Her goal is to encourage something like Trilling's "liberal imagination" that might enable us to address this history for the sake of our national redemption. In *The Painted Drum* (2005), the Euroamerican Faye Travers finds in the estate of a family in her small New Hampshire town a moose-skin drum with magical properties, including the ability to sound without being touched, at least in Faye's hearing.[27] Like the human bodies "found" in the locked cellars and "saved" from the outhouses of Erdrich's other fiction, the painted drum's rediscovery revives its sacred sound, makes it audible again, but in new contexts, as Erdrich's fiction makes indigenous culture representable anew. In *The Plague of Doves* (2008), Erdrich weaves together a complex network of family secrets that would take far too long for me to unravel adequately at the end of this chapter, but it begins with "the discovery in 1911 by two Indian teenagers, Mooshum and Paul Holy Track, of the bodies of a murdered farm family."[28] Falsely blamed for the murders, the two Indian youth are lynched, but Mooshum mysteriously escapes death and survives to tell the story of the original murder in his own wayward fashion. Organized around the plot of a murder mystery, *The Plague of Doves* relies centrally on the revelation of long buried secrets, which have continued to "live" and affect the lives of all the characters, especially those blithely unaware of their long survival in the small town of Pluto in North Dakota where the novel takes place. The *métis* narrator, Judge Antone Bazil Coutts, recalls toward the end of the novel how as a young man he had a job as a grave-digger in the town cemetery, comparing his youthful work of burying the dead with the work of the bees he observes in his maturity: "A bee or two hummed in the drowsy air. The swarm had left the rubble and built their houses beneath the earth. They were busy in the graveyard right now, filling the skulls with white combs and the coffins with sweet black honey."[29] Judge Coutts's image is an apt one for Erdrich's own work of filling the forgotten graves with honey, "black" in its "white" combs of wax and bone, but still sweet to our taste. In *The Liberal Imagination*, Trilling observes that one of the chief characteristics of the great novel is "the unabashed interest in ideas," which for Trilling means "a sign of its 'intellectuality' and specialness of appeal" that makes the greatest novels—*A Portrait of the Artist as a Young Man*, *Don Quixote*, *Tom Jones* are his examples—"works of literary criticism before they are anything else" (*The Liberal Imagination*, 248). In this same context, Louise Erdrich's novels, if we may classify them in this genre, should not be understood as good objects of postcolonial study, but as postcolonial studies in their own rights.

Notes

1. Homi Bhabha, ed., *Nation and Narration* (New York: Routledge, 1990) is the collection of essays by different postcolonial theorists best known for challenging the imperial legacy of the national form, but it draws on Benedict Anderson's critique of nationalism in *Imagined Communities: Reflections on the Origin and Spread of Nationalism* (London: Verso, 1983).

2. Bill Ashcroft, Gareth Griffiths, and Helen Tiffin, eds., *The Empire Writes Back: Theory and Practices in Postcolonial Literature* (London: Routledge, 1999) is a well-known collection that features postcolonial criticism from former British colonies; C. Richard King, ed., *Postcolonial America* (Urbana: University of Illinois Press, 2000), deals with the legacies of internal colonization, especially for indigenous peoples, in North America.

3. C. Richard King, *Postcolonial America*; Cheryl Walker, *Indian Nation: Native American Literature and Nineteenth-Century Nationalisms* (Durham, NC: Duke University Press, 1997); Walter Mignolo, *The Darker Side of the Renaissance: Literacy, Territoriality, and Colonization*, 2nd ed. (Ann Arbor: University of Michigan Press,

2003) and *Local Histories/Global Designs: Coloniality, Subaltern Knowledges, and Border Thinking* (Princeton: Princeton University Press, 2000).

4. Louise Erdrich, *The Master Butchers Singing Club* (New York: HarperCollins, 2003); *The Beet Queen* (New York: Henry Holt, 1986); *Tales of Burning Love* (New York: HarperCollins, 1996).

5. A bumper sticker sold by the Gabrielino/Tongva nation in my area of Southern California reads: "Native Americans of California STILL EXIST."

6. Edward Said, *Culture and Imperialism* (New York: Knopf, 1993); John Carlos Rowe, *Literary Culture and U.S. Imperialism: From the Revolution to World War II* (New York: Oxford University Press, 2000); Amy Kaplan, *The Anarchy of Empire in the Making of U.S. Culture* (Cambridge, MA: Harvard University Press, 2002).

7. John Carlos Rowe, *The New American Studies* (Minneapolis: University of Minnesota Press, 2002), pp. 16–17.

8. Erdrich's maternal grandfather, Pat Gourneau, was tribal chairman of the Turtle Mountain Band of Ojibwe, on whose reservation in North Dakota she spent most of her childhood and the tribe in which she is still a registered member (Julie Maristuen-Rodakowski, "The Turtle Mountain Reservation in North Dakota: Its History as Depicted in Louise Erdrich's *Love Medicine* and *The Beet Queen*," in Hertha D. Sweet Wong, *Louise Erdrich's "Love Medicine": A Casebook* [New York: Oxford University Press, 2000], pp. 23–24).

9. Peter Matthiessen, *In the Spirit of Crazy Horse* (New York: Viking Penguin, 1992), pp. 153–404.

10. See the Heritage Center of Manitoba's Web site on Riel: www.shsb.mb.ca/Riel.

11. Louise Erdrich, *Shadow Tag* (New York: HarperCollins, 2010), p. 13.

12. The Heritage Center of Manitoba Web site: www.shsb.mb.ca/Riel.

13. James Mooney, *The Ghost-Dance Religion and the Sioux Outbreak of 1890* (1896; reprint, Chicago: University of Chicago Press, 1965), pp. 90–92.

14. The German meaning of his first wife's maiden name, Kalb—"calf" or "veal"—suggests that the family follows the logic of its profession. And Eva Kalb does die of a mysterious stomach cancer that seems symbolically if not literally related to a life of butchery.

15. John Neihardt and Nicholas Black Elk, *Black Elk Speaks: Being the Life Story of a Holy Man of the Oglala Sioux* (Lincoln: University of Nebraska Press, 1961), p. 167.

16. Reductive approaches to the relation of the global and local are typified by Francis Fukuyama, *The End of History and the Last Man* (New York: Bard Books, 1992), but there are sophisticated approaches in the work of Frederick Buell, *National Culture and the New Global System* (Baltimore: The Johns Hopkins University Press, 1994) and Donald E. Pease, "New Perspectives on U.S. Culture and Imperialism," in *Cultures of United States Imperialism*, ed. Amy Kaplan and Donald E. Pease (Durham, NC: Duke University Press, 1993), pp. 21–43.

17. Like many other contemporary U.S. ethnic and minority writers, Erdrich mixes literature and history in complex ways. She notes in her "Acknowledgment" to *The Master Butchers Singing Club* that "the picture of the young butcher on the cover of

this book is of my grandfather Ludwig Erdrich," who "fought in the trenches on the German side in World War I. His sons served on the American side in World War II" (*MB*, 389). Nevertheless she concludes that "this book is fiction" (389).

18. Louise Erdrich, *The Last Report on the Miracles at Little No Horse* (New York: HarperCollins, 2001).

19. For a fuller account of Christianity's role in U.S. imperialism of the territories and native peoples of the Great Plains, see Rowe, *LC*, pp. 224–30.

20. I am using the "border" between Native American and Euroamerican in keeping with Scott L. Pratt's definition in *Native Pragmatism: Rethinking the Roots of American Philosophy* (Bloomington: Indiana University Press, 2002), p. 15: "We may refigure the frontiers as borders, as regions of interaction, exchange, and transformation."

21. Louise Erdrich, *Love Medicine*, rev. ed. (New York: HarperCollins, 1993), pp. 248–52.

22. Francis Paul Prucha, *The Great Father: The United States Government and the American Indians*, 2 vols. (Lincoln: University of Nebraska Press, 1984), vol. II, pp. 659–86, 940–69.

23. Erdrich's metafictional joke recalls Don Quixote's discovery in Part II of Cervantes's *Don Quixote* of a "fictional" story of his life, which he is at considerable pains in Part II to refute or correct.

24. Nicolas Abraham and Maria Torok, *Cryptonymie: le verbier de l'Homme aux loups; précédé de Fors par Jacques Derrida* (Paris: Aubier Flammarion, 1976).

25. Derrida, "Fors," p. 53, my (somewhat free) translation.

26. I am taking liberties with Derrida's interpretation, insofar as I am grafting it to a state. Following Abraham and Torok, Derrida is merely referring to subject-formation and its psychic facilitation.

27. Louise Erdrich, *The Painted Drum* (New York: HarperCollins Publishers, 2005).

28. Louise Erdrich, *The Plague of Doves* (New York: HarperCollins, 2008); Brigitte Frase, "A Shot Resounds" [review of *The Plague of Doves*], *Los Angeles Times Book Review* (April 27, 2008), R2.

29. *The Plague of Doves*, p. 291.

[8]

NEOLIBERALISM AND THE U.S. LITERARY CANON: THE EXAMPLE OF PHILIP ROTH

THE FORMAL STUDY of U.S. literature as a specific discipline has a relatively short history, dating from 1900 to 1990. In less than a full century, admittedly "the American century," scholars used a small number of literary texts and major authors to represent the "American experience" as unique and specific to U.S. democracy. This "exceptionalist narrative" was thoroughly criticized by scholars in the late 1980s and early 1990s for its lack of comparative contexts within and outside the United States. Assuming that U.S. liberal individualism was in fact unique and modern, most scholars did not consider transnational examples that would challenge this idea. Accepting the representativeness of a small number of authors and texts, most scholars in this period did not consider the wide range of other literary representations of U.S. experience. In the late 1980s, a multicultural revolution in literary studies of the United States proposed that U.S. culture was not only regionally, but also linguistically, ethnically, sociologically, and politically too diverse to be represented by *any* representative group. At this historical moment during the "culture wars" of the late 1980s, U.S. literary canons were formally dissolved by critics of U.S. nationalism while being vigorously defended first by public intellectuals and then by scholars threatened by the loss of a familiar literary curriculum.[1]

The history of the culture wars has been ably recounted by a number of scholars, but by now the macropolitical issues are relatively clear. Scholars who attacked the literary and cultural canons of what established basic "Americanness" were in the most extreme cases judged to be "anti-American," unpatriotic, and ungrateful critics of American freedoms that had allowed them to speak and write freely in the first place.[2] Public intellectuals as diverse in their views as Samuel Huntington, Alan Wolfe, and Arthur Schlesinger Jr. complained that such criticism of a core or exceptional American identity challenged the basic cohesiveness of the nation and thus could be construed as a threat to national security, because it encouraged the divisiveness and "culture of complaint" such intellectuals identified with multiculturalism. A Nobel prize–winning author, Toni Morrison, was accused of stressing the victimization of minorities, rather than the integrative and redemptive qualities of a shared American identity.[3] While right-wing critics like Newt Gingrich, Rush Limbaugh, William Bennett, and Lynne Cheney demanded blind patriotism, liberals like Philip Roth, Todd Gitlin, and E. D. Hirsch Jr. insisted upon a return to the core values of U.S. citizenship that would enable everyone to participate in democracy.[4] Both political groups viewed social and cultural problems from national perspectives, even as globalization had challenged the discreteness of geopolitical boundaries.

Neoconservatives squarely blamed multiculturalism and cultural relativism for these problems, arguing that new immigrants to the United States were causes rather than effects of transnational forces threatening U.S. national consensus. Samuel Huntington claims that unlike European immigrants who had assimilated quickly to U.S. national identity, immigrants admitted after the 1965 Immigration Reform Act, most of whom came from non-European nations, attempt to maintain strong ties with their native languages and cultures. Huntington terms these new immigrants "ampersands," who wish to "have their cake and eat it too," and thus threaten the legal, political, and economic consensus he considers crucial to U.S. national success.[5] Huntington's sentiments are typical of conservatives yearning for social stability in the past when facing rapid demographic changes. Liberals' complaints about the fragmentation of U.S. society, the breakdown of democratic consensus, and the death of individualism were more unexpected and troublesome, because they often expressed sympathy with the plight of recent immigrants but were unwilling to consider new policies of social, economic, and political inclusion. Many of these liberals argued that previous immigrants had assimilated successfully, so shouldn't these new groups follow their example?

Philip Roth's fiction over the past decade is an intriguing instance of how liberal culture has contributed to these conservative values, despite a self-conscious effort to chart a middle course between right- and left-wing extremes. Roth is an extraordinarily talented novelist and social commentator, whose novels in the past decade have received considerable attention for their subtle treatments of such major problems as the break-up of the middle-class family, the unresolved problems of racial difference, the impact of feminism, and the inevitability of aging in a nation with uneven health care. In Roth's recent fiction, most of his protagonists are "passing" as members of another group than their own: "Swede" Levov in *American Pastoral* (1997) is the blond, athletic high-school hero who just happens to be Jewish; Coleman ("Silky") Silk is the light-skinned African-American classics professor and former dean of Athena College who has literally "passed" his adult life as Jewish in *The Human Stain* (2000); the young Philip Roth tries to grow up in Weequahic, New Jersey passing as a typical American, but during Charles Lindbergh's fictional presidency (in place of Franklin Roosevelt's third term) and his "cordial understanding" with Hitler to keep the United States out of World War II must face the anti-Semitism that marks his family as "Jews" in need of enforced assimilation in *The Plot against America* (2004). Drawing on the philosophical existentialism that has provided the conceptual framework for his works since *Goodbye, Columbus and Five Short Stories* (1960), Roth argues that each of us is alienated, profoundly stereotyped, and misunderstood, but also finally an *individual* who cannot be encompassed by any "we," except the loose collective of such individuals Roth imagines as U.S. democracy.

Like other great novelists, Roth creates protagonists whose lives his readers inhabit, encouraging the sort of identification that allows those readers also to "pass" imaginatively as Jewish-American, African-American, WASP, "red-neck" working-class American, debunking along the way every stereotype about such groups for the sake of shared idiosyncratic, deeply American individualism. Everyone is thus a victim of political correctness, which Roth suggests has a long history encompassing both the political left and the right, so that contemporary feminist extremism has parallels with historical anti-Semitism, the New Left's anti-war protests find parallels with Communist dogmatism and repression, and Black Nationalism's commitment to social justice resembles Nazi fascism. Pitting the ideal America of family values, liberal individualism, secular humanism and its "civil religion" against what he terms "the American berserk," in which inflexible positions and discrete communities war with each other for power, Roth ends up affirming his own fiction as an instance of the canonical American literature that once provided us with representative examples of how to live *as Americans*.

Roth's aesthetic and moral values since the mid-1990s closely resemble Trilling's views in *The Liberal Imagination*, insofar as Roth defends liberal individuals who cannot (or should not) be stereotyped and encourages his readers to identify with human situations that transcend any political party or position. Like Trilling, Roth abhors orthodoxy, ideology, conventionality, dogmatism, as well as political extremism on both the right and left. His characters seek the middle way, even if they generally refuse bourgeois respectability, and they share their author's tolerance of other positions, even those they do not believe. Yet nearly half a century separates Trilling's "liberal imagination" from Roth's; in between, Roth himself wrote a powerful manifesto in which he declared the American social situation had changed. In his "Writing American Fiction" (1961), first delivered in 1960, the year John F. Kennedy was elected president, Roth declares the American writer incapable of making "*credible* much of American reality," whose absurdities continue to outdo "one's own meager imagination" and thus make literary representation impossible.[6] By Roth's own account in 1961, social reality in the United States no longer resembles Cold War society, in which Trilling's concept of the "liberal imagination" was a possible solution based on a long tradition of romantic and modern ideas of liberal individualism. Roth is certainly bitterly nostalgic in 1961 for just these values, but he knows in "Writing American Fiction" that they no longer apply. What, then, is the meaning of Roth's return to such values more than thirty years later, when U.S. social reality has changed even more dramatically? Roth revives Trilling's middle-class liberalism as neoliberalism—that notorious rhetorical cover for conservative politics—in our contemporary period.[7]

Roth's protagonists are complex and impossible to reduce to their family backgrounds, ethnicity, class, and gender; they are characteristically liberal in their politics and critical of extremism of all sorts. Despite his avowed liberal tolerance, Roth himself stereotypes these political extremes, even when he finds their reasons legitimate. In *American Pastoral*, the New Left is reduced to the madness of Swede Levov's daughter, Merry, a Weatherman bomber who kills four innocent people, and to Roth's caricature of Angela Davis as a revolutionary committed to the destruction of U.S. democracy. In *The Human Stain*, Coleman Silk is unfairly persecuted for using the word "spooks" to refer to the apparitional quality of two missing students in his class, who turn out to be African Americans offended by the racial connotation of the term. Vindictive colleagues at Athena College, including the programmatic feminist Delphine Roux, Chair of the Literatures and Languages Department, quickly condemn Silk as a racist and sexist, forcing him into early retirement.

So what is wrong with Roth's advocacy of liberal individualism, which belongs both to the great tradition of the novel in the realization of its protagonist's complex humanity and to the U.S. national mythology, in which the self-reliant American transcends the barriers of history, race, class, gender, and religion to become "himself"? Roth has tapped into the essential features of the American literary canon, whose focus has long been on the development of such a distinctively American individual out of his diverse, often contradictory backgrounds. Cooper's Natty Bumppo, Emerson's "transparent Eye-ball," Melville's isolato, Ishmael, Hawthorne's exile, Hester Prynne, Twain's Huck Finn, James's Christopher Newman, Pound's Hugh Selwyn Mauberley, Wallace Stevens's Crispin, and Ellison's Invisible Man do not begin to encompass the long tradition in which complex, liberal individualism centers American literature. In his influential study, *The American Novel and Its Tradition* (1957), Richard Chase interpreted this literary tradition as adapting the mythic archetypes of the romance to the new demands of middle-class realism, so that the alienation and often contradictory qualities of the American individual might also be considered the ontological foundations of social democracy.[8]

Roth himself acknowledges the cultural legacy of such individualism, tracing it back to ancient Greek tragedy—Coleman Silk is a professor of classics, not African-American studies or Jewish studies or even American literature—and often cites his American antecedents from Emerson and Hawthorne to Dos Passos.

Perhaps the chief problem facing Roth's ideal of liberal individualism is its commodification in the post-Vietnam era, not only by authors like Roth and many scholars nostalgic for a stable cultural canon but also by the U.S. state. Of course, Emerson, Thoreau, Fuller, and other transcendentalists struggled to distinguish their "man thinking" and *Woman in the Nineteenth Century* from the callous frontiersman and selfish entrepreneur in Jacksonian America. Yet the distinction between literary individualism and the U.S. exportation of the American lifestyle, increasingly urged upon other peoples by economic, political, and even military means, is much harder to maintain today. Roth's inspired defense of American identity must be read in conjunction with efforts to revive the Great Tradition of the West as a cultural solution to the social and religious practices of non-European societies, especially in the Middle East and Africa.

Azar Nafisi's bestseller, *Reading Lolita in Tehran* (2003), is a good example of how an Iranian émigré can use the liberal individualism of Jane Austen, Henry James, F. Scott Fitzgerald, Vladimir Nabokov, and Saul Bellow as an alternative to the repressive social policies of the current theocracy ruling the Republic of Iran.[9] In some respects, Nafisi understands the global problems better than Roth, even if her answers serve well the interests of U.S. government officials who favor the United States as a new imperial power. For Roth, "global" issues always smack of a longer history of "internationalism," stretching from the evils of European imperialism to the Communist ambitions for an international hegemony realized perversely in the Soviet Empire. Nafisi understands that economic globalization inevitably means the export of ideas and lifestyles, especially when the new economy depends so much upon the marketing and consumption of means of communication and representation. The post-modern, post-industrial economies of the West and first-world nations of Asia continue to rely on the exploited labor and poor working conditions of many second- and third-world countries, but the products of these new economies focus more on cultural than on material consumption. What is exported in the form of new technologies, popular and mass entertainment, fashion, and high-cultural literature and ideas cannot be ignored in its global circulation. At some level, these cultural exports return to us, whether we live in New York, Paris, or Tokyo, in the form of immigrants drawn both by better jobs and their utopian fantasies of the First World fueled by the cultural products they have consumed. In a parallel sense, the vaunted Americanization of other nations, fitfully resisted and relentlessly marketed, often produces different, unexpected results, so that Sandinista rebels might cheer Sylvester Stallone's John Rambo not so much as the exemplar of a hated American militarism but as an anti-establishment rebel, willing to fight against the military-industrial complex as fiercely as the Sandinistas during their revolution in San Salvador.

Roth is reluctant to acknowledge the inevitable consequences of globalization. Toward the end of *American Pastoral*, Swede Levov seeks out Merry, now hiding from the FBI, and finds her working at a Dog and Cat Hospital in the poorest section of Newark, living in filth and poverty after converting to Jainism. Her father's contempt for the Jainists barely disguises Roth's satire of a religion that is the polar opposite of Merry's earlier advocacy of violent revolution against the U.S. military-industrial complex. The radical pacifism of the Jainists, extending even to their efforts to avoid damaging the air and water, impresses Merry's father as "insane." Swede is particularly intent on knowing how many followers of the religion there are. When Merry answers, "Three million," Swede says impatiently, "I'm not asking you about India. I don't care about India. We do not live in India. In America, how many of you are there?"[10] Clearly the Jainists in India may have their social role to play, but as a tiny minority in the United States they can hardly be relevant, except as further expressions of the "American berserk." Yet what if Roth had written in 1997, four years before 9/11, "Muslim" or "Hindu," instead of "Jain" for Merry's religious conversion? Indeed, given the many anti-war converts to Islam, especially but not exclusively among African Americans in the 1960s, the choice of "Muslim" for Merry's conversion would have better fit Roth's poetic logic. For Roth, it is clearly the "civil religion" that secularizes and defuses the exclusionary qualities of many religions, including Judaism, in the United States. Yet the "civil religion" has hardly prevented formal religions, including Christian sects, from claiming much greater political power in recent elections and lobbying vigorously the U.S. Congress and executive branch.

Liberal individualism and the American "civil religion" are not only characteristic of U.S. democracy, but they exemplify a modernization process that brings intellectual enlightenment as well as economic advantages. American exceptionalism is paradoxically the result of Western progress, which is why U.S. cultural canons are so deeply invested in classical sources. Nineteenth-century U.S. visual artists—architects, painters, sculptors—went through at least two important neoclassical periods, the first in the 1840s and the second in the *fin-de-siècle* enthusiasm for U.S. imperial ambitions. Horatio Greenough's 1841 sculpture of George Washington seated on a Roman throne, draped in a toga, barechested like Zeus, pointing with his right hand to heaven, extending in his left the sword of power, is at first glance an anachronistic representation of a modern, democratic leader, but it typifies how influential American cultural works drew upon the classical heritage while repudiating the despotism and paganism of ancient Rome (Rowe, 107). American neoclassicism persists well into modernity and our contemporary period, both in cultural works and in the liberal-arts curriculum, in which Plato's *Republic* is taught as a clear anticipation of democracy. It is a great historical and categorical leap from Socrates's elite academy, in which philosopher kings are trained to think for and among themselves in a bid for ruling power, to the modern ideal of universal education in the United States. Of course, the modern reverence for Greco-Roman heritage was probably imported in the nineteenth century to the United States from Great Britain, where pretensions to Roman grandeur gave historical precedent to Britain's global empire.

In many versions of the U.S. literary canon, the historical path leads from the Ancients through their revival in the English Renaissance and its new humanism to eighteenth-century English neoclassicism as the prelude to the Enlightenment. Far from breaking with this venerable history, U.S. literary authors repeatedly invoked it for legitimacy. Emerson and Fuller are nearly unreadable today as a consequence of their frequent allusions to this cultural history, even in the moments when each declares most vigorously his or her literary independence. Emerson's *Nature* (1836) begins with epigraphs from Plotinus and Emerson's poem, "Nature," and the famous opening lines acknowledge that "Our age is retrospective. It builds the sepulchres of the fathers" while appealing: "Why should not we also enjoy an original relation to the universe? Why should not we have a poetry and philosophy of insight and not of tradition, and a religion by revelation to us, and not the history of theirs?"[11] Although conventionally interpreted to mean that the new U.S. nation must throw off its cultural ties to European and classical models, Emerson's lines include "also" to suggest how the American must embrace both his exceptionalism and his unavoidable heritage. Margaret Fuller invokes Greek culture in specific revolution against nineteenth-century Anglo-American patriarchy, finding in Greek tragic heroines like Antigone and Iphigenia, and Greek goddesses like Aphrodite, models for modern feminine reformers.[12] Like modern scholars and others committed to ancient "goddess worship" for its political and cultural empowerment of women, Fuller certainly revises the deeply patriarchal values of the Greek tragedians Aeschylus, Euripides, and Sophocles, but she retains the classical aura as fundamental to her American work.

For Emerson and Fuller, the English Renaissance mediates and modernizes the Greco-Roman heritage, providing a cultural foundation for American exceptionalism that the American Revolution did little to diminish. Among his many representative men, Emerson returns frequently to Shakespeare, and Fuller recalls Elizabeth I as a crucial feminine force in the cultural consolidation of the British nation by Elizabethan dramatists and poets. A century later, F. O. Matthiessen would define the American literary canon as "Art and Expression in the Age of Emerson and Whitman," the subtitle of his *American Renaissance*, whose main title explicitly invokes the successful cultural renaissance of the English sixteenth and seventeenth centuries. To be sure, early twentieth-century scholars of American literature, like Vernon Parrington and Perry Miller, were also scholars of the English Renaissance, but that local history is far outweighed by the importance of the English Renaissance for the American Transcendentalists and their New England contemporaries, like Hawthorne and Melville, often considered the figures responsible for the American literary nationalism that would shape literary canons for the next one hundred and fifty years.

In Roth's *The Human Stain*, Coleman Silk is a classics professor, specializing in the Greek tragedians, having first learned to love precise elocution and sophisticated rhetoric from his father, who insisted his family speak correct English and was fond of quoting from his prized, leather-bound folio of Shakespeare's works. Roth hopes to subvert stereotypes about African Americans' lack of erudition and preference for street argot, but Coleman Silk's passion for the classics and for the English Renaissance enables him to pass more than in simply racial terms but also as an exemplary "American," whose reliance on a specific cultural heritage enables his bids for personal freedom through his idiosyncratic and thus *typical* liberal individualism. Silk is infuriated when Delphine Roux, his ambitious, pseudo-feminist department chair, sides with a woman student who complains that Euripides's plays, *Hippolytus* and *Alcestis*, are "degrading to women."[13] Caricaturing Roux as a French intellectual immigrant living in a fantasy world of suspected slights and unfulfilled sexual desire, Roth never challenges the seemingly self-evident importance of teaching American college students ancient Greek tragedies, any more than recent advocates of Shakespeare's being fundamental to the American liberal-arts curriculum have offered justifications more compelling than the usual platitudes about the superiority of his language, as Coleman Silk's father does. Of course, it would be easy enough to teach Silk's offended student how Euripides conforms to or departs from the patriarchal and profoundly sexist social values of ancient Athens, where women and slaves were barred from citizenship.

Yet like his protagonist, Silk, Roth is not interested in how Greek tragedians reflected or opposed the values of ancient Athens. Silk never defends his subject matter, but Roth does by explaining that we read Greek tragedy to understand the universal conflict of the individual with his or her destiny. We may no longer believe in the Greek fates and worship other gods than Zeus and Athena, but we are still captured by the timeless conflict between individual choice and historical determinism. Defenders of the literary and cultural canons usually invoke at some point the "universals" exemplified by the works and authors included, but most of these universals are deeply suspect. The epigraph to *The Human Stain* comes from Sophocles's *Oedipus the King*, in which Creon answers Oedipus's question, "What is the rite of purification? How shall it be done?": "By banishing a man, or expiation of blood by blood" (*The Human Stain*, epigraph). The final section of Roth's novel is entitled "The Purifying Ritual," so we should understand Coleman Silk's life and sacrificial death to involve more than his racial passing and his struggle for individual integrity. The "human stain" is, after all, not racial, sexual, or any other kind of discrimination in our modern world; it is the timeless problem faced by Sophocles's Oedipus and repeated with historically and culturally specific adaptations throughout history. The "human stain" is our shared humanity.

So why do we need "America" at all? Is the conflict faced by the ruler Oedipus against his divinely ordained "fate" applicable to the democratic institutions and liberal individualism so prized by Roth and other defenders of the canon? What happens to these values when the classical heritage and its presumed universals are challenged? Martin Bernal argues persuasively in *Black Athena* that the religious and philosophical ideas of the ancient Greeks were profoundly influenced by African cultures, otherwise forgotten or marginalized in the great Western heritage.[14] W. E. B. Du Bois suggests that Western civilization cannot be disarticulated from the institutionalized slavery and global imperialism on which it depends.[15] What happens when we challenge the progressive scheme that leads from the proto-democracy of the Greek city-state through the formalism of Roman law to the emerging nationalism of Elizabethan England to the French and American revolutions and the birth of democratic institutions? The cause-and-effect links lost in this highly selective history include centuries of slavery, whose nineteenth-century abolition has certainly not resulted in the emancipation of slavery's descendants, and imperial domination and exploitation, resulting in the genocidal destruction by disease and murder of perhaps ninety million indigenous peoples in the Western Hemisphere between 1492 and 1900.

Rightly reminding us that the twentieth century is perhaps the bloodiest in human history, Roth hardly believes in progress, just as most of our canonical literary authors criticize naive beliefs in human improvement. Nevertheless, the criticism of progress from within the West often turns to universals, such as Greek tragedy and its predicates: hubris, hamartia, anagnorisis, catharsis, and other reductive answers. What happens when we step outside this tradition, which is what has irreversibly *happened* in U.S. society as a consequence of new immigration and changing demographics? What is the universal appeal of Oedipus, Lear, and Ahab to a Chinese immigrant to the United States? In her wonderful parody of canonical literature in *China Men* (1980), "The Adventures of Lo Bun Sun," Maxine Hong turns Defoe's English classic, *The Adventures of Robinson Crusoe* (1719), into a "Chinese" story, probably read to her as a child by her mother, who stereotypically mispronounced her *r*'s and *l*'s. Whether Kingston or her mother changed Defoe's story is never explained, but in *China Men* Crusoe's famous Oedipal rebellion against his English father is transformed into Chinese respect for one's parents, so that the estranged Lo Bun Sun and his father are reunited at the end of Kingston's version. Whereas in Defoe, "Friday" is saved, named, educated, and subordinated anew by Crusoe, in Kingston's story he becomes Lo Bun Sun's friend in keeping with Confucian ideals of friendship. In Defoe, Crusoe exemplifies the proto-capitalist values of the Protestant work ethic in his fierce self-reliance; in Kingston, Lo Bun Sun depends on a growing community of outcasts, beginning with Friday, who by the end have established a "maroon" community that serves as a utopian alternative to the modern nation-state.[16]

Who best speaks to the difficulties facing Vietnamese immigrants to the United States, many still suffering their own versions of post-traumatic stress syndrome for being caught between Vietnamese anti-colonialism and South Vietnamese governments propped up first by the French and then by the Americans? Roth's Coleman Silk, like the ancient Oedipus, represents the universality of human suffering, and Roth provides a convincing account of how racial discrimination, which Silk attempts to escape by passing as white, is one important aspect of the human tragedy. Le Ly Hayslip's *When Heaven and Earth Changed Places: A Vietnamese Woman's Odyssey* (1989) is by no means as sophisticated stylistically or formally as *The Human Stain*, but it addresses the specific suffering of Vietnamese caught between macropolitical forces in Vietnam and then in the United States in ways that cannot be universalized. Beaten and raped by the Viet Cong, then beaten and raped by the U.S. military, and finally beaten by her American husband in San Diego, Hayslip cannot be understood by reference to Sophocles's Oedipus or even Antigone. What makes her account worthy of our attention as readers interested in how the United States has changed as a consequence of globalization is Hayslip's representation of that conflictual "contact zone" where several different cultures meet and interact (Rowe, 10–16). Such "border zones" and "border discourse," whether viewed from within a specific community or outside its boundaries, always challenge discrete geopolitical entities, in particular the nation-state. Such border-texts as Kingston's and Hayslip's rarely fit the "standard" of either culture they represent, and therefore their situations cannot be understood in reference to the archetypes of either culture. Encouraging us to think about how certain "universals" are no longer as generally applicable as we once imagined, Kingston and Hayslip help us adapt to our new global circumstances. Of course, their works also alienate and anger those readers committed to traditional aesthetic and philosophical values in the West.

What then of Matthew Arnold's standard of "the best that has been spoken and written," which is so frequently invoked when we debate the merits and revisions of any cultural canon? Only philosophic and aesthetic universals allow us to claim "the best," which means either we abandon the exceptional status of the American experience for the sake of taking all historical cultures into account or that we claim for "exceptional" America, itself the end-point of a progressive scheme of human development, that *its* cultural production, however classified in particulars, is the "best." Neither option makes much sense, of course, in part because claims to American exceptionalism usually reveal their deeply historical, unexceptional sources and because the task of taking all historical cultures into account renders the work of judgment and evaluation virtually impossible. Suffice it to say that Arnold himself never provides even the vaguest definition of "the best," instead offering merely self-evident and deeply Eurocentric examples; Arnold's technique is strategic quotation with a few contextualizing words. Simple as the phrase "the best that has been spoken and written" is, it poses an immense set of theoretical problems, some of which may be insuperable. Merely adding works to what we might term the canon of universal superiority does not really address these theoretical concerns, but instead disguises these problems with an illusory diversity.

Today most would agree that Frederick Douglass's *Narrative of the Life of Frederick Douglass, an American Slave, Written by Himself* (1845) and Toni Morrison's *Beloved* (1987) are canonical texts. Both works are taught frequently in English classes from high school to graduate school; both works enjoy wide scholarly and popular reputations. Both works deal imaginatively and historically with slavery and its abolition, which are central to any understanding of U.S. history. Each work has been interpreted in terms of the liberal individualism and democratic emancipation I have analyzed as being basic to the U.S. literary canon. Douglass "progresses" from an abused, illiterate slave to a self-reliant, literate freedman; Morrison's Sethe rebels against the slavocracy's violence toward her identity and humanity by desperately killing her own child to keep her from the social death of slavery. Sethe may carry self-reliance to its ultimate contradiction, but in so doing she exposes the immorality of slavery and post-emancipation racism. Replete with transcendentalist rhetoric and sentiments, Douglass's 1845 *Narrative* seems to be an African-American elaboration of the individualism advocated by Emerson, Thoreau, and Fuller, all of whom were abolitionists. Written in a style reminiscent of William Faulkner's deliberate confusions of historical time, Morrison's *Beloved* also suggests how each of us relives historical traumas, like slavery and racism, that the community has not addressed. In the great tradition of American narrative, Douglass and Morrison add the African-American self, which has been produced in the struggle to overcome social discrimination greater than that afflicting Hawthorne's Hester Prynne, Melville's Ishmael, Twain's Huck Finn, James's Isabel Archer, and F. Scott Fitzgerald's Jay Gatsby.

Yet the moment we interpret Douglass and Morrison in these canonical contexts, doing so in ways that make considerable sense given the self-conscious efforts of Douglass and Morrison to acknowledge their sources, we lose much of the profound challenge to "liberal individualism" posed by both authors and integral to their criticisms of American society. Douglass may end *Narrative* having achieved a tenuous middle-class respectability with freedom, marriage, a house and job in the North, but his self-reliance has been achieved only as part of the collective action against slavery represented by the organized abolitionists who published his work, his fiancée who helped him escape in disguise to the North, the friends in the South who aid him in his fight against evil slave-masters like Captain Anthony and Mr. Covey, and even the white woman, Sophia Auld, who first helps teach him to read and write until her husband forbids such education of slaves. Morrison's Sethe kills her own child to keep her from schoolteacher and his "slave-catchers," because Sethe is too proud to recognize how much her fierce independence depends upon others, including Sixo, Stamp Paid, Amy Denver, and the Cherokee of Georgia, among many others. By the same token, following her "crime," Sethe is shunned by the African-American women of Cincinnati, and their lack of charity seems to bring upon them Morrison's judgment of a similar hubris they share with Sethe. At the very end of *Beloved*, there is a moment of grace in which forgiveness seems briefly, perhaps imaginatively, offered by the "hill of black people," a collective that appears outside Sethe's home, Bluestone 124, recalling the Biblical "Jegar Sahadutha," "the heap of witness," which prophesies judgment and redemption.[17]

Both Douglass and Morrison challenge the terms of the canon, especially liberal individualism, democratic consensus, and social assimilation and inclusion. They themselves would endorse a revised and expanded literary canon, in which they both deserve central positions, and in doing so they encourage us to interpret canonical writers differently. Morrison argues in *Playing in the Dark* (1992) that the repression of the "Africanist presence" in canonical American literature from Poe to Hemingway suggests the failure of U.S. culture to deal with two of its defining issues: slavery and racism. As she herself points out, it is only in the scholarship of the past twenty-five years that we have been encouraged to address both the troubling racial unconscious of canonical American literature and to look for more direct encounters with these issues in non-canonical works. Is it possible that "the best that has been spoken and written" is sometimes the safest, most ideologically acceptable, and least troubling? Of course, such an extreme, deliberately provocative definition does not cover all canonical works, but there is a measure of truth to the conclusion that canonical works often repress the more troubling aspects of social experience, especially in the diverse, contentious settler-society of the United States.

These problems often cause some scholars who are anxious to defend the literary canon to do so in terms of aesthetic quality, dismissing politics as inappropriate to literary judgments and, in extreme cases, contending that politics has no place in the "classroom," which is to say the formal study of literature. We know that "art for art's sake" is itself a political position, but still scholars argue that perhaps the symmetries and harmonies of aesthetic experience offer us an oblique access to an ethics that encourages identification with other peoples and cultures, even if the aesthetic work itself has nothing to say about such quotidian matters. From Kant's *Critique of Aesthetic Judgment* (1790) to J. Hillis Miller's *The Ethics of Reading* (1987) and Elaine Scarry's *On Beauty and Being Just* (1999), there is support for the canonization of literary works on these philosophically aesthetic grounds. Dubious as I find these arguments, they nonetheless lend themselves to a transnational canon, one that could never be circumscribed within a "national literature." Indeed, the proponents of this standard for literary canonization are often specialists in comparative literature and critical theory, like Scarry and Miller, or philosophical aesthetics, like Kant, who himself considered nationalism the greatest stumbling block to human enlightenment.

In short, the U.S. national literary canon cannot overcome the deeply ideological work most cultural canons serve. We can certainly disguise this cultural work by developing complex theories of "genius" and depoliticized literary genealogies, analyzing stylistic and generic innovations, and gathering repeated literary themes into archetypes and myths. Yet if these distinctive features of "American literature" are not doing political work, then aren't we reading and teaching these texts primarily in order to learn *how to write great literature*? Of course, there is a place for creative-writing instruction in every liberal curriculum, but the discipline of literary study is not primarily intended to prepare new creative writers, but to enable students to understand literature's role in the larger work of social construction. As a pedagogical and scholarly goal, understanding literature's social purposes is far more justifiable than articulating only the formal aesthetic properties of literary texts, even if it also means that the *political purposes* of literature cannot be separated from its social work. There is a great difference, of course, between "politicizing the classroom" by propagating the teacher's specific views and teaching political, social, economic, and cultural history by means of important literary texts.

My teachers taught me Ezra Pound without mentioning his anti-Semitism and dismissing his support of Mussolini's fascism as a "misunderstanding" by U.S. authorities, T. S. Eliot without discussing his misogyny and anti-Semitism and aristocratic pretensions, Mark Twain without addressing the stereotype of "Injun Joe" in *Tom Sawyer* or the racialist humor about African Americans in *Huckleberry Finn*, Henry James by skipping over his anti-Irish, anti-Semitic, racialist assumptions. Today those who address these questions, sometimes defending and other times criticizing these authors for these and other prejudices, are often attacked for their insistence upon a "political correctness" that in these authors' own times would have been an impossible standard and thus the imposition of a "presentist" perspective that falsifies history. Yet when we do understand the pervasiveness of anti-Semitism in American literature, we may begin to understand more about the rise of modern fascism and its genocidal policies toward Jews and other minorities. When we understand how even a writer like Mark Twain, arguably one of our greatest critics of slavery and racism, can himself lapse into racist attitudes toward African and Native Americans, we may begin to understand how unresolved and difficult the problem of racial discrimination is in the United States. Some have argued that "political correctness" has produced its own alternative canon, composed primarily of women, gays, ethnic minorities, all of whom represent the same, tired story of victimization and complaint. Such critics often turn out to be rather poor interpreters of the various literary authors and texts they contend are reductive. John Ellis contends that Toni Morrison focuses obsessively on the victimization of her African-American characters, but most readers recognize the great creativity and imaginative joy of her characters in their diverse efforts to overcome the limitations of slavery, racism, classism, and sexism (Ellis, 91).

There are many specialists in the different ethnic U.S. literatures who in the past thirty-five years have advocated specific literary canons for their respective fields. Given the limited time we have available to teach undergraduate literature majors (two to three years of work in most majors in the United States) and PhD candidates in these fields (two to three years of course work in most graduate programs), we should not be surprised that specializations in ethnic and minority literatures should have produced their own canonical texts. Interesting as it might be to discuss the extent to which these new literary canons follow or depart from more traditional literary judgments, the tendency among such specialists to *reject* canonical methods of classifying and organizing literary studies is to me far more compelling. Many of the most influential ethnic and minority literary texts are written by authors who openly refuse traditional canonical status for their works. Toni Morrison's *Beloved* draws heavily on African-American oral folk traditions, even as it plays on Faulkner's high-modernist literary style. Although unmistakably an African-American novel, *Beloved* is also recognizably a great American novel in its effort to comment on social problems shared by all Americans. Yet if you interpret *Beloved* in only one of these cultural registers, you will miss either Morrison's deep respect for the rhetoric of black preaching or for the complexity of literary modernism's historical consciousness. Gloria Anzaldúa's *Borderlands / La Frontera* is an important avant-garde text for Chicana writers and activists, but Anzaldúa's polylingual style, her deliberate invocation of the *téjano* cultures of the Texas-Mexico borderlands, and her critique of such pervasive Chicano myths as Áztlan and La Malinche make *Borderlands / La Frontera* difficult to identify as a canonical text for either Chicanos or Chicanas. In a similar sense, Theresa Hak Kyung Cha's *Dictée* is considered foundational for Korean-American literature, but its polylingual style, its diasporic settings in Korea and California, and its broad reliance on European post-structuralism make the text difficult to use to define Korean-American identity. Maxine Hong Kingston's *Woman Warrior* (1976) is often cited as a canonical Chinese-American literary work, which is read frequently in high-school and college literary classes, but it is very difficult to treat Kingston's memoirist, who both relies upon and thoroughly criticizes traditional Chinese and U.S. cultures, as a "representative" Chinese American. Even Kingston's publisher cannot decide whether *Woman Warrior* is a "novel" or an "autobiography," classifying the book on its back cover as "fiction/memoir."

Of course, all of these works are avant-garde, whose formal experimentations might be considered little different from those of the literary high moderns, whose works by now are thoroughly canonized. In their own era, Pound's *Cantos* (1919–70) and T. S. Eliot's *The Waste Land* (1922) were considered radical departures from the epic and narrative long poem, respectively, but generations of college students have broadened both poetic genres to include these canonical works. Yet the defamiliarization attempted by ethnic writers like Morrison, Anzaldúa, Cha, and Kingston often goes well beyond formal experimentation to contest the cultural terms informing most formal aesthetic criteria. Pound and Eliot do little to challenge the cultural traditions of Western civilization, in which both were well educated. Pound may insist that the Provençal troubadours deserve our attention as much as Chaucer, Petrarch, and Dante, but Pound still displays his familiarity with the latter canonical figures. Eliot broadens the English literary tradition by invoking in *The Waste Land* international texts ranging from the Hindu *Bhagavad-Gita* to St. Augustine's *Confessions* and the poetry of Gérard de Nerval and Paul Verlaine, but the cultural core of the poem is the English literary renaissance, with frequent references to Shakespeare, Marlowe, Kyd, and Middleton. Pound and Eliot revived a declining English literary canon by adding to it their own international interests, including their U.S. cultural backgrounds, albeit often in disguised and anxious ways.

In many respects, Pound and Eliot's approach to broadening the canon by including "other" traditions anticipates more recent defenses of literary canons and their criticism of ethnic and minority literatures. If a religious or literary text, St. Augustine's *Confessions* or the *Bhagavad-Gita*, can be adapted to the existing literary and cultural traditions, then such a text earns canonical status. But what if such adaptations utterly falsify the original text? Written well before Eliot's conversion to the Anglican Church, *The Waste Land* employs traditional Christian motifs—Augustine's conversion, Christ's journey to Emmaus, the Crucifixion, and the Resurrection—for very secular purposes. Augustine's God is for Eliot the larger cultural tradition to which each author contributes and by which he is subsumed. Christ's pilgrimage is marked in Eliot's poem by the cultural stages through which the attentive reader passes, from the references to Chaucer in the opening "Book of the Dead" to Shakespeare and Middleton in "A Game of Chess." While each of us is sacrificed personally to the larger purposes of cultural and political history, the wise reader discovers his "survival" in the national literature with which he identifies and that also surpasses him. For the Harvard-educated Eliot, born in St. Louis, that national literature is oddly *English*, as were the Anglicanism to which he would later convert and the social values he endorsed throughout his life.

Eliot and Christianity may agree that at stake are the hearts and minds of English readers, which we might broaden to include American readers as well, even though *The Waste Land* remains a deeply *English national* poem with only hints of American sentiment. Anzaldúa rejects the "American" national framework by focusing on *la frontera* where U.S.-Mexican identities are no longer clearly delineated, even in the popular cultures of today's *téjano* communities. Kingston variously endorses and criticizes U.S. literary canons; the protagonist of *Tripmaster Monkey: His Fake Book* (1989) is a literature major (educated at the University of California at Berkeley) whose name, Wittman Ah Sing, both mocks and invokes Walt Whitman while reminding the reader of one of the uglier racist works by two famous American writers, Mark Twain and Brett Harte's *Ah Sin*, the enormously popular play based on Harte's Orientalist ballad *Plain Language from Truthful James*, also known as *The Heathen Chinee* (1870). Wittman carries in his pocket Rainer Maria Rilke's *The Notebooks of Malte Laurids Brigge*, the fictional autobiography by a German modernist poet about a young Dane's adventures in France, and the structure of Kingston's novel draws on the classic Chinese novel *Journey to the West*, about the Buddhist priest Tripitaka, who is sent by the goddess Quan'yin to find the origins of Chinese Buddhism in India. T. S. Eliot incorporates foreign cultures to bolster the existing English ideology, subordinating these international texts to the national mythology. Anzaldúa and Kingston challenge the U.S. symbology, arguing for significant changes in what, who, and how it represents as the nation. By focusing on the "contact zones" between otherwise discrete nations, they also argue for transnational thinking about cultural values, rejecting exclusively national values and knowledge.

Some scholars will undoubtedly argue for the values of the emerging ethnic literary or more broadly conceived multicultural literary canons, contending reasonably that such new canons will continue the practical purposes of older literary canons while avoiding their limitations by providing students with useful frameworks for organizing the otherwise vast literary production of a society as historically and ethnically diverse as the United States. I prefer to follow the leads of the more radical ethnic and minority writers like Morrison, Cha, Kingston, and Anzaldúa, who would prefer to dispense with the very concept of literary canons for the sake of thinking beyond their tacit geopolitical boundaries. We inherit the word *canon* from the Catholic church and its great religious empire of the Latin Middle Ages, and we have transferred the concept of holiness, evidenced by the miraculous works of those canonized as saints, to literary authors capable of "magically" representing in discrete works the operative myths of our modern nation-states. Catholicism and nationalism are still important religious and geopolitical forms, but neither is any longer the prevailing model that defines the relationships of individuals to their communities. The European Union offers a model of political confederation that incorporates and yet exceeds traditional nationalism. New cosmopolitanisms have emerged to account for peoples moved by necessity or choice away from their homelands to work and live in foreign countries, and we are encountering every day new political, legal, economic, and personal situations prompted by such global mobility. Literature and other forms of cultural expression can no longer be understood in terms of a ruling geopolitical state; culture, like the politics it accompanies, must now be interpreted in more flexible terms. Scholars educated in more traditional ways will be troubled by these changes, in some cases deeply suspicious of the new, unfamiliar terms and methods, but scholars and ordinary readers alike will have to change their habits of reading from national to more transnational contexts. Whether or not these new ways of understanding literature will produce new canons of value remains to be seen, but it is certain that the older "national" literary canons are today archaic, their practical values far outweighed by their intellectual contradictions.

Notes

1. See Robert Von Hallberg, ed., *Canons* (Chicago: University of Chicago Press, 1984); Henry Louis Gates Jr., *Loose Canons: Notes on the Culture Wars* (New York:

Oxford University Press, 1992); John Guillory, *Cultural Capital: The Problem of Literary Canon Formation* (Chicago: University of Chicago Press, 1993).

2. Alan Wolfe, "The Anti-American Studies," *New Republic* (February 10, 2003).

3. John M. Ellis, *Literature Lost: Social Agendas and the Corruption of the Humanities* (New Haven, CT: Yale University Press, 1997), p. 91.

4. For a discussion of the conservative positions during the culture wars, see John Carlos Rowe, *The New American Studies* (Minneapolis: University of Minnesota Press, 2002), pp. 4–5.

5. Samuel P. Huntington, *Who Are We? The Challenges to America's National Identity* (New York: Simon and Schuster, 2004), p. 274.

6. Philip Roth, "Writing American Fiction" (1961), in *Reading Myself and Others* (New York: Farrar, Straus, and Giroux, 1975), p. 120. The essay was first delivered in 1960 as "a speech . . . at Stanford University . . . [at] a symposium on 'Writing in America Today' " (117).

7. My argument about Roth's politics follows Ross Posnock, *Philip Roth's Rude Truth: The Art of Immaturity* (Princeton: Princeton University Press, 2006).

8. Richard Chase, *The American Novel and Its Tradition* (New York: Columbia University Press, 1957).

9. Azar Nafisi, *Reading Lolita in Tehran: A Memoir in Books* (New York: Random House, 2003). See my critique of Nafisi, "Reading *Reading Lolita in Tehran* in Idaho," *American Quarterly* 59:2 (June 2007), pp. 253–75.

10. Philip Roth, *American Pastoral* (Boston: Houghton Mifflin Co., 1997), p. 245.

11. Ralph Waldo Emerson, *Nature*, in *Selected Works of Ralph Waldo Emerson and Margaret Fuller*, ed. John Carlos Rowe (Boston: Houghton Mifflin Co., 2003), p. 23.

12. Margaret Fuller, *Woman in the Nineteenth Century*, in *Selected Writings of Ralph Waldo Emerson and Margaret Fuller*, pp. 426–38.

13. Philip Roth, *The Human Stain* (New York: Random House, 2000), p. 184.

14. Martin Bernal, *Black Athena: The Afroasiatic Roots of Classical Civilization* (New Brunswick, NJ: Rutgers University Press, 1987).

15. W. E. B. Du Bois, "Africa and the Slave Trade" (1915), in *The Oxford W. E. B. Du Bois Reader*, ed. Eric Sundquist (New York: Oxford University Press, 1996), p. 637.

16. Maxine Hong Kingston, *China Men* (New York: Alfred A. Knopf, 1980), pp. 224–33.

17. Toni Morrison, *Beloved* (New York: Alfred A. Knopf, 1987), p. 262.

BIBLIOGRAPHY

Abraham, Nicolas and Maria Torok. *Cryptonomie; le verbier de l'Homme aux loups; précédé de Fors par Jacques Derrida*. Paris: Aubier Flammarion, 1976.

Adams, Hazard, ed. *Critical Theory since Plato*. Rev. ed. New York: Harcourt Brace Jovanovich, 1992.

Adorno, Theodor. *The Jargon of Authenticity*. Translated by Kurt Tarnowski and Frederic Will. Evanston, IL: Northwestern University Press, 1973.

Anderson, Benedict. *Imagined Communities: Reflections on the Origin and Spread of Nationalism*. London: Verso, 1983.

Appiah, Kwame Anthony. *Cosmopolitanism: Ethics in a World of Strangers*. New York: W. W. Norton and Co., 2006.

Aristotle. *Poetics*. In *Critical Theory since Plato*, rev. ed., edited by Hazard Adams, pp. 49–66. New York: Harcourt Brace Jovanovich, 1992.

Ashcroft, Bill, Gareth Griffiths, and Helen Tiffin, eds. *The Empire Writes Back: Theory and Practices in Postcolonial Literature*. London: Routledge, 1999.

Barrett, Lindon. *Blackness and Value: Seeing Double*. New York: Cambridge University Press, 1999.

Baudrillard, Jean. *For a Critique of the Political Economy of the Sign*. Translated by Charles Levin. St. Louis, MO: Telos Press, 1981.

———. *The Mirror of Production*. Translated and introduced by Mark Poster. St Louis, MO: Telos Press, 1975.

———. *Selected Writings*. Edited by Mark Poster. Palo Alto, CA: Stanford University Press, 1988.

Benston, Kimberly W., ed. *Speaking for You: The Vision of Ralph Ellison*. Washington, DC: Howard University Press, 1987.

Berger, Thomas. *Crazy in Berlin*. New York: Charles Scribner's Sons, 1958.

———. *Neighbors*. New York: Delacorte/Seymour Lawrence, 1980. (Abbreviated in this text as *N*.)

———. *Reinhart's Women*. New York: Delacorte/Seymour Lawrence, 1981.

———. *Vital Parts*. New York: New American Library, 1970.

———. *Who Is Teddy Villanova?* New York: Delacorte/Seymour Lawrence, 1977.

Bernal, Martin. *Black Athena: The Afroasiatic Roots of Classical Civilization*. New Brunswick, NJ: Rutgers University Press, 1987.

Bhabha, Homi, ed. *Nation and Narration*. New York: Routledge, 1990.

Bloom, Allan. *The Closing of the American Mind*. New York: Simon and Schuster, 1987.

The Blues Brothers. Directed by John Landis. Universal Pictures, 1980.

Brinnin, John Malcolm. *The Third Rose: Gertrude Stein and Her World*. Reading, MA: Addison-Wesley Publishing Co., Inc., 1987.

Broeck, Sabine. "Getrude Stein's 'Melanctha' in den Diskursen zur 'Natur der Frau.'" *Amerika Studien* 37:3 (1992): 512–28.

Buell, Frederick. *National Culture and the New Global System*. Baltimore: The Johns Hopkins University Press, 1994.

Burke, Kenneth. "Ralph Ellison's Trueblooded *Bildungsroman*." In *Speaking for You: The Vision of Ralph Ellison*, edited by Kimberly W. Benston. Washington, DC: Howard University Press, 1987.

Callahan, John F. *In the African-American Grain: The Pursuit of Voice in Twentieth-Century Black Fiction*. Urbana: University of Illinois Press, 1988.

Carby, Hazel V. *Reconstructing Womanhood: The Emergence of the Afro-American Woman Novelist*. New York: Oxford University Press, 1987.

Chase, Richard. *The American Novel and Its Tradition*. New York: Columbia University Press, 1957.

Christian, Barbara. *Black Women Novelists: The Development of a Tradition, 1892–1976*. Westport, CT: Greenwood Press, 1980.

Cohen, Sarah Blacher, ed. *Comic Relief: Humor in Contemporary American Literature*. Urbana: University of Illinois Press, 1978.

De Koven, Marianne. *A Different Language: Gertrude Stein's Experimental Writing*. Madison: University of Wisconsin Press, 1983.

Derrida, Jacques. *Given Time: 1, Counterfeit Money*. Translated by Peggy Kamuf. Chicago: University of Chicago Press, 1992.

———. *Spectres de Marx: L'État de la dette, le travail du deuil et la nouvelle Internationale*. Paris: Galilée, 1993.

Doane, Janice L. *Silence and Narrative: The Early Novels of Gertrude Stein*. Westport, CT: Greenwood Press, 1986.

Dos Passos, John. *Manhattan Transfer*. Boston: Houghton Mifflin Co., 1925. (Abbreviated in this text as *MT*.)

Douglas, Ann. *Terrible Honesty: Mongrel Manhattan in the 1920s*. New York: Farrar, Straus and Giroux, 1996.

Douglass, Frederick. *Narrative of the Life of Frederick Douglass, an American Slave, Written by Himself*. New York: Penguin Books, 1982.

Dubnick, Randa. *The Structure of Obscurity: Gertrude Stein, Language, and Cubism*. Urbana: University of Illinois Press, 1984.

DuBois, W. E. B. "Africa and the Slave Trade." In *The Oxford W. E. B. Du Bois Reader*, edited by Eric Sundquist, 628–37. New York: Oxford University Press, 1996.

———. *The Souls of Black Folk*. New York: Penguin Books, 1989.

Dupee, Frederick W. *Henry James: His Life and Writings*. 2nd ed. Garden City, NY: Doubleday and Co., Inc., 1956.

Eliot, T. S. *The Waste Land and Other Poems*. Edited by Frank Kermode. New York: Penguin Books, 1998.

Ellis, John M. *Literature Lost: Social Agendas and the Corruption of the Humanities*. New Haven, CT: Yale University Press, 1997.

Ellison, Ralph. "Eyewitness Story of Riot: False Rumors Spurred by Mob." *New York Post* (August 2, 1943).

———. Introduction to *Invisible Man*. New York: Random House, Inc., 1980.

———. *Invisible Man*. New York: Random House, Inc., 1952. (Abbreviated in this text as *IM*.)

———. *Juneteenth: A Novel*. Edited by John F. Callahan. New York: Random House, 1999. (Abbreviated in this text as *J*.)

———. *Shadow and Act*. New York: Random House, 1964.

Erdrich, Louise. *The Beet Queen*. New York: Henry Holt, 1986.

———. *The Last Report on the Miracles at Little No Horse*. New York: HarperCollins, 2001. (Abbreviated in this text as *LR*.)

———. *Love Medicine*. Rev. ed. New York: HarperCollins, 1993.

———. *The Master Butchers Singing Club*. New York: HarperCollins, 2003. (Abbreviated in this text as *MB*.)

———. *The Painted Drum*. New York: HarperCollins, 2005.

———. *The Plague of Doves*. New York: HarperCollins, 2008.

———. *Shadow Tag*. New York: HarperCollins, 2010.

———. *Tales of Burning Love*. New York: HarperCollins, 1996.

Faulkner, William. *Absalom, Absalom!* New York: Random House, 1964.

———. *Go Down, Moses*. New York: Random House, 1942.

Feidelson, Charles, Jr. *Symbolism and American Literature*. Chicago: University of Chicago Press, 1957.

Frase, Brigitte. "A Shot Resounds [Review of *The Plague of Doves*]." *Los Angeles Times Book Review* (April 27, 2008). R2.

Freud, Sigmund. *On Creativity and the Unconscious: Papers on the Psychology of Art, Literature, Love, Religion*. Edited by Benjamin Nelson. Translated under the supervision of Joan Riviere. New York: Harper and Row, 1958.

Fukuyama, Francis. *The End of History and the Last Man*. New York: Bard Books, 1992.

Gates, Henry Louis, Jr. *Loose Canons: Notes on the Culture Wars*. New York: Oxford University Press, 1992.

Genovese, Eugene D. *Roll, Jordan, Roll: The World the Slaves Made*. New York: Random House, 1974.

Graham, Wendy. *Henry James's Thwarted Love*. Palo Alto, CA: Stanford University Press, 1999.

Guillory, John. *Cultural Capital: The Problem of Literary Canon Formation*. Chicago: University of Chicago Press, 1993.

Harvey, David. *The New Imperialism*. New York: Oxford University Press, 2005.

Heidegger, Martin. *Der Ursprung des Kunstwerkes*. In *Holzwege*. Frankfurt: Vittorio Klostermann, 1950.

Hughes, Douglas A. "The Schlemiel as Humanist: Thomas Berger's Carlo Reinhart." In *Critical Essays on Thomas Berger*, edited by David W. Madden, 45–60. New York: G. K. Hall and Co., 1995.

Huntington, Samuel. *Who Are We? The Challenges to America's National Identity*. New York: Simon and Schuster, 2004.

Huyssen, Andreas. *After the Great Divide: Modernism, Mass Culture, Postmodernism*. Bloomington: Indiana University Press, 1986.

Hyde, Lewis. *The Gift: Imagination and the Erotic Life of Property*. New York: Random House, 1979.

Irwin, John T. *Doubling and Incest / Repetition and Revenge: A Speculative Reading of Faulkner*. Baltimore: Johns Hopkins University Press, 1975.

Jackson, Lawrence. *Ralph Ellison: Emergence of Genius*. New York: John Wiley and Sons, Inc., 2002.

Jameson, Fredric. *Postmodernism or, The Cultural Logic of Late Capitalism*. Durham, NC: Duke University Press, 1991.

Johnson, Claudia Durst. *"To Kill a Mockingbird": Threatening Boundaries*. New York: Twayne Publishers, 1994.

———. *Understanding "To Kill a Mockingbird": A Student Casebook to Issues, Sources, and Historic Documents*. Westport, CT: Greenwood Press, 1994.

Jones, Carolyn. "Atticus Finch and the Mad Dog: Harper Lee's *To Kill a Mockingbird*." *Modern Critical Interpretations of "To Kill a Mockingbird."* Edited by Harold Bloom. Philadelphia, PA: Chelsea House Publishers, 1999.

Kalaidjian, Walter. *American Culture between the Wars: Revisionary Modernism and Postmodern Critique*. New York: Columbia University Press, 1993.

Kaplan, Amy. *The Anarchy of Empire in the Making of U.S. Culture*. Cambridge, MA: Harvard University Press, 2002.

Kaplan, Amy, and Donald E. Pease, eds. *Cultures of United States Imperialism*. Durham, NC: Duke University Press, 1993.

Keats, John. *Selected Letters of John Keats*. Edited by Lionel Trilling. New York: Farrar, Straus, and Young, Inc., 1951.

Kermode, Frank. *The Genesis of Secrecy: On the Interpretation of Narrative*. Cambridge, MA: Harvard University Press, 1979.

King, C. Richard, ed. *Postcolonial America*. Urbana: University of Illinois Press, 2000.

Kingston, Maxine Hong. *China Men*. New York: Random House, 1980.

Laing, R. D. *The Politics of Experience*. New York: Ballantine Books, 1967.

Landon, Brooks. "The Radical Americanist." *Nation* 225 (1977): 151–56.

Lee, Harper. *To Kill a Mockingbird*. Philadelphia: J. B. Lippincott Co., 1960. (Abbreviated in this text as *M*.)

Lehan, Richard. *A Dangerous Crossing: French Literary Existentialism and the Modern American Novel*. Carbondale: University of Illinois Press, 1973.

Lemke, Sieglinde. *Primitivist Modernism: Black Culture and the Origins of Transatlantic Modernism*. New York: Oxford University Press, 1998.

Luddington, Townsend. *John Dos Passos: A Twentieth-Century Odyssey*. New York: Dutton, 1980.

Lukács, Georg. *The Meaning of Contemporary Realism*. Translated by John and Necke Mander. London: Merlin Press, 1962.

McLuhan, Eric. "The Source of the Term 'Global Village.'" *McLuhan Studies* I:2 (Fall 2000): 12–30.

McPherson, James Alan. "Indivisible Man." In *Speaking for You: The Vision of Ralph Ellison*, edited by Kimberly W. Benston. Washington, D. C.: Howard University Press, 1987.

Madden, David W., ed. *Critical Essays on Thomas Berger*. New York: G. K. Hall and Co., 1995.

Mailer, Norman. *An American Dream*. New York: Dell Publishing, 1970.

Maristuen-Rodakowski, Julie. "The Turtle Mountain Reservation in North Dakota: Its History as Depicted in Louise Erdrich's *Love Medicine* and *The Beet Queen*." In *Louise Erdrich's "Love Medicine": A Casebook*, edited by Hertha D. Sweet Wong. New York: Oxford University Press, 2000.

Marx, Karl. *Capital: A Critique of Political Economy*. Translated by Ben Fowkes. 2 vols. New York: Random House, 1977.

Matthiessen, Peter. *In the Spirit of Crazy Horse*. New York: Viking Penguin, 1992.

Mauss, Marcel. *Essai sur le Don*. Paris: Presses Universitaires de France, 1950.

———. *The Gift: The Form and Reason for Exchange in Archaic Societies*. Translated by W. D. Halls. London: Routledge, 1990. (Abbreviated in this text as *G*.)

Medovoi, Leerom. *Rebels: Youth and the Cold War Origins of Identity*. Durham, NC: Duke University Press, 2005.

Mellow, James R. *Charmed Circle: Gertrude Stein and Company*. Boston: Houghton Mifflin Co., 1974.

Melville, Herman. *Moby-Dick*. Edited by Harrison Hayford and Hershel Parker. Norton Critical Edition. New York: W. W. Norton and Co., 1967.

Menand, Louis. Introduction to *The Liberal Imagination: Essays in Literature and Society*. New York: New York Review of Books, 2008.

Mignolo, Walter. *The Darker Side of the Renaissance: Literacy, Territoriality, and Colonization*. 2nd ed. Ann Arbor: University of Michigan Press, 2003.

———. *Local Histories / Global Designs: Coloniality, Subaltern Knowledges, and Border Thinking*. Princeton: Princeton University Press, 2000.

Mooney, James. *The Ghost-Dance Religion and the Sioux Outbreak of 1890*. 1896. Reprint, Chicago: University of Chicago Press, 1965.

Morrison, Toni. *Beloved*. New York: Random House, 1987.

———. *A Mercy*. New York: Alfred A. Knopf, 2008.

———. *Playing in the Dark: Whiteness and the Literary Imagination*. New York: Random House, 1992.

Nafisi, Azar. *Reading Lolita in Tehran: A Memoir in Books*. New York: Random House, 2003.

Neighbors. Directed by John G. Avildsen. Columbia Pictures, 1981.

Neihardt, John, and Nicholas Black Elk. *Black Elk Speaks: Being the Life Story of a Holy Man of the Oglala Sioux*. Lincoln: University of Nebraska Press, 1961.

Nelson, Cary. *Repression and Recovery: Modern American Poetry and the Politics of Cultural Memory 1910–1945*. Madison: University of Wisconsin Press, 1989.

North, Michael. *The Dialect of Modernism: Race, Language, and Twentieth-Century Literature*. New York: Oxford University Press, 1994.

O'Meally, Robert, ed. *New Essays on "Invisible Man."* New York: Cambridge University Press, 1988.

Patterson, Orlando. *Slavery and Social Death: A Comparative Study*. Cambridge, MA: Harvard University Press, 1982.

Pease, Donald E. "New Perspectives on U.S. Culture and Imperialism." In *Cultures of United States Imperialism*, edited by Amy Kaplan and Donald E. Pease, 21–43. Durham, NC: Duke University Press, 1993.

———. *Theodore Seuss Geisel*. New York: Oxford University Press, 2010.

Pizer, Donald. *Dos Passos' U.S.A.: A Critical Study*. Charlottesville: University Press of Virginia, 1988.

Posnock, Ross. *Philip Roth's Rude Truth: The Art of Immaturity*. Princeton: Princeton University Press, 2006.

Pound, Ezra. *The Literary Essays of Ezra Pound*. Edited by T. S. Eliot. London: Faber and Faber, Ltd., 1954.

Pratt, Mary Louise. *Imperial Eyes: Travel Writing and Transculturation*. New York: Routledge, 1992.

Pratt, Scott L. *Native Pragmatism: Rethinking the Roots of American Philosophy*. Bloomington: Indiana University Press, 2002.

Prucha, Francis Paul. *The Great Father: The United States Government and the American Indians*. 2 vols. Lincoln: University of Nebraska Press, 1984.

Raboteau, Albert J. *Slave Religion: The "Invisible Institution" in the Antebellum South*. New York: Oxford University Press, 1978.

Reising, Russell. "Lionel Trilling, *The Liberal Imagination*, and the Emergence of the Cultural Discourse of Anti-Stalinism." *boundary* 2 20:1 (Spring 1993): 94–124.

Roth, Philip. *American Pastoral*. Boston: Houghton Mifflin Co., 1997. (Abbreviated in this text as *AP*.)

———. *The Human Stain*. New York: Random House, 2000. (Abbreviated in this text as *HS*.)

———. *Reading Myself and Others*. New York: Farrar, Straus, and Giroux, 1975.

Rowe, John Carlos. "The Dramatization of *Mao II* and the War on Terrorism." *South Atlantic Quarterly* 103:1 (Fall 2003): 21–43.

———. "The Economics of the Body in Kate Chopin's *The Awakening*." In *Kate Chopin Reconsidered: Beyond the Bayou*, edited by Lynda S. Boren and Sara de Saussure Davis, 117–42. Baton Rouge: Louisiana State University Press, 1992.

———. *At Emerson's Tomb: The Politics of Classic American Literature*. New York: Columbia University Press, 1997.

———. *Henry Adams and Henry James: The Emergence of a Modern Consciousness*. Ithaca, NY: Cornell University Press, 1976.

———. *Literary Culture and U.S. Imperialism: From the Revolution to World War II*. New York: Oxford University Press, 2000. (Abbreviated in this text as *LC*.)

———. "Mark Twain's Critique of Globalization (Old and New) in *Following the Equator: A Voyage around the World*," *Arizona Quarterly* 61:1 (Spring 2005): 109–35.

———. *The New American Studies*. Minneapolis: University of Minnesota Press, 2002.

———. *The Other Henry James*. Durham, NC: Duke University Press, 1998.

———. "Reading *Reading Lolita in Tehran* in Idaho." *American Quarterly* 59:2 (June 2007): 253–75.

———, ed. *Selected Works of Ralph Waldo Emerson and Margaret Fuller*. Boston: Houghton Mifflin Co., 2003.

———. *The Theoretical Dimensions of Henry James*. Madison: University of Wisconsin Press, 1984.

———. *Through the Custom-House: Nineteenth-Century American Fiction and Modern Theory*. Baltimore: The Johns Hopkins University Press, 1982.

Ruddick, Lisa. *Reading Gertrude Stein: Body, Text, Gnosis*. Ithaca, NY: Cornell University Press, 1990.

Said, Edward. *Culture and Imperialism*. New York: Alfred A. Knopf, 1993.

Sartre, Jean-Paul. *What Is Literature?* Translated by Bernard Frechtman. New York: Harper and Row, 1965.

Sarver, Cynthia Ann. "Seeing in the Dark: Race, Representation, and Visuality in Literary Modernism." PhD Dissertation. University of Southern California. 2004.

Saussure, Ferdinand de. *Course in General Linguistics*. Edited by Charles Bally and Albert Sechehaye, in collaboration with Albert Reidlinger. Translated by Wade Baskin. New York: McGraw Hill Book Co., 1966.

Schickel, Richard. "Interviewing Thomas Berger." *New York Times Book Review* (April 6, 1980).

Schieble, Heinz. *Melanchthon: Eine Biographie*. Munich: Verlag C. H. Beck, 1997.

Schiller, Georg. *Symbolische Erfahrung und Sprache im Werk von Gertrude Stein*. Düsseldorfer Beiträge aus Anglistik und Amerikanistik. Frankfurt: Peter Lang, 1995.

Schlesinger, Arthur M., Jr. *The Age of Jackson*. Boston: Little, Brown and Co., 1945.

———. *The Vital Center: The Politics of Freedom*. Boston: Houghton Mifflin Co., 1949.

Schroyer, Trent. Foreword to *The Jargon of Authenticity*, by Theodor Adorno. Evanston, IL: Northwestern University Press, 1973.

Snead, James. *Figures of Division: William Faulkner's Major Novels*. New York: Methuen, 1986.

Spillers, Hortense. *Black, White, and in Color: Essays on American Literature and Culture*. Chicago: University of Chicago Press, 2003.

Stein, Gertrude. *The Autobiography of Alice B. Toklas*. Harmondsworth, UK: Penguin Books, 1966. (Abbreviated in this text as *ABT*.)

———. *Lectures in America*. New York: Random House, 1935.

———. *The Making of Americans: The Hersland Family*. New York: Harcourt Brace and Co., 1934.

———. *Q. E. D.* In *Writings 1903–1932*. New York: Library of America, 1998.

———. *Selected Writings of Gertrude Stein*. Edited by Carl Van Vechten. New York: Random House, Inc., 1962.

———. *Three Lives*. Harmondsworth, UK: Penguin Books, 1979. (Abbreviated in this text as *TL*.)

———. *Writings 1903–1932*. New York: Library of America, 1998.

———. *Writings and Lectures, 1909–1945*. Edited by Patricia Meyerowitz. Harmondsworth, UK: Penguin Books, 1971.

Stephens, Gregory. *On Racial Frontiers: The New Culture of Frederick Douglass, Ralph Ellison, and Bob Marley*. New York: Cambridge University Press, 1999.

Sundquist, Eric. *To Wake the Nations: Race in the Making of American Literature*. Cambridge, MA: Harvard University Press, 1993.

Swados, Harvey. "An American in Berlin [Review of *Crazy in Berlin*]." In *Critical Essays on Thomas Berger*, edited by David W. Madden, 29–30. New York: G. K. Hall and Co., 1995.

Tilton, Robert S. *Pocahontas: The Evolution of an American Narrative*. New York: Cambridge University Press, 1994.

Tindall, William York. *The Literary Symbol*. New York: Columbia University Press, 1955.

To Kill a Mockingbird. Directed by Robert Mulligan. Universal Pictures, 1962.

Toomer, Jean. *Cane*. Edited by Darwin T. Turner. Norton Critical Edition. New York: W. W. Norton and Co., Inc., 1988.

Torgovnick, Marianna. *Gone Primitive: Savage Intellects, Modern Lives*. Chicago: University of Chicago Press, 1990.

———. *Primitive Passions: Men, Women, and the Quest for Ecstasy*. Chicago: University of Chicago Press, 1996.

Trachtenberg, Stanley. "Berger and Barth: The Comedy of Decomposition." In *Comic Relief: Humor in Contemporary American Literature*, edited by Sarah Blacher Cohen. Urbana: University of Illinois Press, 1978.

Trilling, Lionel. *The Liberal Imagination: Essays in Literature and Society*. New York: The Viking Press, 1950.

———. *The Liberal Imagination: Essays in Literature and Society*. Classic Edition. New York: New York Review of Books, 2008.

———. *The Middle of the Journey*. New York: The Viking Press, 1947.

Truong, Monique. *The Book of Salt*. Boston: Houghton Mifflin Co., 2003.

Twain, Mark. *Adventures of Huckleberry Finn*. Edited by Thomas Cooley. Norton Critical Edition. New York: W. W. Norton and Co., 1999.

Von Hallberg, Robert, ed. *Canons*. Chicago: University of Chicago Press, 1984.

Walker, Cheryl. *Indian Nation: Native American Literature and Nineteenth-Century Nationalisms*. Durham, NC: Duke University Press, 1997.

Walker, Jayne L. *The Making of a Modernist: Gertrude Stein*. Amherst: University of Massachusetts Press, 1984.

Weales, Gerald. "Reinhart as Hero and Clown." In *Critical Essays on Thomas Berger*. Edited by David W. Madden, 76–88. New York: G. K. Hall and Co., 1995.

Weber, Brom. "[Review of *Vital Parts*]." In *Critical Essays on Thomas Berger*. Edited by David W. Madden, 31–33. New York: G. K. Hall and Co., 1995.

Winnicott, D[onald] W[oods]. *Playing and Reality*. London: Tavistock Publishers, 1971.

Wolfe, Alan. "The Anti-American Studies." *New Republic* (February 10, 2003).

Wong, Hertha D. Sweet, ed. *Louise Erdrich's "Love Medicine": A Casebook*. New York: Oxford University Press, 2000.

Wordsworth, William. "Preface to the Second Edition of *Lyrical Ballads*." In *Critical Theory since Plato*, Rev. ed., edited by Hazard Adams, 436–46. New York: Harcourt Brace Jovanovich, 1992.

Wright, John S. "The Conscious Hero and the Rites of Man: Ellison's War." In *New*

Essays on "Invisible Man," edited by Robert O'Meally. New York: Cambridge University Press, 1988.

———. "Shadowing Ellison." In *Speaking for You: The Vision of Ralph Ellison*, edited by Kimberly W. Benston. Washington, D. C.: Howard University Press, 1987.

Wright, Richard. "Between Laughter and Tears." *New Masses* (October 5, 1937): 22–23.

INDEX